A Battalion in Burma

A Battalion in Burma

Second Suffolk in Arakan and at Imphal, 1943–44

Mark Forsdike

Pen & Sword
MILITARY

First published in Great Britain in 2024 by
Pen & Sword Military
An imprint of Pen & Sword Books Limited
Yorkshire – Philadelphia

Copyright © Mark Forsdike 2024

ISBN 978 1 39907 925 9

The right of Mark Forsdike to be identified as
Author of this Work has been asserted by him in accordance
with the Copyright, Designs and Patents Act 1988.

A CIP catalogue record for this book is
available from the British Library

All rights reserved. No part of this book may be reproduced or
transmitted in any form or by any means, electronic or mechanical
including photocopying, recording or by any information storage and
retrieval system, without permission from the Publisher in writing.

Typeset by Mac Style
Printed in the UK by CPI Group (UK) Ltd, Croydon, CR0 4YY.

Pen & Sword Books Limited incorporates the imprints of After the Battle, Atlas, Archaeology, Aviation, Discovery, Family History, Fiction, History, Maritime, Military, Military Classics, Politics, Select, Transport, True Crime, Air World, Frontline Publishing, Leo Cooper, Remember When, Seaforth Publishing, The Praetorian Press, Wharncliffe Local History, Wharncliffe Transport, Wharncliffe True Crime and White Owl.

For a complete list of Pen & Sword titles please contact

PEN & SWORD BOOKS LIMITED
47 Church Street, Barnsley, South Yorkshire, S70 2AS, England
E-mail: enquiries@pen-and-sword.co.uk
Website: www.pen-and-sword.co.uk
or
PEN AND SWORD BOOKS
1950 Lawrence Rd, Havertown, PA 19083, USA
E-mail: uspen-and-sword@casematepublishers.com
Website: www.penandswordbooks.com

To the memory of the five officers and ninety-two men of Second Suffolk who laid down their lives as this story unfolded, this work is dedicated in proud and affectionate remembrance.

Contents

Prologue: Those dirty, youthful faces that smile   viii
Acknowledgements   xi
Author's Note   xiii

Chapter 1	Old Soldier Sahib	1
Chapter 2	Jungle Training	9
Chapter 3	Burma	16
Chapter 4	Bamboo Hill	25
Chapter 5	'Men of the Arakan'	47
Chapter 6	Kohima	72
Chapter 7	The Pimple	82
Chapter 8	Guerrilla Raids	115
Chapter 9	Pyramid	129
Chapter 10	Isaac	145
Chapter 11	Silchar Track	172
Chapter 12	Tomorrow is a Lovely Day	195

Epilogue: They Meet in Twos and Threes   204
Appendix I: 'The sort of man who wins wars'   208
Appendix II: The missing of the battle for the 'Pimple'   210
Appendix III: Honours and Awards   213
Appendix IV: Roll of Honour   215
Notes   219
Index   228

Prologue
Those dirty, youthful faces that smile

*'We were late to the party and then we did not stay to
see it through to the end'*

'Everything, in comparison, favoured the First Battalion', wrote Colonel Walter Nicholson when he completed the third volume of Suffolk Regiment history in 1946.

He managed, in just those few words, to sum up the entire fighting war that Second Suffolk had experienced in the Far East. Compared to their counterparts in Europe, theirs was a war of polar opposites. Where First Suffolk in Europe gained, Second Suffolk in Burma lost. Drained of experienced men, denuded of supplies and denied morale-boosting media attention, the jungle war was not kind to the Battalion.

Though their campaign was shorter than that which would be fought by their counterparts in Europe, it was fought continuously and more intensely. Theirs, too, was a war of ferocity, against an enemy that was erratic, unpredictable and fanatical to the last. Their war was one of small, punitive advances, where the enemy always seemed deathly close and where there was always just one more hill to take.

The terrain over which they were required to fight was tough and unforgiving. It pushed men to the limits of their mental and physical endurance. Miles from home, their link with 'Blighty' was often only a letter from a loved one. The climate, too, was unrelenting. High altitude positions, curious local wildlife and the incessant monsoon all took their toll and sapped their resolve in an inhospitable place. Yet despite these difficulties, the morale of the stolid regular Suffolk soldier and his newly conscripted comrades always remained high.

Open any book on the Far East campaign – even those published in recent years – and you will find just a line or two mentioning Second Suffolk. True, they were but a small part of a massive combined Indian, Empire and Dominion force that fought in the Burma Campaign, but others who fought comparably sized battles to those which were fought by the Battalion always seem to get a mention, yet Second Suffolk's actions went virtually unnoticed in the records of the day.

You may find occasional mention of hills such as Isaac, but you will struggle to find anything else. But they were there all the same, carrying on in the typical, inimitable style of the Suffolk soldier; getting on with the job they were given, with the minimum of fuss or bother.

That invisibility to history has been constant since their service in 1945 when, depleted in numbers and handicapped by illness, the Battalion was removed to western India following their fighting south of Imphal. Below active strength, they were taken off front-line service to be replaced with a new, stronger unit. There was nothing inglorious about their war or their departure from the front line, but they would not recover to fight the Japanese again.

The veterans of Second Suffolk that I knew seemed to wish to remember the times before and the times after their service in Burma. It was the jungle campaign in between that most wished to conveniently forget. Professional soldiers, of whom there was a high proportion in the Battalion, always remembered the 'good old days' – the times of polish, starch and parades. Virtually no one wished to recall the grimy interlude in between these periods that involved their having to fight the Japanese.

Many, too, I believe, felt wrongly that their efforts had been a failure.

'We were late to the party', Lance Corporal Arthur Abbott once told me, 'and then we did not stay to see it through to the end.'

It was perhaps that long-held feeling that made these men not wish to tell of that part of their service. Resentment, too, was something that most Burma veterans of the Regiment felt. They felt, quite rightly, that their tough jungle war, albeit shorter, was always overshadowed by the actions of their comrades in Europe.

For these reasons, very little material in the form of first-hand accounts survives from the men of Second Suffolk. Accounts were requested just after the war, to assist in the compilation of another volume of Regimental History, but these were not forthcoming. The Battalion had by then virtually ceased to exist, and only a few regular officers still serving submitted their memoirs.

In the years that followed, just a dedicated few kept in correspondence with each other and maintained contact in order to meet and talk of their war, but many others remained silent, only making brief mention of their service in the Burma campaign.

In recent years, the Burma campaign has finally and thankfully been readdressed, so that the 'Forgotten Army', as it was previously known, is perhaps not quite so forgotten any more. Moreover, long overdue credit has been given to the troops of the British Indian Army and the Empire that bore the brunt of the fighting and who, without a doubt, secured the ultimate victory in this campaign; but beside them were single British infantry battalions such as Second Suffolk, all playing their part in the overall victory over the Japanese.

This book is intended to be a frank, unvarnished account of the actions of Second Suffolk all those years ago. It is designed to give as much coverage as possible to 'A Battalion in Burma', who deserve, like their counterparts who fought in Europe, to finally have their story told. They have, in my opinion, been long overlooked in the history of the Burma campaign, and it is hoped that this book will now go some small way to rectifying that.

Mark Forsdike
2023

Acknowledgements

Several people have contributed material and photographs to this book, and every possible effort has been made to contact them to thank them for their most valuable contributions. If it has not been possible to name you below, I wish to thank you all for your contributions to this work.

My most sincere thanks must go first to Murdo Duncan, son of Lieutenant Duncan of Second Suffolk. It was Murdo, with his numerous questions about his father's service with the Regiment, who convinced me that a book about the Battalion in Burma was possible and, indeed, was needed by the relatives of those who served within its ranks. He has most kindly allowed me to publish excerpts from his father's taped memoirs, and it is with Murdo's unending enthusiasm that this work has finally come to fruition.

I am most grateful to Richard Partington for permission to use the photograph of his grandfather, Arthur, on the front cover and to include some more of his photographs in this work.

My special thanks must go to Jeremy Archer for his permission to use excerpts from his own book *Burma: The Final Curtain* in this work. Jeremy's tireless efforts with the Burma Star Association, now the Burma Star Memorial Fund, in recording the testimonies of our last living Burma veterans is to be championed. It is due to his tireless efforts that we have a sizeable written legacy from our last surviving Burma campaign veterans.

I am also most grateful to Chris Hulse and his father Kevin, who have most generously allowed me to publish the portrait of Private Fred Hulse taken during the Imphal campaign. With so few images surviving of that period, the inclusion of his portrait in this work is very much appreciated.

I am particularly grateful to the family of Lieutenant Colonel H. R. Hopking. His son, Richard, who also served in the Suffolk Regiment, and his grandson, Henry, have been fantastic in providing access to his archives and have been most helpful in 'filling in the blanks' of his career with the Regiment. I cannot thank them enough for the time they spent with me talking of 'Huffy'.

My thanks are also due to Sharon Van Der Werf for the valuable information on her grandfather, Private David Tod, who was killed during the attack on the 'Pimple' and whose grave was subsequently lost.

I am grateful once again to Owen Van Spall of the Imperial War Museum for his permission to use an excerpt from their interview with Sergeant Bill Watts.

I am most grateful to my wife, Emma, and to my children, Lily and George, who have been forced to wait whilst their father scoured archives, libraries and churchyards for information for this work.

Finally, my most sincere thanks must go to the veterans of Second Suffolk themselves, who have over the past twenty-five years sat and told me their stories and have corresponded with me about their jungle war. Those who contributed to this work were: Arthur 'Gunboat' Abbott, Ernie Bates, 'Jack' Dash, 'Boy' Elmer, 'Reggie' Leeke, Jesse Matthews, Gilbert Mills, Charlie Parr, Clifford Price and Norman Rolfe.

There were many more, including E. G. W. 'Gordon' Browne, Lionel Ruffles and Cyril Wilkinson, who for the passing of time I was not fortunate enough to meet; but through several sources, including the personal archives of the late Arthur 'Smudger' Smith, himself a pre-war veteran of Second Suffolk, and the late Jim Taylor, a Suffolk National Serviceman, correspondence and accounts from them have since come to light which have been included in the pages that follow.

Author's Note

This book is intended to be a factual, chronological account of Second Suffolk's actions in the Burma campaign. It concentrates solely on the actions of that Battalion. Other units mentioned in the narrative are referred to by their shortened titles: e.g. 'Punjabis' and 'Dogras' rather than their full names such as '1/17 Dogra Regiment' or '3/2 Punjab Regiment', or by their official designations in use at the time, such as 'DOGRA'. No offence is intended by these abbreviated forms.

Understanding the exact locations of the various actions the Battalion fought in Burma and India can be difficult for the modern reader to interpret. The maps used at the time were often already out of date, highly inaccurate and relied heavily on incomplete aerial surveys carried out in the 1920s and 1930s by the colonial administrations.

Thus, the names you will read in the text that follows are those which were used at the time and to which the Battalion War Diary made reference. Many of these have now changed, becoming more anglicized, and in some cases entire villages have moved from their previously charted positions. By using the maps that accompany the text, the reader should be able to establish their positions on modern satellite maps with relative ease.

Original 1:25,000 scale maps of the Burma and Imphal campaigns are also comparatively rare, and the Battalion War Diary is devoid of them. Readers should note that some smaller villages and settlements do not appear on maps of the time, and further confusion is added here as the locations and names of villages that are mentioned in the third volume of Regimental History are largely incorrect and often very inaccurate.

An example of this is the village of 'Sabang'. A map in the Regimental History positions it north of Isaac. However, the village was recorded as 'Sedang' in the Battalion War Diary, and despite much searching, the exact location of either named village is yet to be confirmed. It was in all probability just a cluster of huts located east of the village of Sengmai and west of the village of Mapao, both north of Imphal and west of the Nungshigum feature, but south of Isaac.

The 2nd Battalion, Suffolk Regiment is, wherever possible, referred to in the following text simply as 'the Battalion' or as it was known at the time, 'Second Suffolk'. During the war years, when censorship was imposed, the *Suffolk Regimental Gazette* referred to it first as the 'Old Dozen', then 'A Battalion in the East' and finally 'A Battalion in Burma'.

Chapter One
Old Soldier Sahib

'Pathans two - 2 Suffolk nil!'

In January 1929, the 2nd Battalion, the Suffolk Regiment landed at Bombay and entrained for their new home at Trimulgherry. It was to be the beginning of the end of the Regiment's service in India.

The Battalion had been stationed here at various times since the 1860s and had in the early years of the twentieth century been posted to various locations around the great subcontinent on Foreign Service. Their soldiering in India had been one of presence: a presence to maintain law and order and keep the peace between its many races, tribes and peoples.

To many old soldiers, India was a land of adventure and mysticism; a hot, humid outstation of the Empire, where English traditions were still uniquely observed alongside the centuries-old customs of the native population. To younger soldiers, its ancient temples and bustling bazaars were places of fascination. To older soldiers, it was a land of foreign charms, relentless street traders and dubious ladies who responded to the familiar question, *'Do anna, decco?'* – (Pull up your skirt and) two annas for a look?

To many younger soldiers, the country took some getting used to, especially the ways of the locals and their 'dodges', as Lieutenant Kenneth Henderson discovered upon disembarkation:

> At the dockside I was approached by a very tall and distinguished Indian who showed me a chit from an officer of the Regiment recommending him as a servant (bearer). He told me that he had been sent to escort me (all officers had their own bearer). He required an advance of pay and not knowing the form I gave him some money. He also was entitled to a ticket for the journey as my servant so he travelled with me for some 24 hours as far as Rawalpindi where we had to change trains. He then disappeared – so I was quickly learning the facts of life as lived in India![1]

In the twilight of its service overseas, Second Suffolk had come from Shanghai, where for two years it had served as part of the 'Shanghai Defence Forces' with a host of allies, keeping the peace in the International Settlement there. Most men looked forward to service in India, even if it would be hotter than China.

The Regiment prided itself upon its 'family' spirit, and wives and families were as much a part of the regiment as its men. Those who served in these peaceful days remembered with affection that spirit, as Lieutenant W. S. Bevan recalled:

> In spite of everything, the battalion was a big and, by-and-large, remarkably happy family. All ranks (and the families) from the CO to the youngest Band Boy knew everyone else and had no doubt that 2 Suffolk – the 'Old Swedebashers' – was the best battalion in India.[2]

Most, too, remembered the old army custom that everybody had a nickname: 'In the Suffolk Regiment, anyone with the name White was known as 'Snowy' or 'Striker', Roses became 'Bungays', Days were nicknamed 'Happy' and Woods were called 'Timber'.'[3]

Language, too, could sometimes be a problem, especially when old soldiers merged their ancient Suffolk dialect with a smattering of Urdu. Communication for the 'foreigner' could sometimes be extremely difficult, as a newly arrived officer who joined 1 Suffolk in Normandy later recalled on his first meeting with two 'Old Sweats' in a foxhole who had previously served with Second Suffolk in India:

> They introduced themselves and one said in a broad Suffolk burr something to the effect that: 'Would you loike some (rumble) on your (rumble) and (rumble) sir?' I couldn't understand a word. I decided to admit it: 'I'm sorry but I haven't a clue what you are saying.' The speaker looked at his companion in a way which indicated that 'We've got a right one here' and said slowly: 'Would you like some *pozzi* on your *rooti* and *muckin*, sor?' I was none the wiser, and said: 'Perhaps you'd explain, because I'm in a total fog.' He went over each word carefully as if to a two-year-old: 'Would ... you ... like ... some ... *pozzi* (jam, sor) on ... your ... *rooti* (bread, sor) and ... *muckin* (butter, sor)?' It soon clicked, and I realized that this was my first exposure to the mixture of English in a broad Suffolk accent and Urdu picked up by the regiment over the years with service in India. There were other words they used frequently which I had to have explained to me as time went on.[4]

On 25 November 1939, Second Suffolk left Mhow, where it had been based for nearly five years, and proceeded to the fortified camp at Razmak on the North-West frontier, in what is now Pakistan. The camp, which was 7,156ft above sea level, lay on a plateau in Waziristan between two snow-covered mountain ridges.

The 'Razmak Hill Station' was an eerie and lonely place. There were no families here, just the men. The journey of almost 800 miles to reach it had been made by train, with two stops, and finally a journey by lorry to the camp itself. It took four days but passed without incident. The Battalion's presence here was to stop the Waziristan tribesmen coming south to raid the great plains of India.

Razmak had a central camp at the end of the plain. Its huts were of stone, with corrugated tin roofs. There was a bazaar with shops and even a cinema. Outside the settlement were a cemetery and a hospital. The entire camp was surrounded by a ring of sentry posts, inside of which were playing fields and an airstrip. Up on the hills overlooking the position were a series of piquets that were manned at different intervals on different days.

When moving out to occupy one of these positions, the procedure was to liaise with the artillery and machine gun units also based in Razmak, who would select a hill close to the designated piquet and lay down covering fire, allowing the platoon to get across the open ground towards it. Because the country was so open and they could be attacked at any time from any number of positions, the final part of the journey to the piquet would be made at the run.

Each piquet had a stone '*sangar*' – a walled enclosure – and the men would race in and immediately take up firing positions on its parapet. Each *sangar* contained a signaller who, with either a radio or his signalling flags, would keep in contact with the camp. In the summer months, a heliograph would often be used for messaging.

For such physical exertion everyone had to be fit, but warm clothing such as greatcoats was far too cumbersome for the final sprint, as Major Monier-Williams recalled:

> Woollen balaclava helmets, mufflers, leather jerkins and gloves were necessary in the early morning. We had not yet been issued with battle dress, so we used our old-time service dress trousers with short puttees and boots or with *chaplis* (shoes). A somewhat unorthodox dress but the best for the particular job, when we had to run half a mile or more and then climb up a hill as steep as the side of a house. Great coats were useless – too heavy – but we wanted something extra when we got to the top of the hill and had to stop there for four hours in a bitter cold wind, so we took groundsheets in our packs and the platoon had a primus stove with which to make tea.[5]

Each platoon that went out was accompanied by a native '*Khassidar*' or '*Kassader*' – an armed native tribesman in the employ of the British. Sergeant Tommy

Warren recalled his time at Razmak and one particular duty at 'Toady Piquet' when the Battalion came under heavy sniper fire from the local Pathan tribesmen:

> A signal flag waved on Toady. My signaller, reading the message, said someone on Toady had been shot. A little later, another message reported that L/Sgt Polly Hopkins had been shot. Shortly after that, Captain Freeland handed me a piqueting slip and told me to take my platoon and occupy Toady and to send L/Sgt Hopkins' platoon back to the road. I was also to send back the location of the Pathans. Signalling to my platoon to follow, we doubled off towards the hill and began the tough climb, passing L/Sgt Hopkins on his painful way down the road by stretcher, and the usual rude marks passed between us. The rifle fire had now died down to a few odd shots; at this stage we were in view of the Pathans' positions. Pausing just below the summit to crawl forward and take a look, I noted the sections crouched behind their *sangars*, every man looking back at me. Shouting my intentions to them, I sent my VB gun team off to the hut. They knew the drill, we had done this piquet before. The VB team did the 50 off yards to the hut in record time and were inside and up on the roof before the Pathans could open up. With VB gun firing short bursts, the rifle sections were replaced one by one, and the relieved platoon set off downhill to the road. The Pathans were now plastering the hilltop with bullets; it was amazing that so many men could sprint across that short space without one getting hit. It was platoon HQ's turn to run the gauntlet, which we also did in record time. A quick dash into the hut, note the *Kassader* sitting in the corner, rifle between his knees, eyes closed, asleep, scale the rickety ladder, tell them to stop firing, scan the opposite hillside; nothing, not a sign of a Pathan and, despite their rifle fire, not even a wisp of smoke. They were well and truly tucked away deep in a massive jumble of boulders. Heard my signaller's flag being used, then the shout, 'You are to hurry up with the reference to the enemy!'[6]

Back at the road below, a battery of 3.7" mountain guns waited ready to pound the positions and silence the Pathans' fire. Having reported the position, shells pounded the hillside in front of them, and a fierce volley of Pathan fire was returned against the piquet. A correction was made, and their fire ceased, but not before another member of the platoon had been hit, Private 'Tyrone' Power being shot through the right arm. Warren continues:

> Five minutes later, still nothing. Hear movement below inside the hut, slide over to the hole and look down. The *Kassader* was stretching up to his

six-foot plus height, picked up his rifle and ambled out into the sunshine. Our little moment of hate was over. The score as far as anyone knows, was Pathans two - 2 Suffolk nil!⁷

Supplies arrived fortnightly, during which time the road had to be guarded against raiding tribesmen, and the mail arrived weekly by air. After a year there, the Battalion were relieved and withdrawn down to Rawalpindi.

At the end of 1940, Lieutenant Colonel D. R. A. Eley relinquished command of the Battalion and passed it on to Lieutenant Colonel H. B. Monier-Williams. 'Moanie Bill', as he was affectionately known, was a machine gun officer in 1 Suffolk during the Great War and had later won the Military Cross whilst serving with a Company of the Machine Gun Corps. He had also, in the inter-war years, been Adjutant of the 4th (Territorial) Battalion of the Regiment.

Whilst their colleagues in the 1st Battalion were now re-forming in England following their evacuation from Dunkirk, Second Suffolk were keeping up the fine state of physical fitness at which they had excelled before the war. It was noted in December 1940 that a 35.5-mile route march was accomplished in just twelve and a half hours.

In July 1941, the Battalion moved into the Tochi Valley to guard the lines of communication to the hill stations at Razmak and Degen. Sickness was rife, and many men went down with fever, but those who remained were congratulated by the Commander-in-Chief, General Sir Archibald Wavell, when he visited the Battalion in 1942: 'Let all troops know how favourably I was impressed by their bearing and their evident keenness.'⁸

But it was in this time of stagnation, on which as the Regimental History noted, 'no limelight is thrown', that many men of the Battalion became restless; seeing that the war was unfolding elsewhere in the world, and feeling that they wished to play a more prominent part in it, many departed to join other units in India, including the embryonic 151 Parachute Battalion, which was being formed close by.

Back again in Rawalpindi, the Battalion now started to receive its first 2" and 3" Mortars, which were proving somewhat hard to master. The men had been used to working in cooperation with antiquated Crossley armoured cars and squadrons of obsolete Westland Wapiti biplanes across the large flat plains of northern India. Now they had to train to use mortars within the close confines of the hills and valleys.

At this time, the Battalion also handed in its old 'VB' guns and received instead the newer Bren gun that had been in use with the British Army since 1938. The 'VB' gun, or Vickers-Berthier, was the earlier equivalent of the Bren that was predominantly supplied to battalions on Foreign Service.

Back on Internal Security operations in 1942, the Battalion was fighting a rising tide of fifth column actions following the British defeats at Hong Kong and Singapore, but in early March, a draft of three officers and thirty other ranks from the Territorial Battalions of the Regiment, along with many Cambridgeshire Regiment men, arrived to bolster their ranks.

These men were the lucky ones who had either escaped capture at Singapore or had been fortunate enough to find a vessel and sail it to India. Two Cambridgeshire officers, Captain 'Tony' Ennion and Lieutenant George Squirrell, who were part of this draft, would remain with the Battalion until it returned to India three years later.

Another officer, Lieutenant Miles Arrindell of 4 Suffolk, had made a successful escape from Singapore by boat with two other men, as had Lieutenant Peter Hill of 6 Royal Norfolk. He had sailed a captured boat to Ceylon, a distance of over 2,000 miles, but upon being posted to the Battalion, he found the general atmosphere to be somewhat laid-back:

> The Battalion hadn't really realised that the war had started. They were having regular guest nights, with their officers dressing up in their evening blues. We became company commanders – they must have been short of people – and were leading a peacetime army life. A bit boring really.[9]

After spells guarding the railway, the Battalion found itself spread over some 400 square miles, and it was not until October 1942 that it was back together again as a complete unit at Lucknow. The men threw themselves wholeheartedly again into training, but with materiel still lacking, and comrades who had served their allotted time overseas being repatriated, it was only the 'old sweats' that remained enthusiastic.

At the end of the year it was announced that Lieutenant Colonel Monier-Williams had been offered a Staff position at home and would be departing in the New Year. Not long afterwards, his Second-in-Command, Major 'Tommy' Atkins, was also recalled home, and in April more valuable old soldiers were repatriated.

'Moanie Bill' was an exceedingly popular commander. A letter to him from his Brigadier on the eve of his departure noted the unique family spirit that he had fostered within the Battalion during his short time in command: 'I should like to say how impressed I was when I visited your Battalion in Rawalpindi with all I saw. The thing that struck me most was what a happy Battalion you had – both in officers and men.'[10]

Training continued, but men were still being taken for other units. In May 1943, 150 men were detached, never to return. These men were all older, time-served soldiers with many years service. With them went fourteen NCOs, who 'could be ill spared'. Now, many men came from other units to bring the Battalion back up to strength, and though there was now a considerable number of 'foreigners' within the Battalion, its ranks were still predominantly filled with Suffolk men:

> New faces are plentiful as are also new accents, but even though we are a bit of a mixed bag, with the 'Swedes' still the predominating force, all muck in well together. We are looking to the future with confidence as after years of waiting with many disappointments we are glad to be in a position to do our bit to get this lot over.[11]

Age, too, was a problem. Men of the Battalion were on average in their early to mid-thirties. They had been denied drafts of younger men from the Depot at home and from the newly created Holding Battalion (8 Suffolk), and so their ranks still predominantly consisted of pre-war men who had served in India since the late 1930s. Just a handful of Militiamen had joined the Battalion at Razmak in 1939, and now men were being drafted to them from a number of Garrison and Artillery units in India. The Regimental History noted the composition of the Battalion at that time:

> About a quarter of its existing strength had joined during the last fortnight and there was a serious shortage of senior N.C.O.s; the last draft that the Battalion had received consisted of 170 men with only one Sgt. and two Cpls. Most important of all, there was a deficiency of Platoon Officers.[12]

But as soon as men arrived, they quickly disappeared again. The following month, another valuable draft of men was lost to another unit, but in September 1943 a long-standing rumour had been confirmed: that soon the Battalion would be on the move to fight on the Burma Front:

> By this time it was certain that the Battalion was for Burma, and this created a great wave of enthusiasm. The Battalion was in the Ranchi area for final intensive training in jungle warfare. A fairly hectic time was spent, tents being luxury items and a thick bush the acme of comfort.[13]

As the exact date for their posting to Burma was yet to be confirmed, the Battalion prepared to depart for special training. Their greatest sadness, however, was that their Regimental Contractor could not proceed with them. Khan Sahib Haji F. Shaboodeen had loyally served the Regiment in India since 1920, when he was officially appointed as the Regimental Contractor. He had been with the

1st Battalion when they were engaged in the 'Moplah Rebellion' of 1921–22 and had received the India General Service Medal for his services. In his time he had given the Regiment numerous sporting trophies and cups, and men of the Battalion competed annually at boxing to win the 'Shaboodeen Belt'.

The *Suffolk Regimental Gazette* noted his importance and his loss: 'The other loss to us is old Shaboodeen. He was not allowed to come with us. We have called him many names other than the ones he was given at birth, but we will miss him now; we hope to meet you again "Shaboo".'[14]

Posted to the Battalion just a month before they left India, a young Captain from the Royal Norfolk Regiment, Bryan Coward, recalled the still genial family spirit of the Regiment upon his joining:

> I became a Company Commander in the 2nd Suffolks. My first experience was to go into my Company Office which had a low wall and on the other side of the wall there was a Company Clerk and a Company Runner. I heard this conversation; the Company Runner says, 'You seen the C.O. this morning?' and the Company Clerk says, 'No, but I've seen her husband!'[15]

That old order was about to change.

Chapter Two

Jungle Training

'I found them in grand form, full of fun and enthusiasm'

The Battalion were now thrown into jungle training prior to their imminent move to the Burma front. For a Battalion that had predominantly been used to large-scale manoeuvres, the oppressive confines of the Burmese jungle, with its dense bamboo and early morning mists, would be a new experience.

At first, the biggest change was in their appearance. Gone was khaki drill, and in its place a new uniform was issued of jungle green colour. A short battledress blouse or four-pocket shirt of aertex cloth was worn, with a pair of drill trousers in a matching shade. Long puttees that were wrapped around the calf were changed for shorter ones or webbing anklets. The older Great War-vintage '1908 Pattern' webbing had finally been replaced with the newer-style '1937 Pattern', which came from local supply depots in India.

Also at this time, the felt bush hat was issued. The older flat-top *topee* that had been worn since 1937, with its distinctive three-point regimental *puggaree*, disappeared in early October 1943. It had been worn in training, covered with a thick net for camouflage, but in the campaign that was to come the broader-brimmed bush hat would be much more practical and comfortable:

> We have all now been fitted out with bush hats and some of the members look real tough. C.S.M. Stan Winter has chosen a '10 gallon' size hat and with his hat and cigar, he looks like a proper Wild West 'Hombre' – One good point about his hat is that he can shelter the whole of his Company Headquarters under it![1]

As the Battalion moved into a training camp in Bengal to learn how to fight in the jungle, some men of the Battalion did have a few concerns, not least about the wildlife they might encounter. Private Cyril Wilkinson recalled his training and the precautions that were taken should they encounter any 'local' animals:

Reflecting back, I wonder how many of the lads of the 2nd Battalion recall the jungle training camp in Bengal before we went to Burma. What an impression that period of my Army life created with me, we really did live close to nature, if memory serves me right. We were issued with one round of .303, the end of which had been sawn off, to be used, as we were told, in case of attack by Black Panther. The Bengal jungle as experienced proved was really alive with wild animals of every description. Remember we lived on starvation diet to prepare us for the worst, and I think even to this day that the meal prepared and waiting for us, when we had finally finished the jungle training, was the finest meal I've ever tasted. I remember at this camp that we did not have proper coins to tender, as for some reason the native population had hoarded them all, so we were issued with tickets called 'Blue Lights' and even these soon disappeared from circulation, and finally we resorted to the use of postage stamps to replace metal coinage. Remember the difficulty in poor light, at night, trying to buy something with stamps that had become sweaty and sticky! [2]

The Padre, Captain Brown-Moffet, who had joined the Battalion just a few weeks before, noted their high morale, though his broad Irish brogue was difficult to comprehend for many of the slower-speaking men of the Battalion:

Coming from the Inniskilling Fusiliers, whose language was my mother tongue, it was like going to a foreign country to be landed in the midst of men from the eastern counties. The reception I received from the C.O. and officers was very hearty (good omen for the future), and when I was amongst the men we soon got on speaking terms using English and a few signs! I found them in grand form, full of fun and enthusiasm. Training was in progress and the men were keen to learn all they could about jungle warfare.[3]

It was in Bengal that the Battalion would discover its reliance on mules for transport. The conditions they were soon to be fighting in were impractical for trucks or tanks, and any form of re-supply and movement would have to be carried out on foot. The mule was to be the bearer for the Battalion over the next ten months, and the men soon learned to love these hard-working, dependable, if at times stubborn, animals.

Second Suffolk was now running at a strength of around 730 all ranks; almost one hundred men short of the total ranks of the 1st Battalion in England. To add to this, acclimatization to Burma had brought numerous jungle illnesses which temporarily depleted the rifle companies further.

Whereas in 1 Suffolk a thorough weeding-out of men had been insisted upon following their retreat from Dunkirk, in the Second Battalion the case was the opposite. They were glad of any reinforcements they could get, for they had already been 'milked' of most of their experienced officers and fit men for other theatres.

At this time, because of the shortage of men, the Battalion was briefly reorganized from its pre-war four-Company strength into just three. The manpower shortage necessitated 'B' Company being temporarily disbanded, and a much smaller 'Administration' Company was formed with only a skeleton staff. Despite this, the Battalion felt confident that they were up to the job they were now being asked to perform:

> We spend most of our time doing intensive Jungle Warfare Training. We are now adept at getting soaked through in the Monsoon without catching 'pewmonia', crawling through paddy fields on our stomachs (and nearly drowning in the process), keeping dry with only a groundsheet between self and the monsoon and building Basha huts. The Guerrilla platoon under Lieut. Douglas Lee Hunter, have taught us all about 'silent killings' so you see that what I mean is that we consider ourselves really fit and ready to have a crack at the Japs.[4]

The 'Guerrilla Platoon' mentioned here was a unique unit within the Battalion comprising just twenty-five men and a few handpicked volunteers. Armed with an array of weapons including American-made Thompson sub-machine guns and Springfield sniper rifles, these men would be the first members of the Battalion to come into contact with the Japanese:

> This platoon had been formed from volunteers and selected men in the battalion and did very good work. From the outset they had the confidence of the local people by taking out medical stores and rendering first aid, so that the villagers were always willing to help and to give information about the Jap.[5]

Formed in those last few weeks in India, their role was twofold. First, they would be used for reconnaissance and intelligence-gathering, going forward to reconnoitre enemy positions and make plans for future attacks; and second, to maintain an offensive force against the enemy when large-scale attacks were not possible.

In a campaign where advances would often only be made in feet or yards, having a force that could actively harass the enemy positions at any time was a great morale boost to the Battalion. It was not unsurprising that this small unit would go on to be awarded the largest number of gallantry awards won by the Battalion during the campaign.

Jungle patrolling was a skill that now had to be mastered, and it was clear that not everyone was suited to it. Men had to learn the arts of camouflage and observation, and what to do if they came into contact with the enemy. Now, the action would not be at a distance across a plain, but close at hand, within feet.

A patrol would be split into small 'sub-sections', with one man looking right, one left and another up into the trees. The kit they would carry was minimal: belt, pouches, braces, toggle rope for fording streams, and ammunition. With a supply of rations and a cardigan or jumper, they could patrol as far as fifteen (jungle) miles a day and stay out overnight if necessary. It was remarked by one officer that 'Two of the most important factors for successful patrolling were the selection of a good observation post, and silence.'[6]

Pneumonia sadly claimed the life 32-year-old Private Charles Mallett on 4 September. He was a general labourer in Ipswich before the war and had been called up in 1940, serving briefly in the 8th Battalion before being posted to Second Suffolk in India in 1943. He was originally a member of 'C' Company, but had been transferred to Admin Company just a week before his death, joining the Transport Platoon.

The training in Bengal under battle conditions was also not without incident. On 29 September 1943, Lance Corporal Herbert Hunt of 'D' Company and Private Jack Boyden of 'HQ' Company were accidentally killed by shellfire whilst on exercise. Both men had been attached to the Pioneer Platoon for the exercise; another man, Private David Thompson, died the following day from his wounds. The Padre noted the unfortunate circumstances of their deaths: 'A mimic battle, in which live shells were used, finished the period of training. Unfortunately one shell fell short and several men were killed and several wounded.'[7]

The issue of 'Regimental Numerals' for wear on the bush or slouch hat in early October was a high point in their training and an indication that they would be departing imminently for the front. Manufactured locally, these took the form of a small brass 'XII' which was to be worn on the upturned brim of the hat. It was the only piece of Regimental heraldry to be worn by them in action, and two days later, all Foreign Service Pattern helmets and *topees* were withdrawn to stores.

Whilst the training continued, Major H. R. Hopking returned to the Battalion. He had been commissioned into the Regiment in 1919 and joined Second Suffolk in Ireland the following year. He became Adjutant when the Battalion were stationed in Shanghai in 1927/28 and later served as a Staff Officer in Trinidad between 1936 and 1940, for which he was awarded the OBE. Returning home, he commanded the 30th (Home Defence) Battalion, before rejoining Second Suffolk in India.

Major Hopking's posting back to the Battalion was in preparation for a change of command. In late 1943, the Commanding Officer, Major A. A. Ward, who had only arrived three months before, was being moved on to command another unit, and in his place, Major Hopking was to be promoted to Lieutenant Colonel and given command of the Battalion he had joined as a young subaltern twenty-three years earlier: 'His arrival was the best possible tonic at this special time. He at once set to work to fit the Battalion for the strenuous time that was ahead of them.'[8]

Arriving with him from the UK came Major O. K. Leach, who was also returning to Second Suffolk after a period at home serving with another unit. Oswyn or 'Ossy' Leach, as he was affectionately known in the ranks, was a tall Suffolk man, good at sport and a compassionate company commander. He had been commissioned into the Regiment in 1929 and had served with Second Suffolk in India throughout the 1930s, except for the last two years at home.

Then, just a few days later, orders were received for the Battalion to mobilize. A final hurried course of jungle training was rushed through before, on 13 October, the Battalion moved from their training camp to Madras, where they boarded the SS *Ethiopia* for their onward journey to Chittagong.

The Battalion now had just a month to complete their jungle training, though it would at least be under the same climatic conditions as those in which they were shortly to serve. They moved south into the area around Tumbru, fifteen miles south-east of Cox's Bazaar on the Burma border; here intensive training was carried out with the Battalion's mortars and machine gunners, whilst selected representatives from each rifle company went south to gain valuable combat experience with units already in the front line.

The Battalion now became part of 123 Brigade in the 5th (Indian) Infantry Division. It had been the custom, since the days of the Indian Mutiny, to keep a minimum of one British Battalion in each Indian Infantry Brigade in case of unrest, and now the Battalion was to serve alongside men from 2/1 and 3/2 Punjab Regiment, 1/17 Dogra Regiment and 3/9 Gurkha Rifles.

The Divisional Sign that they were later to wear was a red spot on a black rectangle. Officially it went under the nickname of the 'Ball of Fire'. Unofficially it was known as the 'Flaming Arsehole' – in homage to the dysentery that many of its members would suffer whilst serving in its ranks.

In November, the Battalion received orders to move forward into Brigade Reserve to an area around the village of Buywyin, where the Guerrilla Platoon now actively started to hunt for the enemy.

Before going into the front line, one final 'weeding out' of men was carried out, especially of those who had already served their allotted time overseas and were due for imminent repatriation. One soldier, Private Dennis Chaplin, a Battalion Stretcher Bearer, was now going home. 'Arab' Chaplin joined the Regiment in 1937 as a boy soldier, aged fifteen. He joined the 1st Battalion at Plymouth as a Band Boy, before transferring to the 2nd Battalion at Mhow later that year. Upon mobilization, the Bandsmen had all converted to their active service role as Stretcher Bearers.

Heading the other way up to the front were Private Ernie Bates and his chum, Private Les James. They had been Militiamen called up on the same day, 16 October 1939, and had trained together. In India both men served in the MT section, but upon their arrival in Burma there was little use for vehicles and so its ranks were redistributed. Les was posted to 'HQ' Company, whilst Ernie went to 'C' Company.

Some men were sad at having to leave the comfort of their current posting with all its 'traditional' elements of pre-war soldiering, such as the local '*charwallah*', as Private Cyril Wilkinson recalled:

Indian Camp followers, the 'char and wad' *wallahs* of the day, lit a fire and sold egg banjos of a night. I had a craving for these egg banjos and could eat them one after another, washed down with that particular brown paper taste of their char. 'Sung' was this *charwallah* who charged one rupee for his egg banjo.[9]

Major Kenneth Henderson recalled the Battalion's long-anticipated move into the front line:

From Chittagong we marched, about 15 miles each night, for about seven days to arrive at our base camp. The road had been cut through the jungle and rice paddy and by now the rain had ceased so the road was inches deep in sand, with teams of coolies pouring water over it to keep down the dust. We marched at night because it was cooler and because of the risk of air attack. From there we moved to take part in an operation against Japanese positions round Maungdaw, north of Akyab.[10]

The nocturnal march to the frontal positions seemed to many to be an endless one, as Private Cyril Wilkinson continues:

How eerie the night with dust on the track, ankle-deep, swirling chest-high, men staggering in sections either side of the track, the clinking of equipment, the muffled thud of boots and the occasional veiled curse; the sight of the 'bamboo stopes', bamboo huts on raised supports with an endless raised bamboo sleeping platform, quickened the pace, we were fast asleep, no time to take off your equipment, we lay like men of dust, we woke again when it was dark, we marched through the night against the heat of the day.[11]

Burma was quick to claim its first victims. Men of the Battalion fell to various illnesses but were quickly evacuated to hospitals in India for treatment. Many of these cases were, however, 'mad keen' to get back to the Battalion to make sure that they didn't miss out on any of the impending action.

Private Ernie Bates had been taken ill shortly after arrival in Burma but desperately wanted to get back. By a circuitous route, he finally rejoined them at the front:

I was in hospital in October 1943 and worried about getting back to the battalion. I finally made it via Division, Brigade and at last Battalion HQ. Popping my head into CSM Duffy's bivouac: 'Reporting from hospital, Sergeant Major!' 'You haven't shaved' says Duffy – 'Ah well, we must not let standards drop must we? BEARDS!' What a relief, I thought, nothing has changed.[12]

Chapter Three

Burma

'Don't call me sir' he said 'my name's Peter, what's yours?'

The Arakan valley of north-west Burma was to some a beautiful place. Flat, luscious fields of green, interspersed with the occasional steep, densely wooded hill, were set against an often perfect pale blue sky. However, under this beauty a cleverly concealed enemy lay in wait for the Second Suffolk.

In their new positions, on their left flank stood the imposing Mayu mountain range, which had cut the Allied forces in Burma in two. In the centre, along its rocky spine, the Japanese held the high ground together with the two important routes across and through its peaks: the Ngakyedauk Pass in the north and the tunnels in the south.

To the west, north of the small town of Maungdaw, the 5th (Indian) Division were continually pushing south to take the high peaks of the lower range of hills that overlooked the tunnels which carried the road from Maungdaw through to Buthidaung.

The Japanese clung fiercely to these hills, fully aware that those who commanded the tunnels commanded the hills, for this was the only roadway through the mountains, and by taking it the Allies could reinforce and re-supply their beleaguered garrisons on the eastern side. The Padre recalled their arrival and the general situation:

> The big day came when orders were issued to entrain. What rumours went the rounds! Five days later we had landed in Chittagong, so the Arakan Front was our destination. On 7 November 1943, our Brigade took over the front line held by a Brigade from the 7th Indian Infantry Division. The order was roughly, the 5th Indian Division would advance down the western side of the Mayu Range towards Maungdaw, while the 7th Indian Division would advance down the eastern side of the range towards Buthidaung.[1]

Private Cyril Wilkinson also recalled his introduction to 'proper' jungle:

Who remembers the stark black outline of the Mayu range, or when we were told to sleep where you stand, and remembers that early start in the dark to the edge of the jungle proper, with a landscape of terrain the likes of which as far as the eye could see was a mass of rising hills with the density of jungle like a green black wall.[2]

For the Battalion, soldiering in Arakan did present new logistical problems, not least in adapting to the terrain of the area they were now to occupy. For the Battalion Commander, who now found his Companies split over various locations on different peaks and in deep river valleys, calling his Company Commanders to conference was a laborious and difficult affair; but Lieutenant Colonel Hopking, who had been used to summoning men via bugle calls in camp, now took to a unique form of communication in Arakan, as Lieutenant Murdo Duncan, a recently arrived reinforcement from the Welch Regiment, recalled:

I joined B Company of the Suffolks and the O.C. was so typically English that he used to call his Platoon Commanders to his headquarters by means of a hunting horn. We are spread out admittedly over an area of about 300 yards square but that was typical of him.[3]

Not long after their arrival on the Arakan front, the Battalion was visited by the Supreme Commander of the newly-created South East Asia Command, Lord Louis Mountbatten. On 14 December, as the Battalion were settling into their new positions in the front line, Mountbatten arrived:

So it was in a jungle clearing in the depths of Burma, only one mile from the Japs, that our Supreme Allied Commander, Lord Louis Mountbatten, spoke to as many members of the Battalion as could be relieved from their front-line positions. Lord Louis opened his address by explaining that he wished to meet and speak to as many of the men under his command as he possibly could in a limited period, and also as many men as possible could see and meet him.[4]

Mountbatten, who had been made the overall commander in October 1943, was determined to defeat the Japanese. His initial preoccupation upon taking command was to restore morale to the men fighting in the East. The Fourteenth Army had been largely forgotten by the media at home, and many men serving in Burma felt rejected, especially when their counterparts who had fought in the Western Desert and were now fighting in Italy, were receiving so much attention in the press.

Mountbatten set about visiting as many units under his command as possible to speak personally with their commanders and their men and to explain the overall strategic goal that had to be accomplished first: the defeat of Germany. Then, once this had been achieved, all available manpower and materiel could be redeployed against Japan:

> Lord Louis then explained how we who are fighting the Japs came into the picture. He pointed out that Germany must be beaten before we could concentrate everything on Japan. But that until that day we must continue to fight Japan, and fight even harder than before. For if we didn't then Japan would be able to build stronger defences which would be much harder and take longer to beat down. He stated that once Germany was beaten, everything that was used in Europe would be transferred to the East, and then Japan would assuredly and quickly, be thoroughly beaten.[5]

Mountbatten's Aide then told Lieutenant Colonel Hopking that the Supreme Commander wished to speak with men of the Battalion who had fought in other campaigns during the war, along with those who had long service with the Regiment. A quick line-up was hastily prepared for his inspection.

Sergeant Bates, Corporal Stewart, Privates Baker, Brighty, Crossland, Cunnington and Gant were introduced to him in full kit, some wearing the newly issued bush hats, others with steel helmets. They were armed with an assortment of weapons including the recently arrived No. 4 rifle and the Thompson sub-machine gun.

Lance Corporal Lionel Ruffles recalled Mountbatten's visit for a different reason: 'I met Mountbatten once. He was a great man. I was issued with new kit to meet him, but I had to hand it back in again afterwards!'[6]

Sergeant Bates spoke with Mountbatten for some little time. He had served in India since 1937, the majority of his service being with the Royal Norfolk Regiment. The morale of the Battalion was, however, high after just a few weeks in Burma:

> Our morale out here is high, but Lord Louis Mountbatten's inspiring address, coupled with his cheerfulness, personality and high hopes for the future, make us now feel that nothing can or will stop us from getting to whatever we may be told to go.[7]

The Adjutant, however, was distinctly unimpressed by the Supreme Commander's 'pep talk', noting in the War Diary that he 'did not even give a hint on what was planned for this front.'[8]

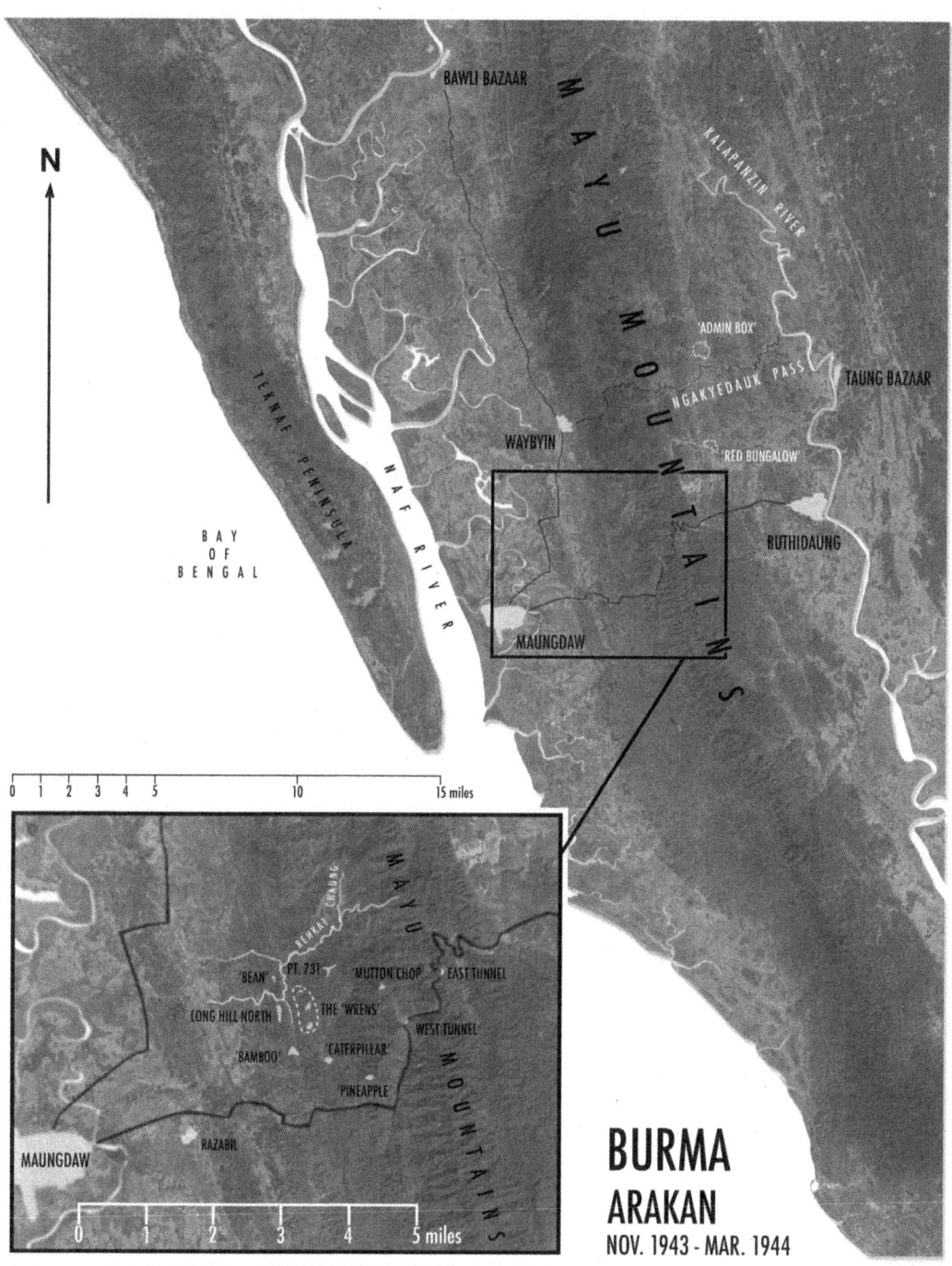

In their new positions, two dominant hill features now presented themselves to the Battalion's front. Looking south, to their left rose a series of shallow peaks forming the overall position known collectively as 'Wrens', whilst to the right was 'Bamboo', a medium-sized hill that rose from the flat green valley below.

Bamboo Hill had a small plateau that looked down upon the important road into the tunnels through the mountains, and beyond it the village of Razabil could be seen. The strategic importance of these mountain features was not to be underestimated. The tunnels through the mountains would, if they could be taken, become a lifeline to re-supply troops fighting the Japanese forces on the opposite side in the precarious positions known as the 'Admin Box' and 'Red Bungalow'.

Here, one thing soon became clear to the Battalion – the absence of any sight of the enemy. The Japanese soldier was a master of camouflage, and it was soon discovered that he would rarely venture off his hill in a direct attack upon yours. He preferred instead a curious form of nocturnal taunting and small-scale raiding. He knew the jungle well and used it at every turn to his advantage. The British at first hated the jungle, but in time they would learn to adapt themselves to its confines. They had to learn the hard way that the jungle was always neutral.

During the Battalion's first few weeks in the foothills of the Mayu Mountains, the Japanese occasionally launched small, daring fighting patrols against them, primarily to test their defences and ascertain their strength. Lieutenant Duncan, who now commanded a platoon of 'B' Company, recalled these early attacks and the accompanying tirade of shouting and wailing that seemed to be the Japanese custom:

My platoon to start with were on a neat little hill only about thirty feet high but with some trees reaching to a greater height. A good position but painfully obvious because it was sticking up among the paddy fields. One night, a party of Japanese came up the river, the Naf River, and they fired a shot or two here and a few more there. We heard it of course and we stood to with every man at his emergency post – an arrangement which we did automatically at dawn and dusk every day these being the most dangerous times, although Japanese attacks came in with wild shouting and shrieking at any hour of the night. Well, we stood to and almost immediately stood down because a Punjabi Battalion behind us fired. We afterwards heard it reputedly had fired thirteen hundred rounds of .303 and eighty mortar bombs, and all we could do was cower in our trenches.[9]

Still well below fighting strength, the Battalion continued to receive a trickle of men from other units. Private Idris Jones, a new reinforcement to the Battalion, recalled his arrival:

> I was interviewed by a senior officer to establish my army trade. I explained that I was a trained Bren gun carrier driver. The officer said that he was sorry but no Bren gun carrier section existed in the battalion. He made an alternative offer of becoming a muleteer. Although I had no idea what he meant, I obviously understood that it was associated with animals known as mules – and immediately rejected the offer. I was directed to 'D' Company, commanded by Major 'Slogger' Leach, and was guided to a section, part of a platoon, and took my place in the front line. Members of my draft were all parcelled out to different parts of the battalion.[10]

The Carrier Platoon had been temporarily disbanded upon arrival in Burma, the terrain making it impracticable to use such vehicles at a battalion level. A few were, however, retained for the ferrying of supplies up from the Battalion's rear areas and for the evacuation of the sick and wounded. Its ranks were redistributed to infantry companies and to the Pioneer Platoon. The non-offensive posture of the Battalion must have seemed odd to some new arrivals such as Jones:

> The area occupied by D Company was criss-crossed by trenches on a sandy hill facing the Japanese front line. 5 Division held the line between Maungdaw and Razabil, while on the other side of the Mayu Range was the domain of 7th (Indian) Infantry Division. D Company was in a holding position, and although there was no immediate attacking action taking place, patrols constantly probed the Japanese front-line areas. Section positions were sometimes mortared and shelled.[11]

The Battalion's first real taste of action came on 21 December 1943 with an early morning patrol of twenty-two men in three sections, under the command of Lieutenant Gray, who set out to reconnoitre 'Point 731' – the highest hill in the locality.

Nearing the position just after midday, the leading section was fired upon by Japanese light machine guns. Scattering into the undergrowth, as was their training, the men moved round on the flanks and made for the pre-arranged rendezvous (RV). In the initial fire, two men had been wounded, and these were being helped back.

Back at the RV, one section was already waiting and was joined by Lieutenant Gray's forward section and the two wounded men, Privates Ward and Watt.

Realizing that they had been spotted and could no longer proceed to reconnoitre Point 731, Lieutenant Gray decided to lay up for the night, in the hope that the missing section would make their way back to the RV. Two of his men now helped Private Ward back for medical treatment, whilst the remainder stayed put. Private Watt, he felt, was too seriously wounded to be moved without a stretcher.

Unbeknown to Lieutenant Gray, the third section, which comprised one Corporal and seven men, had, contrary to their orders, bypassed the RV and made their way straight back to the Battalion area, arriving there around 1600 hrs.

During the night, Private Ward's condition deteriorated, and he died in the early hours at the Regimental Aid Post. Now, the first stragglers started to come back through the Battalion lines. Lieutenant Gray returned with Corporal Wallace and Private MacNaughton at 1600, but another wounded man, Private Hadlow, had since made it to the RV, and he remained with Private Watt whilst Lieutenant Gray and the others returned to get help for them.

Lieutenant Gray now returned to the wounded men with a rescue party, but no trace could be found of either Private Hadlow or Private Watt, and a further patrol by the Guerrilla Platoon the following day also failed to locate the two men. Lieutenant Rod Gray later recalled the event:

> My first patrol in charge of a platoon was eventful. While moving through deep jungle we encountered the enemy whilst we were in a riverbed (*chaung*) and came under heavy fire. One of my men was killed, and we somehow managed to get back to Company HQ. I was immediately told to report to Brigade HQ to give details of my patrol. After this I became liaison officer to General Evans at 5 Division HQ.[12]

Private Bernard Hadlow had originally been a member of the Royal Artillery, before being transferred to the Essex Regiment and then on to Second Suffolk in 1943. Private Peter Watt came from the small Cambridgeshire village of Burwell on the Suffolk border near Newmarket. He had been a journeyman baker, learning his trade but often out of work. He was called up in 1942 when he passed his nineteenth birthday.

The wounding and then the complete disappearance of these two men sharply focused the men's attention on the fact that they had to take care on patrol. Being left wounded and alone in the jungle was a fate that none of them wished to suffer, and overnight, the loss of these men had a profound effect in sharpening the wits of the Battalion.

Despite these two men still being missing, Christmas 1943 was a memorable affair. To many an old soldier who had been used to the peacetime tradition by which officers would serve the men their dinner in barracks, this year under fire in the front line was all quite different, as Private Cyril Wilkinson recalled:

> The afternoon prior to Christmas Eve we got paid. The first Lieutenant sat in his dugout on an ammo box. 'Don't call me sir', he said. 'My name's Peter, what's yours?' I stuffed my rupees in my shirt pocket and wondered! That Christmas, every one of the officers each got a bottle of port, the lads a bottle of Indian Beer, and we stood in our slit trenches as the sun was balanced on the edge of the Mayu Ridge. As a treat 'Admin' cooks had produced a mouth-watering treat in Dixie Lids: jelly with tangerine slices smothered with Carnation evaporated cream. The Dixie lids were placed on the parapets, the lads' eyes and faces lit up with delight. In a flicker rays of sun disappeared behind the ridge, all was dark. The Sergeant's rage exploded, like a madman, shouting 'Stand To! Stand To!' and dashing in front of the parapets, kicking the Dixie lids and contents into the trenches. I don't think the lads of that platoon of 'D' Company will ever forget that incident![13]

Sergeant Nick Carter instantly became the most unpopular man in the Company, and his popularity had not improved by morning, since no Japanese attack came that night. Corporal Bill Skeels of 'D' Company also recalled how unpopular he was following his exploits that night:

> He was a rat to everybody. I will never forget him myself. Massive, black-haired man. Xmas 1943 when men from Admin laid Dixie lids containing jelly and tangerine quarters on the soil of the parapet, and Sgt. Nick Carter, with that despicable look on his face, kicked them all forcefully into the slit trenches.[14]

For some young soldiers, their first Christmas abroad was a happy affair, as yet untainted by action with the enemy. Private Cyril 'Sonny' Mott, a farm worker from Long Melford in Suffolk, wrote home to his sister via airmail: 'It's not too bad out here but nothing like home I'll say!'[15]

After those first few weeks, the Battalion had started to get the measure of their enemy and his habits. The further into the hills their lines now pushed, the more taut the lines of supply and communication became behind them. With no metalled roads, only tracks, all supplies were brought up by mule, placing strain on the men in the front-line, as the Padre recalled:

> We had a most uncomfortable time. The cooks discovered their sites were in the bed of a river, and it was a feat on their part to turn out hot stew

and tea. The mule drivers had a gruelling time, as all supplies by trucks and jeeps ceased, and the mules had to do double journeys to the forward areas. I take my hat off to the drivers and their mules as they brought food, water and ammunition to places inaccessible to jeeps.[16]

However, despite these logistical issues, the Battalion would shortly go on the offensive in the New Year.

Chapter Four

Bamboo Hill

'The spirit of the troops was in accordance with the best traditions of The Suffolk Regiment'

On New Year's Day 1944, orders were received that 'Bamboo' Hill was to be taken as soon as possible by a combined effort of 123 Brigade.

Bamboo was the furthest away of a series of hills to the south of the Battalion's current positions. To the east, a similar series of hills ran in parallel across the valley. 2/1 Punjab Regiment were to occupy the north-easternmost hills, with 1/17 Dogras occupying the series of hills beyond them to the south known as the 'Wrens' – consisting, from north to south, of 'Wrenkitten', 'Middle Wrencat' and 'Wrencat'.

The Wrens took their name from the stream that ran in the bottom of the valley below them known as the 'Rehkat' *chaung*. This, in the parlance of the 'Tommy', became 'Wrencat'. Second Suffolk was given the responsibility of taking 'Long Hill' in the south-west and then Bamboo Hill that lay beyond it.

Long Hill consisted of three peaks, linked by densely wooded slopes and interlinked by narrow tracks known as 'saddles.' By late December the Battalion occupied all three peaks, sharing the northern one with Battalion HQ of the Dogras. The next phase was for the Battalion to take Bamboo Hill itself, whilst in parallel, the Dogras on their left flank would move forward to attack the Wrens.

The operation against the feature began on 2 January, with the Guerrilla Platoon going forward to reconnoitre Wrenkitten on the left flank. This feature had a shallow, semi-circular plateau and was on the northern side of Middle Wrencat.

The Guerrilla Platoon moved across from their positions near Battalion HQ, which was then situated on another hill to the north of Long Hill. They crossed the riverbed in the bottom of the valley and made good progress towards Wrenkitten from the west. In parallel, patrols of 'D' Company now probed the western edge of Wrenkitten, searching for a way to get up and across to Middle Wrencat. Private Cyril Wilkinson, now serving in 17 Platoon, 'D' Company, recalled that patrol and coming face-to-face with the patrol from the Guerrilla Platoon:

> Our section came across a dried-up riverbed. As we moved up it there were sounds of increasing activity from ahead and a bush-hatted officer followed by troops burst into view shouting, 'Every man for himself!' Mortar bombs started falling and heavy machine gun fire added to the confusion.[1]

The following day, in bad weather, Captain Forrest took another section of 'D' Company out on patrol to reconnoitre Wrencat, as Wilkinson continues:

> On an atrociously typical monsoon day, he took a fighting patrol, of which I was a member, to probe the summit of a hill feature, which lay in the region of Point 731. This seemed to be connected by a long saddle to a hill feature known as 'Wren Cat' and the one we were to probe called 'Little Wren Cat' [Wrenkitten]. The rain fell in bucketsful; I dropped the Bren in a raging *'chaung'* with dire consequences to follow. We reached the summit, which was in cloud. It was impossible to stand because of the slope; we propped ourselves by letting the bamboo support us; we were miserably cold and wet. Captain Forrest ordered me to open fire on automatic into the cloud. The gun fired only one round and jammed. The dropping of the gun into the *'chaung'* had jammed it with shale.[2]

Expecting a severe reprimand, Wilkinson waited, but without a word to anyone, Captain Forrest suddenly went forward alone:

> He disappeared into the cloud and rain; we heard the thud of a grenade, then crashing through the bamboo, Captain Forrest appeared, shouting like an excited schoolboy and repeating he had put an enemy machine gun post out of action manned by 'Jiffs', his map case and equipment flapping like a banshee. For many days after I was subject to many inspections of my Bren gun![3]

'Jiffs' were Indians fighting with the Japanese. An abbreviation of 'JIFC' (Japanese Indian Fifth Column), they were predominantly members of the Indian National Army, formed following the British defeats in Malaya and Singapore. Funded and armed by the Japanese, they agreed to fight alongside them in the hope of taking control of India in the event of a British defeat. It would not to be the last time the Battalion would come up against them.

The following day, 4 January, another patrol of the Guerrilla Platoon was operating in an area south of Middle Wrencat when they heard firing. It was a similar patrol of 'D' Company, which had met with enemy fire when crossing the riverbed to reach Wrencat.

From their positions between Wrenkitten and Middle Wrencat, the Guerrilla Platoon could now see 'D' Company's predicament, caught in the open by Japanese fire that could be brought down upon them from positions on Wrencat. Realizing that they now had little chance of retreating without being spotted, a member of the patrol, Corporal Brown, broke cover to establish one of the Guerrilla Platoon's Bren guns on a small outcrop on the Wrencat side of the river.

Bringing down fire on the Japanese positions, he succeeded in drawing away the enemy's fire from Wrencat, allowing the 'D' Company patrol to extricate themselves safely. About an hour later, a party of Japanese tried to make their way round to the south of Long Hill, stalking 'D' Company's route back.

The Japanese now tried to fire upon 'C' Company, who were dug in on the northern side of Long Hill, but once again Corporal Brown, now accompanied by another Bren team, fired upon them and after an exchange of fire forced them to retire. Once their ammunition was exhausted, the team withdrew, but as they crossed the river, Corporal Brown realized that one member of the patrol, Private Heal, was missing. Without hesitation, Corporal Brown went back across the *chaung* alone and along the track to try and locate him.

Brown found Heal lying badly wounded in the dense bamboo and carried him back across the *chaung* and on to the Regimental Aid Post, from where he was taken back to hospital.

Corporal, acting Sergeant Richard 'Dickie' Brown's actions that day would earn him the Military Medal, the first awarded to a member of the Battalion during the campaign. The Regimental History paid tribute to his actions:

> It was here that Sergeant R. Brown got a chance to show his quality. In spite of extremely heavy fire directed on the Company, Sergeant Brown with an L.M.G. silenced three of the enemy machine guns and although an enemy 'cut off' party started to shoot up the rear of his position he continued firing and silenced two more machine guns. He then successfully retired under cover of darkness.[4]

In the firefight three men were wounded and Private Grimes of 'D' Company was killed. Leslie Grimes was a young soldier who had only recently joined the Battalion as a reinforcement from the Royal Norfolk Regiment. He came from Tottenham in London.

Early on 6 January, two more patrols left the Battalion area heading for Wrencat. One under Captain Forrest was approaching the feature from the north-west, from the bottom of the valley between the feature and Long Hill. The other patrol, under Lieutenant Fildes, approached Wrencat from the west.

In parallel to this, Captain Ennion was out with another patrol which managed, unmolested, to reach the summit of Wrencat itself. Here they met a bamboo palisade fence, which they got through with relative ease, but having crossed a single coil of enemy wire, they were suddenly met with a hail of fire and forced to retire.

Lieutenant Fildes' patrol returned at 1800 reporting that they could not reach Wrencat's summit due to poor visibility and enemy fire. By the time Captain Forrest had arrived back at Battalion HQ half an hour later, the Brigadier had arrived and was in conference with Lieutenant Colonel Hopking. Brigadier Winterton, then commanding 123 Brigade, stayed to listen to Captain Forrest's narrative and the intelligence that he brought back about the position. The Brigadier commented on the patrols' activities that both were 'very good, and much useful information was obtained'.[5]

The following day was uneventful as rain continued to fall, but the day after, Lieutenant Watt patrolled to Wrencat, setting off at noon and following the previous route taken by Captain Forrest. He returned the following morning, reporting that the enemy were now digging in intensely and strengthening their positions that had been breached by Captain Ennion two days earlier. Overlapping Lieutenant Watt's return, Lieutenant Inman left the Battalion area at 0930 with a fighting patrol heading for 'Caterpillar' Hill in the east and a small 'Ring' feature beyond. They returned that evening reporting that the Japanese still occupied the Ring.

10 January was quiet, except that 'C' Company were shelled on the southern peak of Long Hill for a quarter of an hour, after which the bombardment promptly ceased. The following morning, the Mortar Platoon retaliated by shelling Wrencat for a quarter of an hour at exactly the same time.

Following their initial actions against Bamboo Hill, on 12 January the Army Commander, Lieutenant General Bill Slim, visited the Battalion and was introduced to 'all available officers', although many were out on their various hilltops or on patrol. The Padre recalled his visit and some ribald remarks from a nearby soldier: 'About that time, General "Bill" Slim came to see the men and gave us a pep talk. Who was it shouted "Char wallah!" just as General Slim walked past? It wasn't meant for him, of course, but then he may not have known that!'[6]

Another soldier later remarked, 'Although his name was Slim, he was actually rather stout.'[7]

Before leaving, the General observed the Mortar Platoon in action shelling Wrencat.

Two days later, Lieutenant Glover took another patrol over to Wrencat in the early hours of the morning. Moving down into the valley with the intention of crossing over the Rehkat *chaung*, they were ambushed by Japanese, and

Lieutenant Glover was shot in the right foot. The patrol were able to extricate themselves swiftly and, with help, Lieutenant Glover hobbled back through the Battalion lines for treatment.

On 15 January, on the Battalion's right flank, a company of the Punjabis attacked a feature known as 'Right Knob' along with its smaller outcrop known as the 'Hook'. Their advance was part of a larger scheme involving an airstrike by twenty-four Vengeance dive bombers and a pounding of these positions by 28 (Jungle) Field Regiment, Royal Artillery, whose guns were based on nearby 'Mutton Chop' Hill.

The action was successful, with the dive bombers hitting all their intended targets, after which an aerial combat ensued in which twelve Zero fighters were reportedly shot down, although one soldier was badly wounded by their fire in the Battalion's area. Though he was swiftly evacuated, Private William Bloomfield sadly died of his injuries in a Calcutta hospital six days later.

Right Knob was successfully captured by the Punjabis, but at 0550 the following morning the Japanese counter-attacked in strength but they were successfully beaten off. Seeing that they were holding their own against a greater Japanese force, the Dogras now attacked Point 731 in the hope that whilst the Japanese were distracted, they could take the position. However, despite their most gallant efforts and the assistance of several Vengeance dive-bombers, they could not take the position and were forced to withdraw.

Just after dark, a party of four Japanese infiltrated through the Battalion lines on the southern end of the 'Mound' – the name the Battalion had now given to the hill where Battalion HQ was positioned. After an exchange of grenades, the Japanese withdrew, but there was 'desultory fire during most of the night'.[8]

After a couple of days of enemy inactivity, on 18 January the Japanese again tried to infiltrate the southern end of the Mound, trying to drive a wedge between the Battalion and the Dogras, but they were again beaten back by grenades. Lieutenant Colonel Hopking was now called away to Brigade HQ to a commanders' conference, at which plans were outlined for the taking of Point 731 and the advancing of the line south towards the Maungdaw-Buthidaung road.

Upon his return, the CO ordered a complete reshuffle of his men in their respective positions and outlined the Brigadier's thoughts to his Company Commanders. The Battalion would be required to take Bamboo Hill as soon as possible and then assist the Dogras in their attacks to take the Wrens. Patrols now went forward again to ascertain the enemy's strength and his positions.

In the reshuffle, 'C' Company was now replaced on Long Hill by 'D' Company, allowing them to become a 'Mobile Reserve' concentrating in the area around Battalion HQ on the Mound. 'B' Company on Wrenkitten was now relieved by 'D' Company of the Dogras.

Now, all Suffolk Companies were concentrated around the Mound and Long Hill on the northern side of the Rehkat *chaung*. The move was completed by 20 January, after which active patrolling towards Bamboo Hill recommenced.

Japanese reconnaissance patrols were now becoming more frequent, particularly at night. In the area of 'Cock and Bull' – between Long Hill in the south and Battalion HQ in the north – the Pioneers laid additional booby traps during the night to guard against any enemy infiltration towards the Mound. Not surprisingly, at 0645 when it was still dark, these traps were set off by a Japanese patrol looking for a route through to Long Hill.

For Suffolk soldiers in their foxholes and observation posts, these hours of darkness were ones of tension and fear, as 21-year-old Corporal Dell of 18 Platoon, 'D' Company recalled:

> Nobody at home seems to know what it is like out here. The newspapers tell you very little, they mention bunkers, but do you know what it is like to stand in a bunker for hour after hour, night after night? Have you ever been afraid of the dark? I have, we all have, only it's a hundred times worse out here. You stand in your bunker in the dark, and it rains and the bugs and mosquitoes come around and it stinks something horrible.[9]

Cyril Dell had enlisted into the Home Guard in 1940 as a boy runner, before joining the 70th (Young Soldiers) Battalion of the Royal Norfolk Regiment. He was then transferred to 1 Suffolk, then on to Second Suffolk.

Throughout the night, numerous strange noises could be heard. The danger lay in not knowing exactly what these nocturnal sounds were. They might be jungle creatures moving, or enemy patrols advancing, or a wounded man trying to make his way back:

> Wild animals slither through the bushes and you think they are Japs, birds flutter in the trees and you think they are Japs, although you know the Japs are only just over there, you dare not smoke lest you give away your position. If your pal falls asleep and begins to snore you sock him. If you snore, he socks you. You dare not use your rifle because the flash shows up your position, you use only hand grenades at night.[10]

At dawn, two patrols were sent forward to reconnoitre Caterpillar Hill, situated to the south-east of Bamboo Hill. Moving round to the southern end of the feature, Lieutenant Lee Hunter of the Guerrilla Platoon, along with one Other Rank, went to observe the east side of the feature, whilst another patrol comprising Lieutenant Hastie and three Other Ranks went to observe the west side.

In conjunction with these, two more patrols carefully took the other points of the compass: Lieutenant Gray reconnoitred the south side, whilst Major Gurney took three more men and skirted along the northern edge of the feature.

Major Gurney spotted a party of Japanese with a wireless set on a small hill beyond Ring Hill, but the Allied artillery in their positions beyond the Wrens had already spotted their movement and now started to bombard the positions.

Lieutenant Gray returned to Battalion HQ the following morning with more definite information concerning the enemy positions on Caterpillar Hill, and based upon this, the CO now felt that he could commence his attack on Bamboo Hill. Lieutenant Gray's patrol had one man, Private Moody, missing and despite returning to try and find him, no trace of him was ever found.

Private Herbert Moody was twenty-four years old. He was, as far as can be established, the only member of the Royal Armoured Corps to join the Battalion in Burma. He was part of a mix of reinforcements who were posted to the Battalion in early December 1943 from various units, including the RAC, the Pioneer Corps and the Royal Artillery.

On 24 January, the attack recommenced. 'A' Company now advanced towards Bamboo Hill from Long Hill, whilst their counterparts, the Dogras, pressed forward on the left flank to try and take Wrencat.

During the initial advance onto Bamboo Hill, one platoon made good progress pushing forward up its steep, thickly wooded slopes to get to a position just thirty yards from its summit; but moving around onto its flanks, unbeknown to them at the time, the Japanese had machine guns situated in shallow, connected bunkers in the shape of a horseshoe on its rearward face. These now barked into life, halting any further advance to the summit.

With casualties mounting, Captain Gray, commanding 'A' Company, now decided that he would consolidate where they were and dig in as best as possible. His men lay on a small plateau about 30 yards wide by 15 yards in depth. Using their entrenching tools, since no picks or shovels were carried in the initial advance, within minutes his men were down below the surface, using what they could of the scrub to cover their actions as much as possible. The soft sandy soil made it relatively easy to dig down fast.

When a lull in the enemy's fire came, Captain Gray sent runners back down to Battalion HQ with information on the enemy dispositions. As darkness fell, 'A' Company remained on the plateau in their foxholes, and overnight they deepened them further. Amazingly, the Japanese did not harass them.

Meanwhile, back at Battalion HQ, the CO, armed with 'A' Company's information, revised his attack plans to now assist Captain Gray and push the advance forward to the summit. Together with Major Richards, who commanded 'C' Company, they formulated a plan to restart the attack the following morning.

Major Richards now planned to take all three of his platoons and Company HQ forward. With two platoons leading, Company HQ and the reserve platoon would follow in the rear. They would follow the route of 'A' Company's initial advance to link up with them at the plateau. Then they would all advance from there to the summit. With 'A' Company giving covering fire, when the summit was reached Major Richards would split his two platoons and move around the flanks of the hill to attack the machine guns in the bunkers of the horseshoe trench beyond.

Watching 'C' Company's advance from Long Hill was American war correspondent and artist Millard Sheets. In an article that was later published in several magazines and periodicals in the US, though never in Britain, he wrote of how he watched their determined advance to join 'A' Company at the plateau for the final assault. But they had been spotted, and soon the Japanese brought fire down on them:

> The Bamboo was still getting it half an hour later and you wondered how those fellows you had seen slip off so quietly into the jungle below were making it. The shelling drowned all other sounds. Were they up to schedule? Had they run into trouble and we couldn't hear? The jungle remained a silent screen to our eyes but could not screen our thoughts. Having climbed a well-cut trail through similar growth, through the same grasping, sweating tangle of vines and grass, you know the difficulty of their every step in the uncut tangle. You can see them falling from creepers that tug at their feet – falling in mud hidden by grass so tall it almost smothers you, partly by its density and partly because it may hide sudden death. They struggle towards their objective – direction particularly frightens them; twisting, turning, climbing, crawling – going around an impassable two or three yards confuses them. They can't see out through the taller shrubs and trees above the grass and vines. The sour stench of unaired rotten growth combines with the itch and the crawling of little black bugs in their sweat to sicken their already aching bodies. Fear that the moving grass may bring sudden death increases with every step. But, if blindly, they must go on to climb the last steep distance to the top.[11]

Then came a moment's silence, before the Battalion's solitary machine gun opened fire:

> The artillery has now ceased, to be replaced a moment later by the machine-gun fire. This fire rakes the summit and serves to guide the men below. This must be moving well along by now. One has stopped to check his time – he

finds he is slightly ahead – he must pause, but only for a moment. He wishes to God he could have kept going while he was stunned by the confusion. In the last hour it has seemed as though he were someone else following a strange body through the jungle – as though the body has been in mortal danger but he was not. Muscular effort has nearly ceased to be an effort and the only real physical sensation had been the enormous pounding of his heart. Otherwise his body has seemed to float unguided but with power to resist the dragging creepers, as if propelled by some powerful drug. The slight pause destroys this illusion and things have come back into focus. Everything has become real again as the agony of great weariness sweeps clear through his body. He wonders if he can ever drive that body out of its great inertia into action. Visions of home and everything important there sweep in front of him. Tenderness mixed with bitterness clouds his already blurred eyes as he wishes he could rip the bellies of the bastards who think war is noble and that it solves everything. He doesn't want to look at his watch – he's afraid it's almost time to move up again. It is time and that sick, horrible feeling in his gut turns him into rubber. The firing stops suddenly – no more excuses now. He has checked his tommy gun a hundred times already but he checks it again and starts his last climb ...[12]

As 'C' Company disappeared down into the bottom of the valley and out of his sight, Sheets wondered how they were getting on. As they came back into sight on the slopes of Bamboo Hill itself, he continued to watch their difficult ascent:

From our perch high above we waited anxiously for the final plunge to the summit. Minutes dragged by. A tommy gun broke the silence and then all hell broke loose. Machine guns with a slower beat than ours dominated the bedlam. They were the Japs – damn them. After all the pounding from the air and from our guns, they were still there. Rifle fire, a muffled shout to 'come on' were drowned by mortar fire lobbed from behind their hill into our advancing men – mortar fire disastrously accurate. Japs appeared in the very bunkers and positions that had been erased by our fire. They had come out of the holes dug too deep to destroy. Our advancing infantry was too close now to risk firing on the Japs although the Japs could sweep the jungle below them with fire. After a long time it was quiet again. No one said very much. The Japs disappeared into their hill. I could hear the tired and monotonous voice of the observer in the foxhole above me describing over the telephone to company headquarters the thing that had happened ...[13]

Upon reaching 'A' Company at the plateau, Major Richards now decided not to head directly for the summit but to start from the plateau and move first around to the south side of the hill, whilst 'A' Company gave him covering fire. In parallel to this, 'A' Company agreed that they would now advance once again from their positions to try and take the summit itself, then assist 'C' Company by providing fire from the summit down into the bunkers of the horseshoe trench beyond.

As soon as 'C' Company set off, 'A' Company tried again to advance to the summit. However, just a few minutes after they set off, 'C' Company's advance around the hill met with a hail of fire from the bunkers. They had been advancing steadily, but now the enemy fire was so intense that they were stopped dead.

Out in front with his leading platoon, 'C' Company's commander, Major Richards, was hit in the shoulder. As he prepared to set off back to the Regimental Aid Post for treatment and stood up from the undergrowth, a shot from a Japanese sniper killed him. With little prospect of advancing further, it was decided by Lieutenant Lawrence that 'A' Company would now remain where they were: midway between the plateau and the summit.

Despite the loss of Major Richards, 'C' Company tried again to complete their 'sidestepping' move around the feature, this time slightly lower down its slopes on the opposite side, pushing between the bunkers on the reverse slopes and the enemy foxholes on the summit in an attempt to circumnavigate the summit and join up again with 'A' Company on the plateau.

Under continuous sniper and rifle-grenade fire from the bunkers, and with several men wounded, 'C' Company did, however, succeed in making their way around to effect a link-up with 'A' Company.

Meanwhile, to the north-east, a single Vickers medium machine gun of the Battalion was positioned on 'D' Company's hill – north of Long Hill – and was giving covering fire to assist 'A' Company's advance. Firing over the men on the plateau, when the infantry had advanced far enough the crew packed up their precious gun and swiftly departed from their hill. CSM Kevin Duffy of 'D' Company recalled the event:

> Well I remember that single MMG, two other members were Privates Earle and Barber and one more name I cannot remember. When we carried in 'A' Company to Bamboo as far as we could with safety, we made rather a quick old move off that hill in 'D' Company area. So fast, in fact, that one of the crew lost his footing and got to the bottom in double quick time! No bones were broken, so we just carried on.[14]

That single Vickers gun was something of a 'treasured' object in the Battalion, but it showed the acute lack of adequate medium machine guns, weapons that the infantry desperately needed to support such advances. However, unlike some units in their Brigade, Second Suffolk were already well-trained in the use of MMGs in close quarters infantry support, as CSM Duffy continues:

> Before Bamboo, the 2nd Battalion were the only unit in 123 Brigade who had men who knew anything about an MMG. When I took over and was told to select a crew, I will always remember the words of our Commanding Officer: 'To be put to its fullest use'. I believe my Company Commander, Major Henderson, was present at that time. That gun, at the time, seemed to be a personal present from Brigadier Winterton to our Commanding Officer. I am sure (I know, really) that the gun crew and myself treated it as such. That gun in honour of our Commanding Officer was 'put to the fullest use'.[15]

Whilst 'A' Company stayed put on Bamboo Hill for a third night, Lieutenant Thursby took two teams of stretcher-bearers forward to bring the wounded in under cover of darkness. Behind them, carrying parties from 'A' Company HQ brought up ammunition to re-supply those in the frontal positions.

This initial attack on Bamboo Hill had cost the Battalion eight killed, fifteen wounded and five missing, in what was the first major action for Second Suffolk. It gave them a taste of what was to come and of the enemy that they had come here to fight.

On the morning of 27 January it was decided that 'C' Company would leave 'A' Company on the feature, move to another feature on the right of Bamboo Hill and try to attack the bunkers from there. This second feature was known as the 'Hook', but to reach it, 'C' Company would have to undertake a dangerous side-step in full view of the enemy bunkers on Bamboo Hill; however, it was thought possible. For a third day, with food and water almost gone, 'A' Company were left alone on the plateau.

Not long after 'C' Company set off, Captain Mitchinson, who had assumed command of the Company following the death of Major Richards, was himself badly wounded in the arm by a grenade and had to be evacuated. He had been engaging a party of Japanese who had infiltrated across the Battalion's lines of communication lower down the slopes of Bamboo Hill behind 'A' Company on the plateau. In going to Captain Mitchinson's assistance, Lieutenant Inman, who commanded a platoon of 'C' Company, was also wounded by a grenade, but his men pressed onwards without him and reached the Hook shortly afterwards.

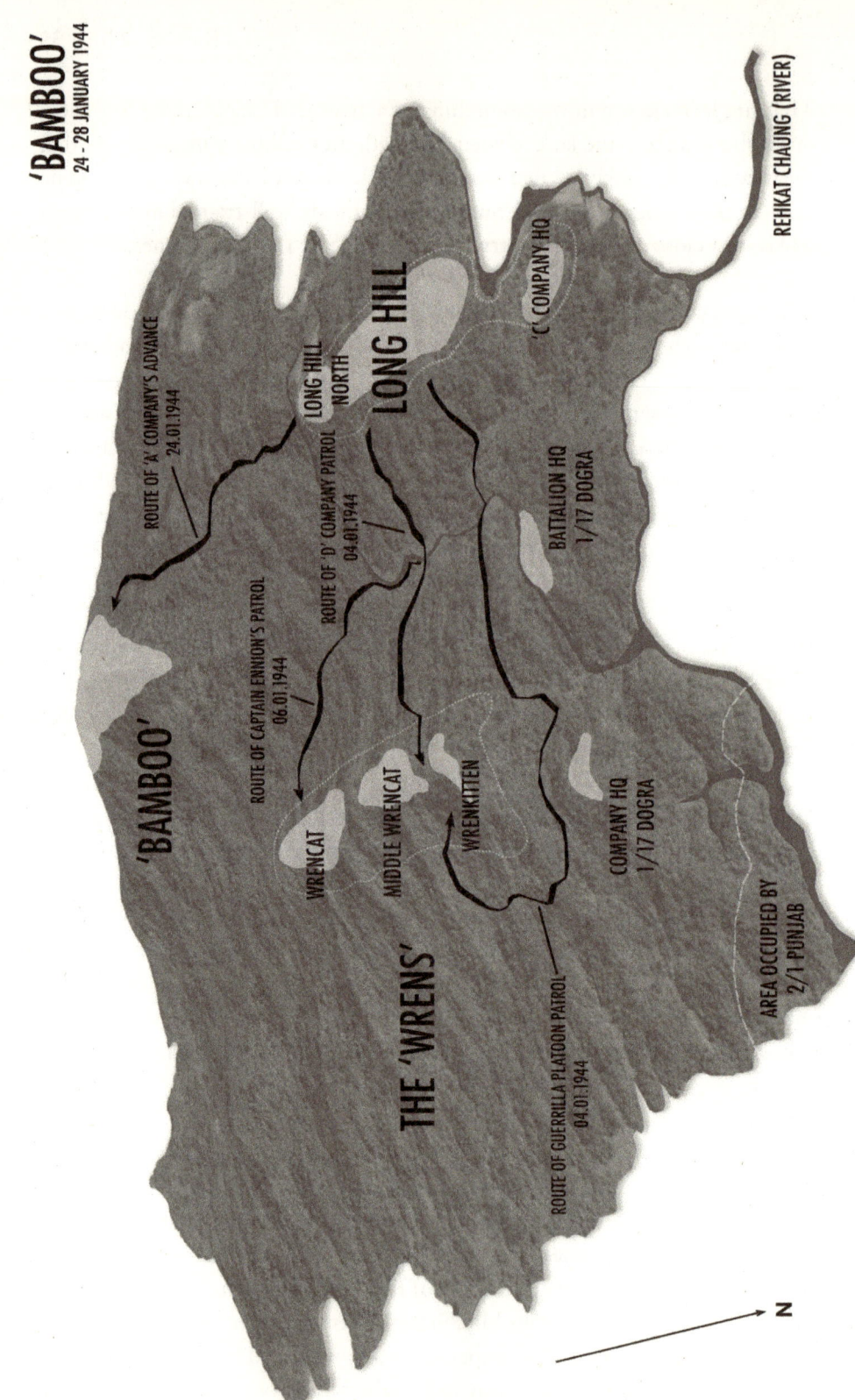

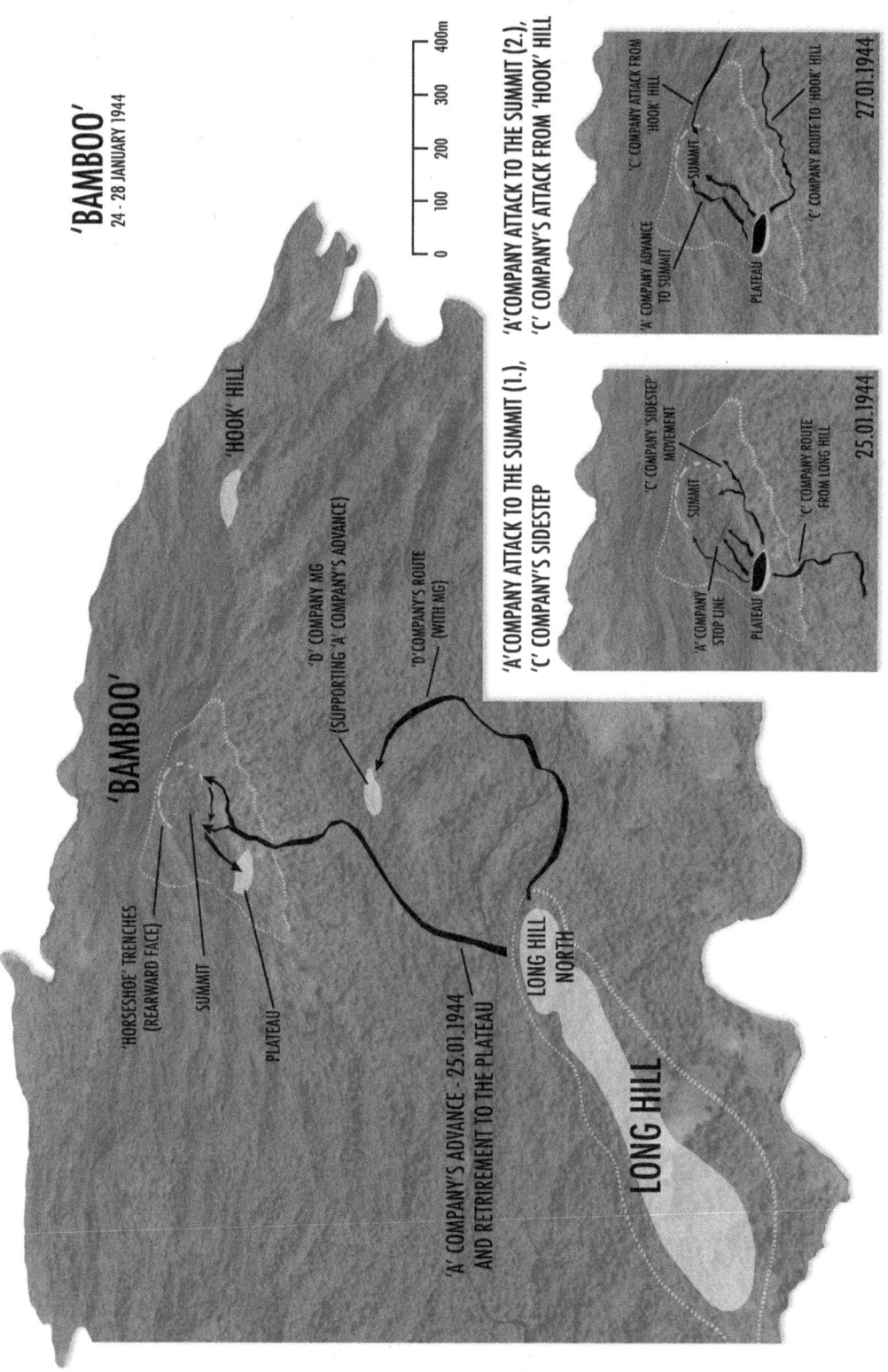

As Captain Forrest came forward at dusk to assume command of 'C' Company, the men out in front were already consolidating their position on Hook Hill. Though shots were exchanged and the odd grenade thrown, the night was described as 'quite stable'.

'A' Company on Bamboo Hill were mortared and machine-gunned by the Japanese just after noon on 28 January, then came a frontal assault upon them by the Japanese on the summit.

In a frenzied attack lasting just less than half an hour, the Japanese tried again and again to advance on 'A' Company's positions. Each time they were beaten off, but each time they came back stronger. As the final effort was again rebuffed, and seeing that to their left the Dogras were attacking Wrencat, 'A' Company's commander, Captain Gray, decided to advance in the hope of taking the summit whilst the exhausted enemy's attention was partially distracted.

Leading his men, Captain Gray now pushed forward. It was tough going, with heavy enemy mortar fire and dense bamboo that made it difficult underfoot, yet they kept up a steady pace. Soon they had visual contact with the enemy and they increased their fire upon them. Moving forward, Lance Corporal Salter led his section on regardless of the heavy Japanese grenade and mortar fire that was directed upon them. Single-handed, he destroyed two bunkers using grenades as they advanced up Bamboo Hill's northern face. Then, when his stock of bombs was exhausted, he moved round to the east to assault another position that had not previously been spotted. With accurate and steady fire he subdued this position as well, allowing the advance to continue. For these gallant actions he was awarded the Military Medal.

Lance Corporal Salter's efforts ensured that the Japanese positions were temporarily silenced. This allowed one platoon to make it to the summit, but in the advance Captain Gray was shot and had to be evacuated. As he was carried away from Bamboo Hill he died on the stretcher before reaching the Regimental Aid post.

Back out in front, Second Lieutenant Tomkinson had reached the summit with a small party of men and a few Sappers who were engaged in 'stiff hand-to-hand' fighting with the Japanese. Having successfully forced away the enemy, they were now being subjected to heavy machine-gun fire from Japanese positions on Wrencat. The Sappers had successfully laid a pole charge down towards the horseshoe trench. Blowing it had the desired effect, and it was noted that they 'blew the Jap occupants to pieces'.[16]

Despite the supporting artillery fire from 'Ant' and 'Bean' Hills, and a troop of Lee tanks now in a position close to Wrenkitten that could fire armour-piercing shells directly onto Bamboo Hill's summit, the Japanese machine-gun fire was too intense, and with casualties mounting, Second Lieutenant Tomkinson decided to withdraw.

Beating a hasty retreat, some made it back to their previous positions on the plateau, others dropped down the steep slopes of Bamboo Hill deep into the valley below. Many of the wounded had to be left around the summit, the stretcher-bearers being unable to reach them due to the intense fire: 'The enemy in position on the reverse slopes brought such heavy mortar and grenade discharger fire to bear that the platoon was forced off the summit, slithering down its precarious sides to the bottom. On their left the Dogras' attack had also failed.'[17]

It was those dreaded dischargers, the 'Type 10', that the men learned to fear the most. Like the British equivalent, the 2" Mortar, this form of mobile artillery could cause havoc when fired at close range; the grenades burst overhead, sending down shards that tore through anything in the vicinity.

Despite their 'extraordinarily determined attack',[18] the Battalion's third major attempt to take Bamboo Hill had failed.

It was now a time of bitter dejection for those men of the Battalion who had fought so hard to try and take the hill. It clearly showed the Battalion how fanatical the enemy was in his determination to retain the position. He had constructed deep, comprehensive defences in which he could shelter from the blast of artillery, only to re-emerge after it had passed and resume the fight. His camouflage was excellent, and he hid those defences well.

Now in a final act of retaliation, the Japanese brought down their artillery and mortars onto positions behind Long Hill. Though the positions were out of sight of the Japanese, their shells still found their targets, as Millard Sheets recalled:

I was down in a little ravine behind the hill where I was living with some Tommies, and they used to bring tea up twice a day, with open buckets tied onto the backs of burros [donkeys], one on each side. Of course the so-called tea was always filled with saccharine, and you had grasshoppers and bugs of various kinds. You never had a lid on anything. I was standing there with two Tommies, who were about six feet away from me. We were talking, and they gave me some of this lousy tea, then they started right down our ravine. From Bamboo Hill, the Japanese were lobbing shells over the hill where the trenches were, right into this ravine. They knew the terrain so well – they'd been over it; they knew it – and these shells came bing, bing, bing, just like that. A shell hit the ground about twenty feet away, just absolutely cut off the face of one of the men. The other guy was killed, but I wasn't scratched, never even scratched. It killed the donkey. I was standing on the other side of the donkey and I think it shielded me. I don't remember what it was, but such things happened so many times in the war that I just couldn't believe it.[19]

Private Idris Jones also recalled that bombardment and its aftermath:

I remember one horrendous battle vividly. An attack was made by 'A' Company of the Suffolk Regiment on a hill which was held by the Japanese, but they failed to take the hill. A mortar bomb landed in the cooking area and killed all the cooks. I was part of the burial party. We buried nine men that day, and thirty more were wounded in the attack.[20]

Two days later, looking out from his foxhole over to Bamboo Hill just a couple of hundred yards away or so, Major O. K. Leach was writing a brief piece for the *Suffolk Regimental Gazette*:

Further to the fact that we are in the 14th Army – and proud of it – we have been in the front line for 2½ months without rest. In that time we have made what War Correspondents call 'local advances' as well as doing the famous 'local patrols'. The date is now January 29th and there is a slight lull in our battle which started on January 24th. It has been a spell of intense activity and full of never to be forgotten memories. 'A' Company went in first, then 'C' Company the next day. These two companies have certainly done their bit. Although we have not actually gained the actual high features which were our objectives, it has not been for lack of effort.[21]

Not far away, Captain Hildesley was sending his final intelligence summary of the month to Brigade HQ, reporting the Battalion's final actions against Bamboo Hill. He recalled the importance of the supporting fire that had been rendered by the troop of tanks that had supported the Dogras in their attack on the Wrens; that had later assisted 'A' Company in reaching the summit of Bamboo Hill, but it was in those crucial final yards to the objective that the covering fire ceased and the infantry had to press on alone:

A Coy moved off 1450 hrs and when the tanks and artillery had finished the platoon were well up the hill. The shelling drove the Japs to the south end of the hill and all our men got on top all right. Japs got an M.G. into a trench and the first two Japs to man it were shot. But they eventually got the gun into action. There then came a shower of grenades from the south. The Sappers got a pole charge off in a trench where 3 or 4 Japs were. One Cpl. shot 3 Japs with his T.S.M.G. [Thompson sub-machine gun] who hid in a trench. By now we has sustained a few casualties and 2/Lt. Tomkinson decided to withdraw fast off the top for 3 minutes in order to re-organise. They tried this but it was so sheer that they found themselves about 40ft. down in one step, so they came off Bamboo driven off by M.G. fire from a flank.[22]

Commendation of their determined actions was now received from the commander of 123 Brigade. In a signal to the Battalion Commander, Brigadier Winterton wrote to Lieutenant Colonel Hopking congratulating his men on their actions:

> The Brigade Commander wishes to congratulate Suffolk on the gallantry displayed in to-day's operations, which could be witnessed by all. The spirit of the troops was in accordance with the best traditions of the Suffolk Regiment.[23]

Further commendation was received from the Commander of Fourteenth Army, Lieutenant General Bill Slim, via the Commander of 5th (Indian) Division, Major General Harold Briggs. A signal received stated:

> The Army Commander and Divisional Commander are very proud of the magnificent show put up by your Battalion during the past four days and again today. It was beyond compare. Please give wide circulation to this message.[24]

Praise was also given to the gallant actions of the two Company Commanders who were killed in the action. Captain Douglas Gray was a pre-war Territorial officer with 5 Royal Norfolk Regiment, joining them in 1938. He had narrowly avoided capture at Singapore in February 1942 and managed to escape to India, where he was posted to Second Suffolk. His fellow officers thought highly of him:

> Throughout four days of hard fighting, his personal example and leadership were outstanding. His was a happy Company, one can say no more. His many friends in Norfolk and Suffolk who knew him well, in happier days, will mourn a good friend and a fine officer. We, who have served with him, will continue the fight inspired by the memory of his passing.[25]

Major Patrick 'Dickie' Richards had been with Second Suffolk for over five years. In an appreciation of him, Captain Philip Papillon, a fellow officer who had just returned to England, wrote:

Since the war he held only one objective in life and that was to get into action and to do his bit to finish the war at the earliest possible opportunity. The smaller points of peacetime soldiering only annoyed him during a war, and it was thus with delight that, at long last, he was able to lead the Company which he had commanded so long into the front line. He was killed as he himself would have wished – at the head of his troops. As was only too well known by those who served with him the men he commanded would have followed him anywhere under the most adverse conditions. Suffice it to say that the Suffolk Regiment has lost a regular officer whose inspiration and leadership set to those of us who remain to carry on his work an example which will be hard to attain.[26]

It was a bitter irony that just five months later, Philip Papillon would himself be killed in action commanding 'D' Company of 1 Suffolk at the Chateau de la Londe in Normandy, and from their jungle positions, others of Second Suffolk would then be paying a similar tribute to him.

Major Richards was held in high esteem by his men, so much so that one man, Private Michael O'Conor, a recently arrived reinforcement from the Oxfordshire and Buckinghamshire Light Infantry, wrote a poem which he dedicated to him:

> He died in the path of duty
> Leading his men to attack,
> The bullets that got him were many
> They hit him front and back.
>
> In his death there lies a story
> Has been told full many a time,
> A tale of courage and valour
> By which his soul may shine.
>
> His body lies in the jungle
> Mid grass and trees, to wit,
> They buried him as a soldier
> A soldier of valour and grit.[27]

It was Private O'Conor who had bandaged Major Richards' first wound before he was hit fatally for a second time, and he later volunteered to bury him in the Battalion Cemetery.

Following the battle, a tale of comradeship emerged that, due to the loss of Major Richards, would have gone unrecorded were it not for a letter home from a young soldier.

Private Whetnell, who lived in Perry Barr, Birmingham, wrote to his mother following the action at Bamboo Hill telling her of one of his comrades' actions. She later sent his letter to her local newspaper, which published it:

> They made the top of the hill but were heavily mortared. George refused to leave under fire and had to be kicked off the ridge by his officer. He had seen one of his mates fall and wanted to go back for him. For three days they held on under the Japanese position and were then ordered to withdraw, as men were being sniped while getting supplies to them. A few days later, I saw George staggering into our H.Q. with a sack on his back. I asked him if he had the rations. 'No', he replied. 'I've got my mate.' George had volunteered to look for his mate's body to bury him decently in a cemetery we had made. He had staggered over three miles of tough jungle under the terrific mid-day sun with just a rifle and ammo. That was George, and his name wasn't mentioned as the O.C. was killed in the action.[28]

Private Leslie Whetnell was originally a member of the Royal Warwickshire Regiment, having been drafted to Second Suffolk in 1943. He later served as the Intelligence Section Clerk and had, amongst his other duties, the important task of mapping the numerous jungle burials of men of the Battalion. The Padre also recalled the action at Bamboo Hill and its aftermath:

> Bamboo Hill was the first feature where the Battalion drew blood. The thick jungle made it very difficult for the men to spot the enemy, and losses, grievous losses, were incurred in killed and wounded. The little cemetery which was named 'XII Military Cemetery' became the resting place of officers and men – those who had laid down their lives for a just and righteous cause. Before we left the area a concrete plaque was made by one of the men of the Pioneer Platoon. Then on a Sunday morning, a never-to-be-forgotten day, we held a Memorial Service in the cemetery. Our C.O., Lieutenant-Colonel H. R. Hopking, read the lesson. With bowed heads we remembered our fallen comrades and gave thanks to God for them. They were dead and yet one felt they still lived. The loved ones of these men were remembered, and we prayed that they might be given the grace and strength needed for the days which were ahead.[29]

Another man killed at Bamboo Hill was Lance Sergeant Daniel Edlin. He had been serving with 'C' Company, but his body was never found. Born in Chobham, where his parents kept a public house, he was a recent arrival to the Battalion, having been transferred from the Buffs (East Kent Regiment) in mid-1943. He had been called up in July 1941, having previously served as a gunner on a Defensively Equipped Merchant Ship, being responsible for shooting down a German bomber at sea, for which he received British Empire Medal. He had previously served with Admin Company before joining 'C' Company in India on 2 October 1943.

Badly wounded during the attack on Bamboo Hill was Private Jack Barfield, who sadly died of his injuries six days later in hospital. Jack had lived in the village of Bramford just outside Ipswich all his life until he was called up. He worked for the local fertilizer firm of Fison, Packard & Prentice and had been captain of the works football team.

Another man who would die of his wounds in the days that were to follow was Private Vincente DaCosta, who had been wounded with 'A' Company during the initial attack on 24 January. Of Portuguese origin, his parents lived on the island of Macau which, throughout the war, the Japanese respected as a colony of neutral Portugal.

The exploits of Lance Corporal Frederick Salter made the news in his home city of Exeter with an article entitled 'Exonian's Gallantry on Burma Front'. Frederick lived with his parents in Parr Street, but their house was badly damaged by incendiaries during a German air raid on the night of 4 May 1942 and later had to be demolished. The mention of his award in the British press was the first public notification of the Battalion's actions on the Burma Front.

Following these battles, two of the Battalion Signallers, Privates 'Jack' Dash and 'Maxie' Mattin, now had the unenviable job of communicating between hilltop positions using the age-old method of shutter signals and flags which were employed when the radios failed to work. In sight of the Japanese snipers far forward on Bamboo Hill, it was a dangerous business, as Jack recalled:

> We were sitting ducks to the few Jap snipers that remained on the next hill. Maxie's signal flag – for we used flags when the radios didn't work – was well and truly peppered and I suffered a stray shot to the heel of my boot. The Jap was a pretty lousy shot we found, but I was glad to get off that hill. You never seemed to be away from the Jap in Burma, and you always got the feeling that he was watching everything you did.[30]

The Mortar Platoon's correspondent to the *Suffolk Regimental Gazette* shared Jack's opinion of snipers: 'Many of us have now had an opportunity, at some time or other, of being a target for a Jap sniper. They are rotten shots.'³¹ It was noted later that:

> The advantages which might have been gained by their skill and patience in concealment were largely nullified by their poor marksmanship. Even snipers, who were specially trained, showed a general inability to hit moving targets at much more than 50 yards' range. As machine-gunners and mortarmen, however, they were very capable, and their artillery was often used imaginatively, particularly the little infantry guns which frequently opened fire from unexpected positions at point blank range, to great effect.³²

Many of those wounded in the attacks on Bamboo Hill recovered quickly to return to front-line service with the Battalion. Some, however, were old soldiers who had already served their time, having been with the Battalion for over five years, and their hospitalization led to a swifter repatriation than was planned for them.

Among the wounded in the first attack was Private S. R. B. Abbott, who had the distinction of being wounded with two Battalions, on two fronts. An old soldier who had served in India since 1933, he was wounded attacking Bamboo Hill with 'C' Company on 25 January and after recuperating was repatriated back to the UK to serve with 1 Suffolk in Europe. He was wounded a second time in the cold winter of 1944/45 when the 1st Battalion were dug in along the River Maas in Holland.

Another man of 'C' Company wounded that day was Private Herbert Satchell. He had been promoted to Lance Corporal in India, and then on the eve of their departure for Arakan to full Corporal, but just days later, he requested to be allowed to revert to the rank of Private, not having a liking for the increased responsibility.

The Battalion would not launch another attack on Bamboo Hill. It sat there taunting them with their failure to take it. However, despite their losses, the lessons learnt here were invaluable: intelligence on enemy positions was key, and frontal assaults were not the way forward. The Battalion had learnt the hard way how to fight the Japanese, and their learning curve was short and steep, but they were now thinking like their enemy and starting to use the jungle and the terrain to their advantage:

> These frontal assaults against strong and consolidated bunker positions, supported as they were by equally strong flanking positions, had been costly; it was decided that the Brigade on the right should launch an

attack against the flank and the rear of the Jap defensive lines from the direction of Maungdaw.[33]

The Battalion now reverted to active patrolling. The order of the day was encirclement, and pincer movements around and through the enemy's flanks were now favoured. If one could get at the Japanese rear areas and cut their lines of supply, one could then encircle and besiege their positions. Stealth and infiltration were the watchwords of any future attack.

Artillery, too, now began to play an important role in supporting the infantry attacks. In order to get their artillery pieces into position in the jungle, various Royal Artillery regiments were now positioned within infantry 'Boxes'. Thus, after the attack on Bamboo Hill, the 28th (Jungle) Field Regiment, Royal Artillery were positioned on Long Hill in the newly created 'Suffolk Box'.

Whilst artillery was a morale-raiser, it was also much distrusted by the soldiers in frontal positions. When the two sides were sometimes just yards apart, an incorrectly ranged barrage could cause unnecessary casualties by 'friendly' fire, as had been seen during training in India. Daily, the gunners sent F.O.Os and F.O.B.s (Forward Officer Observation and Forward Officer Bombardment) into the frontal positions to range for targets that were to be attacked, sometimes with mixed results, but often highly successfully. (See Appendix I)

As January drew to a close, the Battalion lost a further draft of thirty-two men who were being repatriated. At a time when morale was low, the loss of these 'old hands' was greatly felt.

Despite the costly and determined fighting of the preceding week, the actions of the Battalion occupied just four lines in the official history of the 5th (Indian) Division, which noted that 'The 2nd Suffolks shared Bamboo Hill with the enemy, and on January 28 made very determined effort to capture the hill. They reached the top, only to be forced to withdraw.'[34]

Like many who fought here, CSM Tommy Warren recalled later the disappointment at their failure to take Bamboo Hill: 'Many will recall our bitter fighting in our endeavours to dislodge the enemy. They may relive the disappointment felt when we realised we would never stand on that southern bank of the *chaung* as its new tenants.'[35]

In concluding a piece for the *Suffolk Regimental Gazette*, Major Leach struck an upbeat tone for its readers at home. Sending copies of the two congratulatory signals, he noted: 'We are all in great heart. Our casualties are about 55 and nearly all these wounded. We are sending back two messages – not because we want to boast – but just to show you that we *are* doing our stuff. And now on with the battle.'[36]

Chapter Five

'Men of the Arakan'

'Johnny Johnny, over here!'

February opened for the Battalion with a sizeable draft of reinforcements arriving to bring the depleted 'A' and 'C' Companies back up to strength following their actions at Bamboo Hill. Seventy-six men arrived from the Base Camp at Deolali, fifteen of whom were from 1 Lincolns direct from a Transit Camp in India.

A reshuffle of officers was now carried out, with Captain Squirrell becoming Second-in-Command of 'B' Company, Lieutenant Calver taking command of one platoon in 'B' Company and Lieutenant Keft becoming M.T.O. (Motor Transport Officer).

On 4 February, as Vengeance dive-bombers swept in low over them to attack Wrencat and the Ring feature once again, the 'Support Platoon' was being formed. It had been experienced in the recent attacks that, with all three platoons of a company committed to battle, should any difficulty arise or a situation present itself in which additional men were required, there was no mobile reserve at hand. It was therefore decided to create a platoon that could follow in the rear of an advance and be at hand if called upon.

Lieutenant Box now commanded this new unit, which would comprise one sergeant, two corporals and twenty-one other ranks. Weapons were varied but included two recently arrived .303 Vickers medium machine guns, four Bren guns and two Boys .55-inch anti-tank rifles; the latter was a cumbersome, unwieldy and highly unpopular weapon which was most unsuitable for jungle use.

The following day, Lieutenant Arrindell took over command of the Intelligence Section, whilst Lieutenant Ellis took over command of the Mortar Platoon.

On 6 February, Lieutenant Gray returned from patrol just before a heavy shower of rain fell, making the roads impassable. Now, in awful weather, the Battalion took over all of Long Hill, with the Dogras vacating their positions there. The rain eased just before dusk, and during the night an unsuccessful Japanese raid resulted in Corporal Kirk and Private Bullock of 'A' Company being wounded by grenade splinters.

Documents taken from enemy dead by the Guerrilla Platoon now confirmed that their opponents around Bamboo Hill were the 112th Japanese Infantry

Regiment, largely assisted by 'Jiffs'. A 'mock' attack was now planned by the divisional artillery against Bamboo Hill to 'entice Japs from their positions'. It was hoped that this would reveal the enemy's positions and bunkers, allowing the infantry to attack once more and finally take the position. However, the Japanese, seemingly wise to the ruse, attacked first and brought down heavy mortar and grenade fire on the Battalion's positions. Later that afternoon, an enemy sentry was seen bobbing up and down from a trench line that crossed the summit of Bamboo Hill, but it was thought to be a dummy.

With no major advance planned for the Battalion, now came days of 'tit-for-tat' fighting, and for the next few weeks neither the Battalion nor the enemy would take any great offensive action. Instead, each side limited itself to small punitive raids, making 'token' attacks upon each other in their rear areas, just to ensure that the element of fear of an impending attack was maintained. It was a frustrating time for the Battalion, who yearned to go on the offensive and take Bamboo Hill from the enemy once and for all.

The Battalion, still dispersed on various hills, continued to follow its daily routines as normal. Supplies could only be brought up to within a mile of the front line positions by vehicles, so the remainder of the journey had to be completed by pack mule, and finally by the men themselves.

Though boxes of mortar bombs, ammunition and rations were crucial to keeping up the fight, it was the tins of clean drinking water that were essential to the safe and healthy survival of the Battalion. Water had to be rationed, and whilst water bottles had to be kept filled by order, the remaining personal allotment for washing, shaving and the brushing of teeth had to be closely monitored.

Whilst shaving daily was mandatory, the rules were 'bent' somewhat when supplies of water became scarce. CSM Tommy Warren recalled the predicament of many a newly arrived soldier who had to be strong-willed enough not to guzzle his drinking water too quickly: 'Those young soldiers, many not long from England; brave young men, raw, and still apprehensive of the jungle, judging when to take a sip of water from a bottle that has to last 24 hours.'[1]

On 8 February more old soldiers left on repatriation. Major G. T. O. Springfield, who had not long been with the Battalion in Burma, received orders for his own return home, together with CQMS Kerridge and Sergeant Nice. All were time-served old soldiers who had been with the Battalion before the war.

CQMS Harry 'Kate' Kerridge had joined the Regiment on 3 January 1923 and had now attained his '21' with the Colours. A labourer from Witnesham near Ipswich, he later served with the Royal Army Service Corps, before retiring from the Army in 1952.

After their departure, enemy movement was reported from 'B' Company's positions on Long Hill. Down in the Rehkat *chaung* below them, Japanese patrols were seen and grenades were thrown in response. The following morning, as air battles continued overhead, 'Point 731' was shelled by the artillery.

On 10 February, Major Leach took a patrol of 'A' Company out to their previous positions on 'Pipe' Hill. They found several of their booby traps that had been blown, and a considerable number of enemy dead lay about in various stages of decomposition. It was clear that the Japanese had not wished to recover their dead for burial.

In parallel to this, 'C' Company now moved out from Long Hill with their place being taken there by 'Admin' Company, who now shared the hill with 'B' Company. The following morning, a platoon of 'D' Company withdrew from nearby 'Sickle' Hill and were sent onwards to 'Sausage' Hill. 10 Platoon of 'B' Company under the command of Sergeant Bissell were now detached and detailed off from Long Hill with orders to occupy a small hillock in the southeast. From here, they observed artillery fire being brought down upon Bamboo Hill in the early evening, and after the fire had ceased, the Battalion's mortars continued the bombardment for a further half hour.

On the morning of 16 February, Lieutenant Colonel Hopking returned, having spent the previous night at Brigade HQ, with new orders that now the Battalion were to fall temporarily under the command of 161 Brigade in their Division.

As another platoon of 'D' Company changed places with its counterparts on Sausage Hill, an unfortunate accident occurred. The Mortar Platoon accidentally fired at the hillock that was still occupied by 10 Platoon. Sergeant Bissell who had remained there with a section of men, was killed, and six of his men were wounded.

Sergeant Arthur Bissell had joined the Battalion in 1942 and served with 'B' Company in India, before moving to 'C' Company for their final training. When they arrived in Arakan, he was sent back to 'B' Company. He was buried later that afternoon in the Battalion Cemetery.

Within the Battalion area, the pathways between the various positions were soon worn brown with continual tramping, and any form of movement between them became physically demanding. CSM Stan Winter recalled the topography and how it prevented the establishment of any form of centralized Sergeants' Mess: 'You see, we never "get together" these days. The reason being that the Companies are dotted about on the hill-tops of the Burma Jungle, and the routes to and from these hill-tops are both numerous and deadly, thus the Sergeants' are isolated from one another.'[2]

In the humid conditions the radios seldom worked, and often it was easier to send a man with a message to Battalion HQ. Cables laid out for field telephones never seemed to hold for any great period, since enemy patrols would routinely sever them in the hours of darkness. Runners would therefore have to make journeys of over two hours from one peak to another, thoroughly exhausted and caked in mud when they arrived at Battalion HQ with their messages.

In an attempt to keep the essential areas of administration clean and free of mud, large coconut mats were pegged out at Battalion HQ, the Regimental Aid Post and the Cookhouse, but the fast-growing jungle shoots always had a way of finding their way through these mats.

The men now settled down to live a hermit-like life, in some ways not unlike what their fathers had experienced during the Great War. Behind front-line positions, small caves were dug out of the muddy hillsides, each occupied by two or possibly three men, with maybe just a small shelf carved out for a pack and a few home comforts. Private Ernie Bates of 'C' Company recalled his quarters:

> You had what we called a 'cubbyhole' where you would put a picture of a loved one or your shaving items. Later, when we saw direct hits on these scrapes and men's bits and bobs being strewn across the hillside, we took to keeping everything in our packs. If you were lucky, you'd have a groundsheet or a tarpaulin to cover the entrance.[3]

In between these positions the bamboo was left to grow tall, often to over six feet. The men created covered pathways through it, and it shielded their movement between the various positions from the enemy. The onslaught of the monsoon rains meant that drainage was paramount to ensuring that their 'scrapes' were safe from collapse, and hasty revetments often had to be made with wood from ration boxes and crates:

> Life has been a little uncomfortable recently, but at least we have had plenty of washing water. The climatic conditions have also caused a noticeable improvement in design and building of 'Jagas' and bashas or whatever you call your 'sleeping berth'.[4]

The Padre also recalled life in those days. Between the local wildlife and the unexpected arrival of local children, it seemed that there was never a dull day:

> Reconnaissance parties were sent out to get information about Jap positions and 'digging for victory' was begun in earnest as the men prepared for the struggle that lay ahead. There were the usual false alarms until the men got used to the noises of the jungle. Even so, one solider swears that a small bear got into his bed at one end while he made a quick exit at the other! There was one nerve-shattering, but amusing, incident in one platoon, where three youths arrived from no-man's land each triumphantly carrying

an unexploded bomb, and asked for buckshees for them! The English language was inadequate, even for the sergeant, in telling the youths what to do with them and in double quick time too!⁵

These small scrapes and dug-outs had numerous names, many of which had a familiar theme: 'Several of our temporary homes have been given names such as "Pin-up Villa" and "Repat. Avenue" – "repat" of course, being the most-talked-of subject among the old hands.'⁶

The monotony of daily routine without action soon began to wear down the men's morale. During the hours of darkness all sorts of strange noises could be heard which made most soldiers feel uneasy. Amid the chorus of howling animals and buzzing insects, many men felt isolated and entirely alone, despite having a comrade just feet away, each taking his turn to sleep whilst the other kept watch.

These men knew there were no 'rear areas' here and that those same strange sounds could easily be covering the stealthy advance of an enemy patrol that might suddenly attack at any moment. It was perhaps the sense of isolation that preyed most upon their minds; that they had to stick it out as best as they could and that there could be no retreat. Corporal Cyril Dell described those Arakan days in a letter home. His resentment at being part of a forgotten battlefront was evident:

> There are no entertainments, NO, not anything of the kind, you would lie under your mosquito net and listen to strange noises. Your pal in the next bunker is doing the same. Night after night, day after day, we stick to the same ordeal but for victory we are praying may it all soon come to an end so instead of sitting in bunkers, we can sit in our homes.⁷

Despite the seriousness of the situation, there were, however, times when amid the routine ordinary soldiers found time to joke. Private Arthur Partington, who was called up in June 1940 and had served first in the 8th Battalion, was a great joker. One of the Battalion's Buglers, his son recalled some instances of his father's humour:

> My father served in the 2nd Battalion of the Suffolk Regiment in India and Burma and he never seemed to take the war seriously and was always in trouble. One of many jokes involved cutting a swastika in the drill sergeant's hair. Another was to blow on his bugle the American reveille and almost give the Sergeant-Major a heart attack! Not surprisingly, he never rose above the lowest rank of private! ⁸

On 14 February the day started quietly, with only spasmodic fire being brought upon the Battalion by random Japanese patrols crossing the valley floor below them in the direction of Bamboo Hill. Overhead, Vengeance bombers were active all day, whilst the Battalion waited for a large-scale enemy attack that was expected that evening.

Captured intelligence had suggested that the Japanese would attack that night, and because of this, the Battalion were 'stood to' earlier than usual, but as darkness came and the hours ticked away, the enemy failed to materialize. With no attack forthcoming, at 2330 the 'stand down' was given.

Daily patrols went out to given hills to check for any enemy movements, whilst overhead the fighter-bombers seemed to be taking the only offensive action. As the artillery pounded Bamboo Hill once more, Private Sharpe of 'A' Company, who was out on patrol in the valley below, suffered slight shrapnel wounds from being too close to one explosion.

As more and more barrages fell on Bamboo Hill, the position was carefully observed. With each close strike, additional bunkers were spotted that had been unknown when the Battalion attacked three weeks before. The Japanese had hidden these well, and it led to a belief that deep within the hill the positions might be interconnected by tunnels.

On 19 February, Lieutenant Calver took a patrol out towards Long Hill South in the hope that they could 'bag' a prisoner for interrogation. Footprints had been spotted in the area the previous day, but despite having spent several hours covering the spot in the hope of a return visit by the enemy, no one passed by.

The following evening, two Japanese soldiers were seen crossing the *chaung* from Bamboo Hill heading towards 'B' Company's positions. Grenades were thrown, and they retired. Upon inspection the following morning, bloodstains were found in the area indicating that at least one had been wounded.

On 21 February Mitchell medium bombers passed low over the Battalion, heading east to attack the area of the tunnels through the mountains. Escorted by Hurricanes and Spitfires, they were quite a morale-boosting sight. However, that afternoon, the enemy on 'Chimney' Hill retaliated with a barrage against 'D' Company; thankfully, there were no casualties.

Two days later, it was now the Guerrilla Platoon's chance to try and bag a prisoner. Moving off early towards 'A' Company's old positions near 'Pipe' Hill, they too met with failure, for no enemy came their way.

That afternoon, the CO decided that in view of the inactivity on the Battalion front he would invite the officers, NCOs and a party of other ranks from their comrades in the Dogras to a 'tea party' in the area behind Battalion HQ. The gathering was a 'great success', as was later recalled in a newspaper article at home:

In the clearing was a gathering of soldiers, British Tommies, lean and sun-tanned, seated beside short, well built men of the famous Indian Regiment. In the centre was a gramophone from which came the strains, one minute an American swing band, and next, a song of ancient rituals and customs. The men present were chatting and laughing, frequently clearing their throats, with the contents of tin mugs clasped in light and dark hands alike. To the casual observer the whole atmosphere was one of peaceful goodwill and friendship. He might even imagine that it was all taking place in a quiet corner of a cantonment somewhere in far away India. And so well it might be apart from the distant thump of artillery and the high-pitched whine of shells passing overhead, bound for a billet in the homes of the enemy, where they could be seen sending up clouds of smoke and dust into the clear blue sky. This was no peacetime station, but merely a brief interlude in war, for a matter of hundreds of yards away sat little yellow men, the invaders of peaceful Burma. The very members of the gathering had only a short while back been fighting side by side to oust the enemy from his fox-holes in the surrounding hills, and probably some of them would in a few hours hence be pitting their wits against the soldiers of the Rising Sun, or patrol far into enemy country. This was indeed but a brief interlude in the chaos of war. It signified more than a short period of rest; it told a tale of comradeship, a mutual trust between men who in nature and looks were as far apart as the Poles, but in their hearts was a mutual bond, that of soldiers fighting for a cause dear to them both. That surely is what makes soldiering even under the worst of conditions bearable to man.[9]

The correspondent noted the close affinity between the Dogras and the men of the Battalion:

Now a few words about the Regiments and men taking part in this party; and party it was; for in the tin mugs was rum and on plates were heaped cakes which looked strangely akin to a mince pie, but were in fact an ingenious invention produced from ration biscuit and fruit and nuts! To get back to the point, the British soldiers were members of a famous East Anglian Regiment; men who before the war had lived in small villages and towns in Suffolk, Norfolk and the surrounding counties, but here and there one detects the voice of the indomitable cockney, who has the honour of gracing, sometimes in infinitesimal strength, every known unit in the British Army. To the Indian soldier in the party runs an almost parallel tale; they, too, were soldiers of the land and their Regiment. The Dogra

Regiment holds an equally high reputation for doggedness and offensive spirit in military circles. They had fought their way to Donbaik in the first Arakan campaign and were now back again fighting just as valiantly over country from which they had previously been forced to withdraw due only to lack of numbers.[10]

Despite the language barrier, these two battalions still found a unique way to communicate:

> As one stands and watches these men of different countries and language it strikes one how amazingly well British and Indian soldiers can converse. The Tommy using all odd words that he knows of Urdu, usually under a camouflage of extraordinary pronunciation! The Sepoy in his turn mixes his few words of English in with his native tongue; between them they carry on a perfectly intelligible conversation.[11]

The party over, the routine continued, with patrols venturing out into unpatrolled areas of the jungle. Lieutenant Murdo Duncan recalled the 'virgin' terrain which they had to traverse:

> Perhaps I should try and clarify the term jungle as it applied to much of Burma and certainly to our part of the Arakan. Nothing like the Amazon Jungle, or a tropical jungle. On our maps it was shown whitish, white jungle we called it, and it was composed of, and I don't know what the botanical term is, it was very thick scrub, perhaps about six to ten feet high and, although one could always see the sky and distances, if you were above these bushes, you could quite often patrolling, or marching, take two or three right angled compass bearings to be sure of maintaining your direct line. There was also a lot of bamboo on the hills and that was an absolute pest. Once you bent it to get through, it sprang back and trapped your pack.[12]

Writing home to the *Bury Free Press*, Major O. K. Leach recalled the stagnation of the advance, but also the important work that was being done behind the Suffolk positions:

> We have made a dent in the Jap line, and have built up tracks through the jungle to our forward Companies. All their maintenance has to be done by hand, and some of the way is fairly well sniped. The Battalion has bagged six snipers in the last ten hours and this has now become quite a sport.[13]

The following morning, Captain Anslow was evacuated with yellow jaundice to 45 Indian Field Hospital for treatment. He was temporarily declared 'S.O.S.' (Struck Off Strength), but later that afternoon, it was reported that the Ngayedauk Pass had been opened, and now the first casualties from 7 Division's area on the other side of the mountains were being evacuated away behind the Battalion's area for transportation back to hospitals in India.

The air offensive continued on 25 February as Second Lieutenant Stephens and Lieutenant Thursby went out to the south-west to place more booby traps. Back in the Battalion area, command of 'A' Company now passed to Captain Forrest, as patrols continued to venture out towards 'Sickle' and 'Pipe' Hills.

As the month drew to a close, the Dogras on the Battalion's left flank were being withdrawn and replaced by 1 Royal Scots Fusiliers (R.S.F.) from 29 Brigade. That day, too, Lieutenant Duncan with Privates Dixon and Risebrow took off on a reconnaissance patrol to the south, looking for a route to advance round and take Bamboo Hill.

On the last day of February, Major E. G. W. 'Gordon' Browne rejoined the Battalion and was given the role of Adjutant. He had been away for a period of almost a year, serving with Wingate on his first expedition. He had originally been commissioned into the Regiment in 1936 from Sandhurst and had already seen fighting in May 1940 with the 1st Battalion in France, where he had managed to row out from the beach at Dunkirk to a waiting ship with what remained of his platoon. He recalled the situation that now confronted him in Burma:

> The battalion were spread widely in company localities each on a dominating hill feature. The hills were very steep-sided and actually with a knife-like crest at the top. Positions had to be hollowed out of the sides and platforms built up. Except in a few clearings, ground visibility was no more than a few yards. The area was covered with dense scrub growing to a height of ten to twelve feet and was usually elephant grass or bamboo. Water was fairly plentiful in steam beds but was beginning to dry up. The climate was hot by day but reasonably cool at night and there was no rain. Sickness was well under control though the malaria rate was higher than it should have been. I took over A Company after a short time and from now on I shall write mostly of them. The war was very gentlemanly just then. We had already tried to dislodge the Japs from their positions opposite, but for various good reasons had failed, and were now waiting for operations elsewhere to develop. We were at extreme small-arms range (700–800) [yards] and saw very little of each other. Anything we did see we 'beat up' with mortars and machine-guns, and the occasional patrol went out. The Japs fired a few shells but they didn't worry anybody. An inexperienced unit would

have had lively nights as the area was stiff with small bears, deer and other game which sounded like Jap patrols. Elephant had been in the area but had been cleared off. Soon other formations attacked on our right and left with very heavy artillery and tank support, and we had a grand-stand view which would have made a most exciting film. The Japs opposite us were forced to clear off with hardly a shot being fired.[14]

Lieutenant Lawrence, who had been wounded during the attack on Bamboo Hill, returned from hospital in early March and was immediately out on patrol again. However, within a couple of days he was wounded again near 'Leach' Hill – another feature to the south-west of Bamboo Hill. A Japanese soldier was seen and a stick grenade was thrown, wounding Lieutenant Lawrence in the face and Private Southgate in the back.

The patrol made a cautious return to the Battalion area through 'B' Company's forward positions. Later, Lieutenant Lawrence was evacuated to the Regimental Aid Post, where the Medical Officer, Captain Schwatz, removed most of splinters from his face, before he was sent onwards to the Advanced Dressing Station to have the remainder extracted.

As a result of the intelligence that Lieutenant Lawrence had brought back, the Battalion's Mortars now opened up on Leach Hill and Pipe Hill, with retaliation coming from the Japanese on the slopes behind the Battalion Cookhouse. No one was injured, and cooking continued throughout the bombardment, with Cook Sergeant Cropley standing in his white apron with his hands on hips, unperturbed by it all. Despite his giving the Japanese snipers a good aiming point, they never fired at him, and that night all was quiet.

The following morning, whilst Vengeance bombers again flew over the Battalion's positions to attack Bamboo and Ring II Hills, two public relations officers arrived at Battalion HQ. One was a photographer and the other was the former BBC correspondent, Paul Chadburn, who was then writing a series of articles on British units serving on the Burma front.

Many items of captured Japanese equipment were now brought out for them to view, and whilst Chadburn started to interview members of the Battalion, his photographer took several pictures of the men in their various Company areas. The photographs he took that day included one of a group of men eating dinner, whilst another was of Major Leach at the entrance to his dugout catching up with news from home in a recent edition of the *Suffolk Regimental Gazette*, which he had just received by post. The following edition, received a few weeks later, would contain the official notification that his wife had given birth to their son back home in Surrey on 15 February.

Chadburn's article appeared later in the April 1944 edition of the Army weekly magazine *Parade*. Chadburn was himself a Suffolk man and had much in common with the men he interviewed:

The men live on jungle-covered hills; East Anglia in arms is removed into scooped-out cells. Like a colony of cenobites, the gigantic beard of the jungle hanging all over and around. Furniture is two blankets and a mosquito net; laid in neat rows on niches within hand reach are things like small iron pineapples [grenades]. Nearby holes lead into dark, cold galleries underground, pale shafts of light penetrating the sandbagged slits. In narrow gulleys from time to time, three men gather in monotonous tableaux; crude-looking pieces of iron piping there bark, quiver, smoke a bit. The group disperses. At intervals comes an urgent rushing noise, a sinister singing over the tree-tops. Now and then, a thing about the size of a corpulent bream – if you were to see it whole – drops out of the sky and bamboo crackles up in flames. Or, as a drone screeches into a roar and a shadow of wings races over a clearing, bits of jungle fly apart in bamboo splinters, roots, dust and smoke.

These are the sheltered places. There are other hills not far off, barer, more blasted, bleak as sugar loaves. You reach them over open, undulating ground, alternatively dipping into cover and rising into full view of the Jap across the valley. Nine times out of ten, he'll let be; the Jap's a bad shot anyway. Mortar bombs, shells, have torn jagged holes in the ground. Incendiaries cleared blackened patches. At the foot of the pimple men loiter smoking – one is having a hair cut where a dozen mortar rounds fell short a while ago. You soon get the knack of recognising the bang across the way and getting your head down in time; well-behaved shells do not drop sharply enough to hit the gulley. A board beside the track leading across a lower slope at the floor of the steep stairway says 'Harley Street'. At the top of the steps a trench curves round in a semicircle facing the Jap bunkers opposite. The outer sides are pierced like the walls of a castle. Men sit in niches, cleaning tommy guns, playing nap. A small mortar on the parapet bangs, sending a thing like a lump of coal spinning high into the air, curving, knocking up a puff of smoke across the way. From time to time, a shell lands there, beating up the dust. Twelve Vengeances drone high overhead; the crump of bombs comes from the Buthidaung crossroads; in a few minutes the dive-bombers are back again, heading north.[15]

The article continued:

This is a quiet day. It is not always so. A short while back the East Anglians made an expedition; they met a host and quelled it; they forced a strong position, and killed the men who held it. That was at Bamboo Hill. Infantry attacks on the foothills of the Mayu range are tough. Your approach is narrowed at times to a sheer upwards track. Japs, sitting pretty above, just lob grenades down. Attacks are made by day, for concealment and surprise are impossible where the rustle of a leaf will draw a volley of machine-gun bullets. Yet movement at night there is. In a cell on a hillside, drinking a mug of char, with the Oxford Book of English Verse beside him and a dozen men in bottle-green jungle dress sitting amongst the bamboos round about, we came upon 'The Monk'. He is the officer in command of the Guerrilla Patrol, picked men who go out, sometimes for six nights on end, probing the Jap lines, blowing up dumps, and by stealth piously performing every sort of devilry they can contrive. They may not risk the valleys (*chaungs* they are called); by roundabout ways they must proceed along the heights. They must not speak except in rare whispers. By day they lie up, mumchance. Twenty-nine times already these men have gone out into the night of the jungle. When they return, the 'vow' may not be broken; the brotherhood become sitting instead of creeping cenobites. Their daily newspaper 'Seac' they do have, and mail from home, except when they are on the move, is as a rule quick and regular. There are wireless sets, but the position, as to repair, is not so good as it became eventually in the Western Desert. The rest, as far as the outside world goes, is silence. There are no towns behind the lines. Two hundred miles away, there is a circus and a cinema, but these men have not seen either. There is a projector at Brigade H.Q. but the men in the forward lines and at Battalion Headquarters stand to until dusk.[16]

When it was published, the front cover featured a full-page photograph of Sergeant Parr of the Mortar Platoon, who was reputed to have the longest moustache in the British Army. At over eight and a half inches, it filled the front cover almost from edge to edge. The 'Monk' that Chadburn alluded to was undoubtedly Captain Lee Hunter.

The article, which was entitled 'Men of the Arakan', concluded with a cheery postscript delivered by a Suffolk soldier as Chadburn departed: 'Tell them', one of the men shouted after us, 'that the Eighth isn't the only Army – Monty's lot had to sit around, too, until the stuff came along!'[17]

The following morning, as the Battalion's Mortars harassed Leach Hill again, together with the adjoining Chimney Hill, an 'O' Group was held at Battalion HQ, during which it was announced by the CO that the Battalion would once again be reverting to 123 Brigade, and that Lieutenant Gray had been officially appointed the Battalion's new Brigade Liaison Officer.

The previous Liaison Officer, Lieutenant Yonge, returned from his last conference with the Brigadier bringing the news that Private Thurston, who had been badly wounded attacking Bamboo Hill on 26 January, had died from his wounds in hospital. Cyril Thurston had previously served in the 8th Battalion from 1941 to 1943, when he was transferred to 'B' Company of Second Suffolk in India.

Late on the afternoon of 29 February, Lieutenant Duncan took another patrol out towards Bamboo Hill via Long Hill South. He recalled their efforts to get into position and the Company Commander's detailed instructions for their offensive action:

> My Company was ordered to attack a particular hill over 700-foot high. It was to be an evening attack so the Company moved forward by platoons in the afternoon, hid up, and our own group had climbed to a higher, well-wooded mound, lay down, and listening to the Company Commander's plan and orders. 'We must get up that hill, we must get up that hill'. Suddenly, there was a distant 'poop' and the Company Commander yelled 'get down!' We were flat on our bellies of course, and a couple of seconds later there was a tremendous bang to our right, and the Company Commander yelled 'back to your platoons and get out of here!' Some firing came our way as we re-joined our platoon where we, at last, I and my sergeant and section commanders had a quick discussion – 'You must get up that hill.'[18]

Leaving the remainder of his platoon there, Duncan and his batman set off alone for the summit:

> I led the platoon forward along a dry stream bed, found a perfect place to lie up, and then took my batman/runner, Casey from Dungannon, and cautiously eased forward towards the original observation point. There were a number of empty cases, brass bullet cases lying around, so we moved up the hill more slowly, then suddenly froze for there was somebody at the top. Lying flat, his boots facing me, I saw at once that he was a British soldier, and after observing him for a minute, decided that he was either dead or asleep. It was the former. He was a Guerrilla Platoon sentry and he had caught the full blast of that mortar bomb and must have died instantaneously, for he was lying there, his Bren gun still slung over his shoulder. Now with the evidence that the Japs had been around and might still be in the vicinity, I decided that the body, or gun, might have been

booby-trapped. Perhaps I should have taken the chance and immobilized the Bren, I certainly had no intentions of carrying him back to our lines, so I left everything as it was and went back down the hill to deeper shadows and a rest – back to back, and rifles across our knees.[19]

Refreshed by a brief half-hour 'catnap', the pair set off again back to where they had left the remainder of the platoon, but upon arrival they found them gone:

Disappeared! Without a trace! But where to? And why? I afterwards learnt that in the general shambles, the Guerrilla Platoon, in retiring to our own lines, spotted my platoon and the officer ordered them to follow him back to camp. There I learnt that he had reported everything correct, all his men back safe and unharmed and all weapons intact. So much for us, the platoon officer. How my Company Commander explained to the C.O. the aborting of the mission, I just do not know.[20]

In the failing light, getting back through the Battalion's frontal positions would be a problem, for any movement brought a shower of grenades:

Well, Casey and I, absolutely stuck, set off for our lines. It was now dark and we had great difficulty. It was only a question of a quarter of a mile to go; did it with much effort and, in fact, in climbing up to our positions of the last hundred feet or so, we had to stop because grenades were being thrown down at us. Understandably perhaps, because our morale was not all that high, especially that of Indians, not only them but British troops, any noise at night was liable to bring reprisals and any movement at all and any strange noise was liable to alert the whole front. So, we dropped further down the hill and waited till daybreak. When climbing once more we were recognized for what we were.[21]

On 5 March sentries on 'Little Wrencat' [Wrenkitten] reported seeing a Japanese sentry on Wrencat itself. Captain Lee Hunter now took a Guerrilla patrol out south from Long Hill into the valley bottom to harass the enemy on Bamboo Hill from the south-west.

Communications were, at best, difficult in the jungle, and like their counterparts in Europe who suffered from ineffective valve-operated sets that refused to work in damp weather, Second Suffolk experienced similar problems in the oppressive humidity of Burma. However, sets were carried on such patrols, and although Lieutenant Lee Hunter's patrol had left the Battalion area at 0530, it was not until at 1930 that a garbled message was received from them over the radio to request that Bamboo Hill be immediately bombarded by mortar.

The Battalion's Mortars on Long Hill, together with Mortars of the Frontier Force Regiment (F.F.R.), went straight into action, pounding the hill in the failing light. During their bombardment, two enemy patrols moved out to attack Allied artillery positions on the right flank. They were, however, spotted by the forward lines on the eastern slopes of Long Hill, and fire was brought down against them. One Japanese Officer, one Warrant Officer and five Superior Privates were killed, but the second Japanese patrol managed to get through, making for 29 Brigade HQ, although many were killed before they could reach it.

The following afternoon, a 'Mock Battle' was carried out in co-operation with air units and tanks, but it met with mixed success. The aircraft were unable to attend, and the troop of tanks accidentally fired upon 15 Platoon, 'C' Company, causing Lieutenant Watt to extricate his men swiftly from their hilltop. One tank lost its track and was left out in the open. After the tanks' unfortunate shelling of 'C' Company, it was not unsurprising that no one was prepared to venture out to assist them.

After his successful efforts the week before, Lieutenant Duncan was now requested by Lieutenant Colonel Hopking to lead another party out on patrol:

> The C.O. sent for me again and said to me, 'Duncan, I want you to take out a 36-hour patrol. Go out at night, observe the whole of the next day and come back the following night. Take as few men as you like.' Well, my goodness. There were no, admittedly, continuous Front Lines, but the Japs were only a couple of hundred yards away. 36 hours! Perhaps the C.O. had been impressed by what I had done before or perhaps he wanted to get rid of me once and for all.[22]

That night, a massive barrage was heard in support of an advance the following morning by units in 7th (Indian) Division, who were attacking positions on the eastern side of the mountains. The enemy retaliated by shelling the Mortar Platoon on Long Hill, but no one was injured. In the early evening, 'B' Company reported that the Japanese were in position on Chimney Hill, and the Mortars were asked to harass their positions.

It was now just over two months since the Battalion's first real action against the Japanese, and they had finally got the measure of their enemy. Though they had suffered losses at Bamboo Hill they were in fine spirits, as one officer recalled: 'We are deeper into Burma, with the Fourteenth Army, and "doing alright".'[23]

Repatriation now claimed the Quartermaster, Lieutenant 'Vic' Allum, but RSM Jasper took his place as temporary Quartermaster with ease. George

Jasper joined the Regiment in 1930 along with his brother. The pair initially served with the 1st Battalion at home, before being posted to Second Suffolk in India. Later, George would be commissioned and would serve again as QM in Malaya and Germany.

On 7 March, 'A' Company spotted several Japanese walking about on Point 731. Suspicious about this unusually open behaviour, Lieutenant Bradley took out a reconnaissance patrol to Wrenkitten to view them from there. Wrenkitten had only recently been vacated by the Dogras, and during the handover, the CO left to visit the left flank Battalion, 2/1 Punjab, positioned on a hill to the east of Long Hill.

Lieutenant Bradley's patrol returned later that evening with nothing to report, except that they had observed a new Japanese bunker that had been built on the eastern slope of Bamboo Hill since their previous attacks in January.

On 9 March, the enemy started shelling the Battalion positions with a 75mm gun that had been brought up and dug in on Bamboo Hill itself. The Battalion's Mortars again took the brunt of the enemy's fire, the majority of the shells falling on them at Long Hill. This heavy shelling caused a fire to break out in the area of Battalion HQ, and Second Lieutenant Stevens and his platoon had to swiftly vacate their foxholes, sheltering in the valley bottom until dark, when they could return. As the hillside caught alight, Lieutenant Duncan recalled the humour of the situation:

> One day there was a fair amount of Jap shelling, which didn't often happen, and we were quite amused to find that the shells not only were landing short, but with not much of a bang, no terrain damage, and what sort of shells they were using or not, I do not know but, very soon afterwards, the bush, scrubland, went on fire to a width of about 60 or 70 yards. And as it was obviously coming towards our lines, our booby-traps, wiring, we didn't have a lot of wire actually, and slit trenches, we had to get out and fight it. And there you had the extraordinary spectacle of 40 or 50 white men, stripped to the waist, running about and beating out these flames. Extraordinary sight and a perfect target and the Japanese fired not one other shot or shell.[24]

As darkness descended, large fires could also now be seen on Wrenkitten and Wrencat, and the Japanese could be seen running about in a panic. Ammunition was heard exploding, and light machine-gun fire was also heard from the direction of Razabil in the south. The Japanese looked to have suffered a taste of their own medicine.

As the situation quietened down, in the early hours a reinforcement draft of thirty men were brought up and distributed to the various Companies in their hilltop positions.

The following day, 161 Brigade attacked on the Battalion's right flank along the Maungdaw and Buthidaung Road. As part of their advance, the Battalion covered their left flank by putting down smoke and high explosive around the Wrens. Such was the rate of their fire that it was recorded that the Battalion's Mortars fired 302 rounds of high explosive and 16 rounds of smoke onto these positions in just one hour; an average of one bomb exploding every eleven seconds.

As Vengeance bombers attacked the 'Razabil Fortress' the Japanese were seen again openly digging in on Chimney Hill. Lieutenant Hastie now took a fighting patrol out to Leach Hill to harass them with light machine guns, whilst Captain Lee Hunter took a patrol of the Guerrilla Platoon to Wrenkitten and opened up on the enemy from there.

Unfortunately, Captain Lee Hunter's patrol were spotted, and the Japanese brought down heavy rifle-grenade fire on them, but luckily there were no casualties. The Japanese also fired three rounds of high explosive onto the north-west corner of Long Hill, but luckily the Mortars were well back, and no casualties were suffered.

On 11 March, more Vengeance dive-bombers returned to attack 'Pineapple' Hill, a prominent feature near the village of Razabil, but with only limited success. Major Browne now assumed command of 'A' Company, having been given the temporary role of Adjutant, whilst Captain Forrest now reverted to being Second-in-Command of 'D' Company.

Firing was heard all day to the south of the Battalion's positions around Razabil, and at 1800 Second Lieutenant Gauld and Corporal Salter went forward on a reconnaissance patrol to the east of Bamboo Hill. Most of their route was devoid of cover, and the Battalion's Mortars, which were then situated in 'D' Company's frontal positions, harassed Chimney Hill as a distraction.

At dusk, a Japanese patrol was sighted between 'B' and 'D' Companies' positions. Allowing them to come on, 'B' Company observed them crossing the Rehkat *chaung* in the bottom of the valley, before a member of the Support Platoon threw a grenade down at them, forcing them to retreat. The Dogras now attacked and occupied 'Propeller' Hill to the south of Wrencat.

One of the reinforcements that arrived the day before was Private George Sands, a young soldier from the Royal Berkshire Regiment. He was comparatively new to the jungle and all that fighting there entailed, but he quickly discovered what a deadly place it could be. He later recalled the viciousness of the enemy that they faced and his constant taunting, particularly at night, designed to wear down their resolve:

> When you fought the Japanese in the jungles of Burma, you didn't take prisoners. It was hand-to-hand with the bayonet ... and you really did wait to see the whites of their eyes. The jungle was brutal. We saw what the Japanese did to their prisoners. Even to this day I don't like to talk about it. We saw our people that they had killed. So we didn't take prisoners. We'd be in slit trenches and hear them call out 'Johnny, Johnny, over here!'[25]

This nocturnal jeering from the Japanese was designed to provoke a verbal riposte, whereupon they could pinpoint the position and bring fire upon it. Maintaining one's temper and controlling the natural reaction to reply with a tirade of bad language was a skill that had to be mastered by many a young soldier.

The following day was quiet, with only Captain Lee Hunter taking out his Guerrilla Platoon to patrol around Bamboo Hill and Ring Hill at dusk. 'Harassing' fire was brought down on 'Hundred Foot Feature' after dark by the Battalion's Mortars, and those of the Frontier Force Regiment pounded Wrencat until 2200, when three Japanese were seen running from their positions there. A party of Gurkhas on its western slopes fired upon them but failed to bring any down.

Whilst the Gurkhas were investigating around Bamboo Hill, Captain Forrest now led a patrol to Leach Hill and 'Pampus' Hill and reported back in the early hours that both were now unoccupied. The Japanese looked to have vacated their positions there only recently.

Then, just after dawn on 13 March, the Signals Office beside Battalion HQ came alive, radio sets buzzing with traffic from the Gurkhas, who stated that they were 'now going in to capture Bamboo'.[26] Ready and eager to assist in taking the prize that had eluded them before, Lieutenant Watts moved his platoon up in support and prepared to advance.

From the bottom of the valley on their right flank, the Gurkhas steamed up the western slopes of Bamboo Hill from positions to the left of Battalion HQ. Lieutenant Watts now moved his platoon across from Long Hill round to the eastern slope of Bamboo Hill and, with the Gurkhas moving swiftly up its western slopes, both units reached its summit at 0600, whereupon success signals were fired by Very pistol to indicate that the hill was now in Allied hands. Finally, after six weeks, men of Second Suffolk stood upon the summit of Bamboo Hill.

The swiftness of this action now prompted the Adjutant to suggest that the Gurkhas should push on to 'Biscuit' Hill a little further south, and this was also declared free of the enemy a few minutes later. Now as the Battalion dug in on Bamboo Hill, the Gurkhas left to patrol to Ant and Bean Hills. They returned an hour later to Ring Hill, reporting that no enemy were sighted. The Japanese had gone.

This action, which finally saw the taking of Bamboo Hill, was the culmination of some weeks of careful planning to launch a major offensive to the south by 161 Brigade to take the Razabil Fortress once and for all and secure the southern tunnels through the Mayu Mountains. For their part, 123 Brigade continued to attack the key hilltop positions that confronted them, diverting the enemy's attention as far as possible, whilst their counterparts moved around behind to attack the enemy from the rear:

> Evans' 123 Brigade were to simulate a major attack against Razabil from the north, while 9 Brigade would remain in reserve to hold the front, to delay enemy reinforcements from reaching the battleground, to protect our convoys, and thus to relieve the attacking troops of anxiety about their rear and flank.[27]

The Intelligence Officer and the Pioneer Officer now went forward to record in detail the abandoned enemy positions on Bamboo Hill. Making a thorough check for booby traps, they discovered the bodies of Privates Brooks and Grace, who had been killed in the attack on 28 January. Their remains were removed and buried in the Battalion cemetery.

Kenneth Brooks and Joseph Grace had been called up in 1940. Both men had previously served with 2 West Yorks in 9 Brigade before being transferred to Second Suffolk in early 1944.

As the morning passed, the Gurkhas were replaced on Bamboo Hill by 'C' Company. As soon as all was declared clear, the Brigadier came up to inspect the ground that had been contested for almost two months.

Whilst the Brigadier spoke with Lieutenant Colonel Hopking, working parties continued clearing the scrub around the summit. The remains of another body were discovered in Rehkat *chaung* near a small outcrop known as the 'Parson's Nose', but it could not be positively identified. It was removed by the Medical Officer the following morning and reburied in the Battalion Cemetery.

In parallel to these actions, it now fell to Captain Tony Ennion to finally plant the Battalion Flag on the summit of Bamboo Hill. It had been carried into action by Major Richards in January and had been recovered with his body. The flag, which was nothing much more than a small yellow 'duster' with the Regimental device of a Castle and Key, was already much faded. It had been brought out from England by Lieutenant Colonel Hopking and had '30' sewn in one corner, from the days when he had commanded the 30th (Home Defence) Battalion, and a '2' in the other, for his current command. He wrote home:

> It may interest late members of '30' Battalion to know that this same Regimental Flag is once more flying proudly in the breeze, but this time in the Burma jungle. Only a few days ago this flag was taken into action by a Company Commander of another Battalion of the XII Foot, who, unfortunately, lost his life on the field of battle.[28]

In the afternoon, Wrencat was attacked unsuccessfully by the Dogras, whilst 1 R.S.F. unsuccessfully attacked Point 731. The Dogras on the slopes of Wrencat were harassed all night, but the Battalion front was quiet. The Battalion now occupied a salient out onto Bamboo Hill, but the flanks and hills either side of it still remained in enemy hands.

The following morning, the Intelligence Officer recorded and removed a Japanese mine from a point north of the 'Hundred Foot Feature'. It was of a type unknown to the Battalion, hence its careful and recorded removal. That afternoon, the Dogras attacked Wrencat again, now supported by a platoon from 'C' Company. A party of four Brens under the command of Lieutenant Box gave covering fire, and the Battalion's mortars assisted in covering their advance. From Long Hill the CO could see the Dogras tenaciously crawling up Wrencat's steep slopes.

After a last charge at the point of the bayonet, Wrencat was finally taken just before noon by the Dogras, with some assistance from Second Suffolk, and as men of the Battalion stood upon its summit, the Japanese could be seen fleeing from its south-eastern slopes. The R.S.F. attacked Point 731 again in greater force, assisted by two troops of tanks, but for a second time their attack failed.

Back on Bamboo Hill, in the early evening, the advance party of 8 York and Lancs arrived to reconnoitre the position for their impending relief of Second Suffolk in the forthcoming days. Whilst conferences went on between the senior officers of both Battalions, daily routine continued.

That evening, news reached the Battalion that 4/7 Rajputs had finally taken 'Point 1079' – the highest feature in the locality – and were now pushing south towards the tunnels through the mountains between Maungdaw and Buthidaung. With Bamboo Hill and Wrencat secure, Lieutenant Duncan now took his platoon to occupy Middle Wrencat, relieving the exhausted Dogras there. After their dogged and persistent efforts to take the hill, 'WRENCAT' was a Battle Honour that rightfully only the Dogras would be awarded.

On 15 March, with elements of Second Suffolk spread out across Bamboo Hill, Middle Wrencat and Long Hill, a party under Lieutenant Hastie, accompanied by two Signalmen from the Royal Corps of Signals equipped with a No. 48 Wireless set, moved around the eastern side of Bamboo Hill and headed south towards Pineapple Hill.

Upon reaching this hill at 0700, they found it free of the enemy and reported back by wireless. There were no signs that this feature had been occupied; the Japanese had chosen instead to construct defensive positions at Bamboo Hill and other higher features in the locality.

With orders received that the Battalion was now to be relieved imminently, a flurry of activity ensued, packing up equipment and stores. For over three months they had leap-frogged from hill to hill in less than a quarter of a square mile of jungle. Everyone was now looking forward to being relieved and worked feverishly to be ready to depart as soon as their relief arrived.

Writing on the eve of their departure, a sergeant of the Battalion recalled in a letter home their state of flux and how every possible mode of transport, including the dependable mule, was employed to move the Battalion's kit:

> We have been conducting a war of movement, moving ourselves and a few tons of kit from hill to hill with the aid of mules of course. (A mule is a horsey, donkeyish animal – not like one of your 15 cwts.) C.S.M.s and C/Sgts have become expert on mule loads. Before a move, C.S.M.s can be seen checking over loads. One was heard to remark to a platoon sergeant, 'This load is too heavy for a mule, you will have to carry it yourself', and so life goes.[29]

Early the following morning, the Intelligence Section set to work recording, then dismantling, another Japanese bunker on Bamboo Hill. Whilst there, they discovered the remains of a Sapper, later identified as belonging to 74 Field Company, Royal Engineers, who had assisted 'A' Company in their attack on 28 January.

His body could not be removed straight away, for beside him lay an unexploded pole charge that he had carried into action, and this had first to be disarmed. As this task was being completed, Battalion HQ received the news that Point 731 had finally been taken by the 1 R.S.F. at their third attempt with the assistance of more tanks that had crossed the Rehkat *chaung* to bring down fire upon the position.

With the changeover now due within twenty-four hours, the Battalion stood ready to depart. However, away in the jungle to the south, Lieutenant Duncan was out on a patrol which had both terrifying and humorous consequences:

On my very last patrol in the Arakan, I went out one night with two men. We didn't know what to expect of course, so we had a bullet up the spout, and we had our safety catches forward. We were climbing up a rather steep, stony path with dark bushes on either side and, just as I came to a sharp bend, there was a blinding flash and a colossal bang right in front of me! And I thought, 'I'm dead. I'm dead.' Felt no pain. Turned around and there was one man spread-eagled on the path, arms and legs out, and I thought, 'My God, what a mess.' No signs of the other fella, for he had taken a header into the bushes. Well, before two or three seconds I realized that I was pressing a trigger and it was I who had fired the shot, and I can only suggest that my foot having slipped, there was a little extra pressure on the trigger. So, I went down on this chap on the path and buried my face in his chest. Not to listen for his heartbeat but to smother my laughter and to assure him that everything was all right. And he didn't want to get up, so I had a look for the other guy whose feet were up and his head was down in a ditch and tried to pull him up but failed, and had to get the first fellow and the pair of us hauled him out by the legs. But they didn't see the funny side of it at all! But of course, that one shot would have alerted both fronts, the whole area, and so the homeward journey, was taken much more slowly, and much more cautiously.[30]

The following day, the York and Lancs arrived and the Battalion was withdrawn from their various hills, back over a mile and a half to the nearest metalled road, where a convoy of trucks was waiting to take them across the border into India, to a rest camp at Dohazari, south-east of Chittogram.

The journey of over a hundred miles was completed through the night, with the first elements of the Battalion arriving in the camp at 0700 on 17 March, while the last arrived at noon. Lieutenant Duncan's men, then on Middle Wrencat, were among the last to leave: 'Our relieving unit – the 8th Battalion Yorks & Lancs, absolutely spotless, 100% fit, 100% up to strength, took over our position and tried to crowd into the fox holes which were dug for about half the number.' Major Browne also recalled the joy at hearing they were to be removed from the Arakan front:

There had been indications that we were about to be relieved and were suddenly told to move out and go north by Motor Transport. The men were in high spirits as they thought they were due for a rest – little did they know! We kept going all night over a shocking road and arrived the next morning at Dohazari, where we went into a transit camp.[31]

After a bath and the first night in three months during which they did not have to 'Stand To', the men relaxed, but the following morning, firm orders came to pack up their kit and be ready to move immediately to new positions. Moving to a nearby airstrip, the men were being rushed with the rest of their Brigade to a new battle front that had opened in the north-east of India, where the Japanese now threatened the garrisons at Imphal and Kohima.

Major Kenneth Henderson, then commanding 'HQ' Company, recalled their swift departure:

> Suddenly we were ordered to vacate our positions in the front line, an order we did not in the least mind obeying. We were quickly moved back to the airport at Chittagong and the whole brigade, including mules, transport and guns, was flown in American aircraft to Imphal, a few hundred miles further north. This was the first time that a whole formation such as ours was moved by air. The reason was that the Japanese had launched a major attack further north towards Imphal and Kohima and reinforcements were urgently needed to meet it.[32]

The Padre remembered the speed of their redeployment to Imphal, but also how pleased they were to be rid of the dreaded Arakan dust:

> We ate dust, we breathed dust, we were covered in thick layers of dust, but what did it matter, soon we would be away from it all. Alas, we were certainly going to get away from it, but it was by plane to Dimapur! [Manipur] So instead of a rest, it was more fighting we had to do. Both the 5th and 7th Indian Divisions were well versed in Jap tactics and they were better able to deal with this new menace. The Battalion, lock stock and barrel (except the big transport) including mules and jeeps were emplaned and within four hours were taking up new positions to stave off the Japs.[33]

All surplus kit now had to be left behind. With weight critical, each man was allowed just 17lbs of personal kit for the short flight to India. Minimal ammunition was carried – just fifty rounds of .303 and one grenade each. The men held their large packs on their knees, with their groundsheets, mosquito nets and rolled blankets tied around them.

Some men had never been in the air before, and the flight in mainly USAAF C-46 and C-47 aircraft was noisy and uncomfortable. During its one-and-a-half-hour duration, Cook Sergeant Harry Cropley sat on the floor at the back, quietly puffing away on his pipe. Cropley had literally just completed twenty-one years service with the Regiment, having served with the Battalion since 1923. Major Browne also recalled the flight:

> Fortunately I knew a bit about air transportation, so the organisation of loads was not too much of a job. We spent a night on the aerodrome and piled into transports at dawn the next morning, my own being a Curtiss Commando piloted by Americans. The trip was uneventful except that everybody was very cold, and we didn't like the look of the country underneath at all.[34]

Sergeant Cropley's calm and cheerfulness was a tonic to those who felt nervous, and just over four hours after setting off from Burma, they were in their new positions around the Indian town of Imphal.

But not everyone was leaving Dohazari by air. Yet another draft of 'old' soldiers was being repatriated to England, many of whom would subsequently join the 1st Battalion. Among them were Corporal Leeke and Lance Corporal Mowle, both of whom had seen fighting at Bamboo Hill and who were now leaving for home with another 'old sweat', Lance Corporal Barber.

Corporal Reginald 'Reggie' Leeke had enlisted into the Suffolk Regiment on 12 June 1935 and joined the 1st Battalion at Plumer Barracks, Plymouth. In 1936, as a young private, he had won the 'Long Siberian Range Competition' at Bisley, shooting over 1,400 yards and carrying off a prize of £300. He promptly brought all his mates a drink then went around the corner to buy a brand-new Panther motorcycle.

Lance Corporal Don 'Spitter' Mowle later joined 1 Suffolk and landed with them on D-Day. He would be photographed on a snowy December morning later that year at Geijsteren in Holland. The caption accompanying the photograph noted that he

> saw service and action with the (2nd Bn Suffolks) on the Horakin [*sic*] Front, Burma, (with the 5th Indian Div.). He returned to England on 18th April 1944 and after one month's leave, he joined the 1st Bn Suffolks and landed in Normandy on D-Day with the 3rd British Div. and is now looking forward to his next leave.[35]

'Horakin', which is yet to be found on any map of the Burma front, was in all probability the photographer's scribble for 'Arakan' as delivered by Mowle in his broad Suffolk accent.

Lance Corporal Alec Barber had originally enlisted in the Northamptonshire Regiment in the mid-1930s and had already served his five years overseas with Second Suffolk. Barber would, like Mowle, join 1 Suffolk for D-Day but would be wounded with 'A' Company as they advanced to take the crossroads at Coquard near Tinchebrai on the night of 13/14 August 1944.

The Arakan campaign left bitter memories in the minds of those who had served there. For some, that bitterness never vanished, but others, such as Captain Bryan Coward, would later look back philosophically on those days:

> You see Burma was unlike any other war, you were completely isolated. You were in the jungle, you had your soldiers around you, you had the Japanese around them and you knew what a nice lot of chaps the Japanese were. They were damned good when they were dead. We always felt that we were doing a good job to get these chaps through the Pearly Gates so they could meet their maker. Well you got the opportunity every now and then, when you had the opportunity you killed him, it didn't happen every day. Anyway, it was a bit of a nasty war.[36]

Sergeant Charlie Parr held a similar view, based upon his experiences in Burma, though he never expressed it in such humorous tones: 'The first Japanese we came across surrendered, but then they killed my mates who were closest to them with grenades. We took no prisoners at all after that. It was a filthy business.'[37]

As the first chapter of their service in the Far East closed, the Battalion could be pleased with their efforts, even if they did not at the time think that they had been particularly successful. They had acclimatized and adapted well to the terrain in which they were called to fight and, more crucially, they had got the measure of their enemy:

> The Battalion had been in continuous contact with the Japanese for four months; an unsuccessful period it may have seemed to many officers and men. But in fact, they had proved their stubborn quality; they started lacking experience and training, they ended veterans, confident in their superiority in every respect to the Japanese.[38]

From the dust of Burma, the Battalion now marched onwards, back into India.

Chapter Six
Kohima

*'One had the feeling that those in command
did not quite know what to do with us'*

The Battalion's arrival on the Imphal front underlined the grievousness of the situation in that area. The 5th (Indian) Division had been pulled from the Arakan front in great haste to be redeployed in defending the beleaguered garrisons at Imphal and Kohima that were now under Japanese attack.

Upon their arrival on the airstrip at Imphal, whilst platoon commanders checked that all was present and correct, Lieutenant Colonel Hopking was called to a conference at Brigade HQ. After his return he sent all the company commanders and their seconds-in-command out by truck to reconnoitre the positions that they were now to take over north-east of the town on the Imphal-Ukhrul road.

The Battalion had in the past weeks been in semi-static positions, so these swift movements by truck were a welcome change. Some, however, like Captain Coward, hoped that after their six months in Arakan they might be allowed a short period of leave:

> I was in the 5th Indian Division and our first show in Burma was in Arakan and we came out of Arakan thinking we were going on holiday and what a good idea it would be to have a nice bit of leave and instead we were transferred to Imphal! Actually I was in charge at that time of the mules. I had 50-odd mules and we flew them by Dakota from Dohazarri to Imphal.[1]

The terrain of Imphal was similar to that which they had recently vacated in Arakan, except for the absence of the much-hated 'Arakan dust':

> Here again were many of the little pimply hills up-cropping from the plains, and it was towards a group of these that the Battalion was moving to dig the first of many defensive positions against the threatened attack on Imphal. These hills on the Padel Road were covered with sparse low scrub and occasional pineapple plantations; into the distance in all directions stretched long uninterrupted views of plains. In front of their defensive

line was an expanse of low-lying flooded ground, a fine blue colour, very inviting; it was not long before the whole battalion was swimming and paddling, revelling in this opportunity of washing the last traces of the Arakan dust from their bodies.[2]

Unlike Arakan, where only an occasional native was seen, here the locals were more forthcoming. Major E. G. W. Browne recalled their cheerfulness at seeing reinforcements such as Second Suffolk arrive:

> The people at Imphal seemed very glad to see some new faces and seemed to us to be pretty 'windy'. We were full of confidence after beating up the Japs in the Arakan and were ready for anything, and the fresh atmosphere made us feel very much more energetic than we had been for some months.[3]

However, with the rapidly deteriorating situation in the north around the town of Kohima, the Battalion were now preparing to move again; they were soon placed on six hours' notice to be ready to 'move to any scene of operation'. The following morning, that was changed to just one hour's notice.

That afternoon, the situation at Kohima worsened. Determined Japanese attacks had pushed the Allies back, and now the Battalion was being sent north as urgent reinforcements to assist the beleaguered garrison.

During the morning of 20 March, as the men stood ready for their one-hour call, orders were received that later that afternoon they would travel by truck in convoy to Kohima. Having left Imphal at 1515, the 85-mile journey north was accomplished without incident, and all elements of the Battalion arrived by 0030 on 21 March. Major Browne recalled their move:

> My company was motorised in 8 cwt. lorries. We arrived on 19th March, and on the 21st March set off post-haste for Kohima at an hour's notice. We arrived in the middle of the night, as usual, having had a hair-raising drive with Indian drivers over a most tortuous road. My driver was a Pathan who had fought against the battalion on the frontier some years before! We really hadn't a clue as to what was going on and thought Kohima looked a very nice place the next morning. However, we sent out patrols towards where there were supposed to be Japs and proceeded to dig ourselves in on what later came to be known as 'hospital hill'.[4]

Whilst the infantry moved northwards, the equine elements of the Battalion were now being reallocated for use by other units on the Imphal front. The Battalion had brought its mules and their harness by air from the Arakan front, and Captain Coward was now detailed to take them from the landing strip to a depot south of the town. As the newly created 'Officer Commanding Mules', he now set off on foot with his charges:

> When we got to Imphal we arrived on the Palel Road and we marched sixty-five miles or seventy miles in three days with all our kit and one thing and another including these damned mules. And when got to the Headquarters of some Corps we were told we had to 'dig in' the mules. Now, just imagine the brainpower needed of the Staff Officer who decided that the mules should be 'dug in'! You imagine, you dig a hole for yourself you only need it so deep and so long. But a mule, it stands as high as you do and it puts its head up anyway and the head is the thing you have to keep – and you have got to dig a down pit and an up pit! I mean it would need two bulldozers per mule![5]

Upon arrival in Kohima, the Battalion had been allotted an area in the already evacuated 49th Indian Base Hospital, and the following day, 'B' Company was placed at fifteen minutes' notice for operations. For a brief few hours the Battalion were comfortable, and 'the C.O. enjoyed the luxury of the Matron's bed, only vacated the day before.'[6]

Whilst Captain Lee Hunter took the convoy of vehicles back to Imphal to collect the last elements of the Battalion remaining there, Lieutenant Lawrence set off on patrol to try and make contact with elements of 1 Assam Regiment, who were in positions around the village of Jessami, east of the town.

Back in Imphal, Lieutenant Box was now tasked with delivering seven carriers to the Battalion's new positions at Kohima. The vehicles he took receipt of were not in the best mechanical condition and they had to make several stops along the way due to overheating, shed tracks and various other mechanical issues. He arrived in Kohima with just one carrier at 0100 on 22 March, the rest having broken down en route. Two more and their crews arrived later that afternoon, having managed to limp up the road.

Lieutenant Lawrence made progress towards Jessami. He encountered no enemy, but heavy rain fell all the next day hampering their advance. Making it into Jessami that evening, he had some difficulty in finding the exact positions of the Assam Regiment but remained there awaiting orders.

Back in Kohima, the Battalion's rifle companies were spread out in various locations around the hospital's grounds. In the afternoon, Lieutenant Colonel Hopking returned from a conference with orders to send a patrol south towards the 98th Milestone on the Kohima-Imphal Road. They returned some hours later with nothing to report. However, the situation now looked to be getting very much worse. A large Japanese force had almost encircled the town and were now in danger of severing the road between Kohima and Imphal behind the Battalion's current positions.

On 24 March, the CO received orders to evacuate two Companies south by road. With no available transport, 'B' and 'D' Companies set off on foot, halting for ten minutes in every hour, with one longer stop for dinner. In parallel, the Intelligence Officer, with all the available vehicles that could be pulled out, travelled on ahead to their destination. They arrived there in advance of the marching troops but had suffered a fatality en route.

The Battalion ammunition supplies were completely lost when the truck they were being carried in left the road near the 13th Milestone (from Kohima). The R.A.S.C. driver was killed, but two Indian and one British soldiers managed to jump clear. 'C' Company's ration truck was also lost off the road into a deep valley, some half a mile back from the ammunition lorry.

Orders then came to the two companies that remained in Kohima, that they were being withdrawn; elements of 2 West Yorks would replace them in their defensive positions, allowing them to pull back and rejoin the remainder of the Battalion moving south. The West Yorks had, like Second Suffolk, been flown in together with the remainder of 9 Brigade from the Arakan Front. Major Kenneth Henderson recalled the chaos and confusion of those days:

> No sooner had we arrived from Imphal than we were ordered to move about 100 miles north to Kohima by truck. As soon as we arrived we started digging defensive positions but after two or three days we were ordered back to Imphal, having been relieved by fresh troops from India. The next day the Japanese cut the road and Imphal was under siege. For the next three months or so there were Japanese attacks at various points around Imphal whilst we were being supplied by air from India.[7]

CSM Tommy Warren also recalled the uncertainty of that time:

> One had the feeling that those in command did not quite know what to do with us, for after appending defensive positions along the Padel Road, we were moved to Kohima, only to return to Imphal a week later. The fact that the Japanese attacked Kohima the next day might indicate that our feelings were not misplaced! Hearing a battle going on ahead as we proceeded some 20 miles down the Ukhral Road, we quickly returned and took up positions in the high hills east of Imphal. By this time the Japs had cut all routes to India, our only means of supply being by air to the Imphal airstrip.[8]

Major Browne also recalled their retreat:

> The next day a battalion of the [Royal] West Kents arrived and we were ordered back to Imphal at speed. Once again a night move, and this time with the unpleasant possibility that there were Japs on the road. We spent what was left of the night just off the road and tension mounted slightly when we heard an apparent battle going on quite close, which later turned out to be an ammunition lorry that had caught fire! At crack of dawn we moved again and started to work our way down the Ukhrul road, eventually digging in, and then moved again to protect some guns. Off again the next morning and dug in at the village of Yainganpokjoi where one company covered through some troops who were retiring and actually saw some Japs. We had been chasing around so much and getting so little sleep that we were quite exhausted. The next day we moved yet again.[9]

The retreat was at times chaotic, but it did have moments of hilarity:

> A platoon under Lieut. T. E. Watt, maintaining a forward standing patrol, lay up for the night in some scrub, and woke next morning to find themselves in the midst of a Company of Japanese. Discretion is the better part of valour. They endeavoured to slip away unobserved. But the Jap officer raised the hue and cry and as they broke cover Watt found himself being chased by the enemy commander, a fellow over six feet tall brandishing his sword, while the rest of his company stood and stared. One or two parting shots and our patrol was clear![10]

However, coming from the opposite direction was Major George Squirrell. He had not left Arakan by air but had instead made a precarious overland journey to Imphal by road, bringing the Brigade's vehicles to the new battlefront. No sooner had he caught up with the Battalion just south of Kohima than he was forced to turn about for Imphal once more:

> We were hardly out of the line when I had to report to 123 Brigade. 'Major', he said 'I have a job for you, Squirrell, you will take 123 Brigade transport to Imphal. There are no maps to find your own route, make daily contact with the Colonel at Army HQ to arrange a drop point for rations and fuel. What are you waiting for – get going!' We were soon away. Jeeps to ambulances, the heat was terrific, and the dust stifling and even at low speed distance between vehicles was up to 1 mile. After 4 days of driving, we had one day to stop and clean up, check vehicles and rest. Four more

days driving and having covered over 1000 miles we arrived at Imphal. The last vehicle cleared Kohima less than one hour before the Japs cut the road. All vehicles in good order. It was a great team effort everyone else gave of their best with most satisfying results.[11]

There were also an unlucky few who did not make it through. Private Tom Dunnett, who had been a member of 'B' Company but had been transferred to the Transport Section, was in charge of a carrier that had broken down. Cut off with the crippled vehicle, he remained in Kohima with the garrison there: 'We had just got through Kohima when the Japs cut the road behind us. We were isolated and had to be supplied by air. We were completely cut off for several weeks and the road wasn't reopened until after the terrible battle there.'[12]

In times of uncertainty food was a constant preoccupation for the British soldier, who always worried where his next meal would come from. In Arakan the diet came predominantly from the British 'Compo' ration, but when the battlefront shifted back to India, supplies came from both the United States and Australia. Until a firm base could be established and a cookhouse created, all ranks ate from one or the other nation's ration packs:

> Of these three, the British produced the best variety but was bulky and the tin required an opener. The American 'K' was slightly less bulky and very easy to handle. The container soaked in paraffin wax was useful to cook on. The Australian was small and easy to carry but not very palatable. Of these three, the 'K' was best, but all tasted pretty awful after a few days![13]

It was the monotony of the menu that most soldiers remembered, but also the dreaded flies that seemed to swarm about your mess tins when you were trying to eat your dinner. Corporal Cyril Dell recalled the monotony of the tinned bully beef – the British 'Iron Ration':

> Our food was not too good, bully beef and biscuits, but we had to eat it, then come the flies, in swarms they settle all over you, settle on your food, by the time you have got your spoon to your mouth it is covered with flies, you knock them off, but then they are in your mouth before you can close it.[14]

Cigarettes were always welcome, but the locally produced 'Victory' brand that were issued in the ration packs were much despised, and one old soldier remarked, 'They only gave 'em away because no bugger would want to buy 'em!'[15] Private Norman Rolfe of 'C' Company recalled just how much they were disliked: 'My God they were awful! Wood shavings that with the slightest draw fell apart

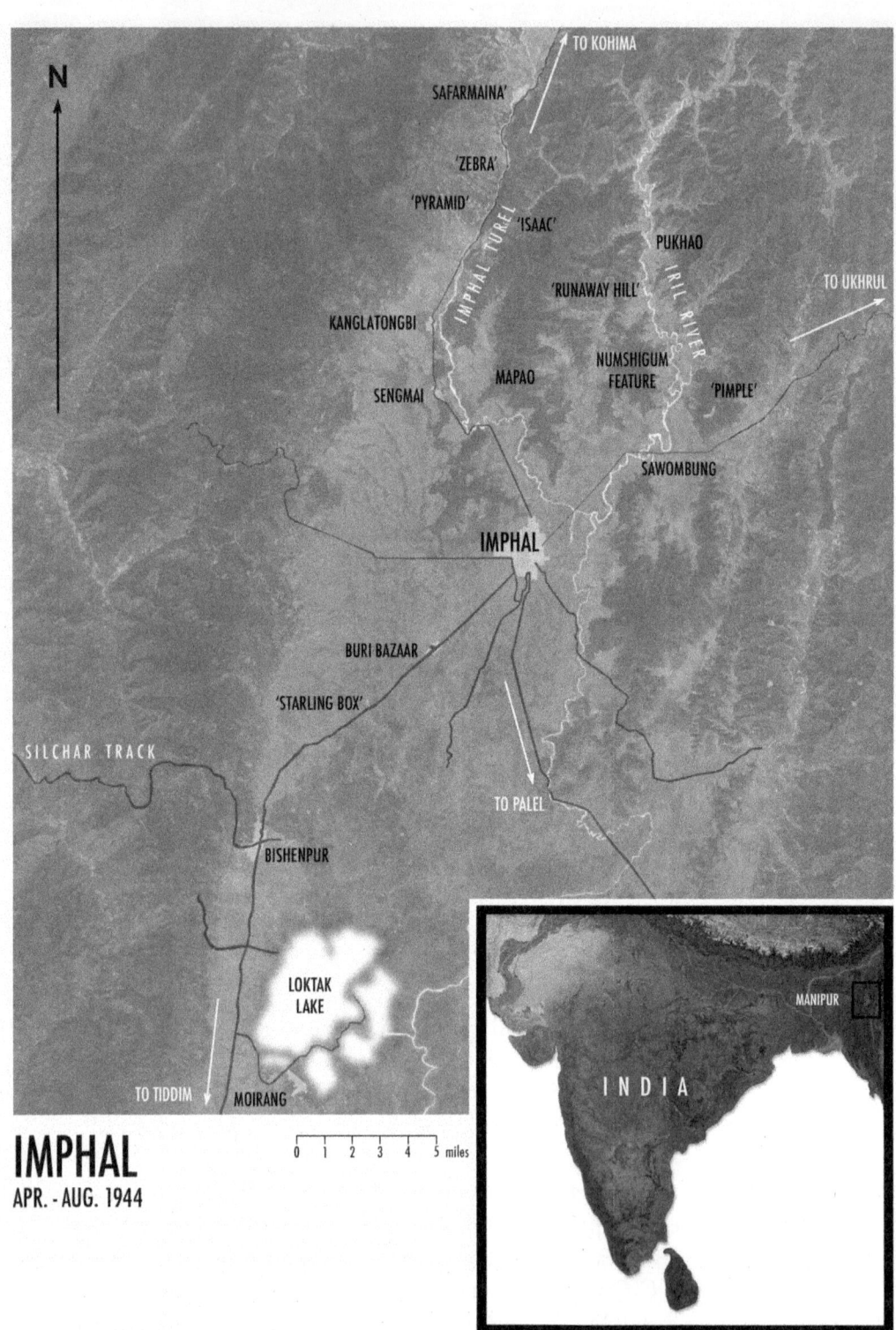

and you ended up setting fire to your shirt. We were always pleased when we got parcels from home and we found English cigarettes inside. Many of my friends took to smoking a pipe instead.'[16]

After three days without communication, Lieutenant Lawrence's platoon returned from positions near Jessami and rejoined 'D' Company, making their way south to catch up with the Battalion. Upon arrival in their new positions north-east of Imphal, 'D' Company's Commander, Major Gurney, decided to lead a platoon patrol out himself towards Lamboida Khut, whilst Captain Lee Hunter led his Guerrilla Platoon out towards Yaingangpokpi.

No sooner had Major Gurney's patrol started up the track towards Guanthabi than they were fired on from enemy positions on the hills to the south of the road. Skilfully concealing themselves in the ditches on either side of the road, they captured two suspected 'Jiffs' and sent them back to the Battalion area for interrogation.

Later that afternoon, the Guerrilla Platoon reported a party of more than sixty Japanese coming down the road into their positions. They held their fire until the enemy were within range, at which point they could see that the leading man, an officer, had been wounded and was marching with his arm in a sling. Waiting until the last possible minute, they were about to open fire when the Japanese suddenly fled. Not a shot had been fired, and soon the reason for their disappearance became apparent, when a member of the platoon spotted a party of stragglers from the 50th Parachute Brigade advancing in the direction of Imphal from their positions around Sangshak. They could not see the Japanese, but the Japanese had seen them and fled. In the confusion, the Guerrilla Platoon held their position in the ditches along the road.

The following morning, 29 March, the Intelligence Officer, Captain Arrindell, went out to try and contact a troop of Stuart light tanks belonging to 7 Cavalry from 254 Indian Tank Brigade to ask them to assist him in pressing onwards and making contact with Captain Lee Hunter, who was still believed to be near Yaingangpokpi with the Guerrilla Platoon.

In the meantime, however, Captain Lee Hunter and his men had been pushing north-east along the road in the direction of Sangshak, where they had met a refugee from the village of Guanthabi. This man told them that the Japanese had raided his village the night before, taking away rice and salt; they had also taken hostages.

In parallel to these actions, Second Lieutenant Gauld now moved north-east towards the village of Chingdal (Chindai). His platoon were detailed to enter the village and remain there, keeping in radio contact with Battalion HQ. They regularly reported that more stragglers from 50th Parachute Brigade were passing through their positions heading for Imphal, along with several civilian refugees.

In a remarkable twist of fate, reporting at Brigade HQ for orders, the Second in Command, Major Menneer, found a sleeping Captain W. S. Bevan, who had left the Battalion in 1942 to join 151 Parachute Battalion in 50th Parachute Brigade and who had been in action to the north-west. In the withdrawal from Litan, Captain Bevan had become separated from his unit on the Ukhrul road, as he later recalled:

> After withdrawing from Litan I reached the forward positions of Geoffrey Evans's 123 Brigade at five in the morning, just as it was getting light, flopped down all-in on the ground and was instantly asleep – I'd not had much rest for the past four days. The next thing I remember is waking up with a start – someone was shaking me by the shoulder. Coming to my senses, I realised whoever it was was wearing the brass numerals XII on the turned up brim of his bush hat. He asked if I was alright, I replied, 'Yes, but who are you, why the XII on your hat?' (The Suffolk Regiment, being the 'Old Twelfth of Foot, still used the Roman numeral XII). To my surprise he said he was second-in-command of the 2nd Suffolk. I explained I was a 'Suffolk' and knew everyone in the Regiment – I couldn't think who the hell he was! He said he was a Suffolk Territorial Army Officer – which accounted for my not knowing him – his name was Ken Meneer (he took over command of 2 Suffolk temporarily not long after). I had a lot to do, so was unable to visit 2nd Suffolk.[17]

On 30 March, Captain Forrest left with five men to relieve Second Lieutenant Gauld's patrol near Chingdal, whilst a second party under Lieutenant Watt moved out to relieve Captain Lee Hunter's positions near Sangshak. Lieutenant Watt found Captain Lee Hunter in position at the foot of a hill feature known as 'Point 4241' and, changing over, Captain Lee Hunter set off back to the Battalion area, arriving there at 1000. Lieutenant Watt reported back by radio that the hill to their front was still occupied by the Japanese and that he was remaining in his current position to keep it under observation.

That evening, as the CO was gathering intelligence from Captain Lee Hunter's patrol, the Brigadier arrived at Battalion HQ. He was eager to hear of the enemy's dispositions, and Captain Lee Hunter reported that he had patrolled as far as Sagolmang, encountering a disabled truck in Yaingangpoki as they passed through, but that apart from those occupying Point 4241 he had not seen any other enemy.

The last day of March started with a small road patrol returning from Sagolmang with nothing to report. Lieutenant Duncan now took a patrol of five men out to relieve Captain Forrest near Chingdal, where contact was re-established with Lieutenant Watt via wireless, but he had nothing to report from his positions.

The Japanese were strangely quiet, but as the Battalion now moved up into new positions north of the Yaingangpokpi Road they knew their enemy was still there and that this was just the calm before the storm.

Chapter Seven

The Pimple

'A steep and rather bare mountain'

The Battalion now found itself dispersed in various locations both down on the valley floor and up in the hills to the north of the Imphal-Ukhrul road. Here, they occupied a high peak shown on maps as 'Point 4057' but christened by the Battalion the 'Mound'.

This peak was a small plateau where a defensive position had been established, but at its north-eastern end a small ridge connected it to another higher peak that was still in enemy hands. This further peak was known as the 'Pimple'.

The entire feature resembled an octopus, with rocky tentacles spreading out in all directions from its summit. To the west stood a similar series of hills known as the 'Nungshigum' feature. Nungshigum was due north of the Brigade HQ, then situated in the village of Sawombung on the Imphal-Litan road. The Regimental History noted the topography:

> The position which the Second Suffolk held was a high feature named the 'MOUND'; a steep and rather bare mountain consisting of a large mound with a small pimple on its northern perimeter. 'B' Company, under Major P. J. Hill, had constructed an elaborate system of defences, with communicating trenches, fire bays and dug-in sleeping quarters. The company held the mound excluding the pimple, which lay some 100 yards outside the perimeter. Extensive belts of wire from 15 to 25 yards in depth surrounded the whole position and crossed the small saddle separating the mound from its neighbouring pimple.[1]

However, CSM Tommy Warren recalled the reality of the Battalion's vulnerable and thinly deployed defences and the lack of material to construct forward defensive positions that were often 'embellished' in official histories as above:

> The lack of supplies, the enemy having taken the supply dump for that front; the strict rationing of food, of water and of ammunition – particularly grenades; the pitiful supply of barbed wire, restricting my Company's trip

wire to a few single strands – NOT the extensive belts of wire 15 to 25 yards wide as stated in the Regimental History.[2]

From the Mound the feature sloped back down towards the road in the south. Here, astride a stream, other elements of the Battalion held various positions as Major Browne recalled:

> Now began a really energetic period. The battalion took up a defensive position on the high ground dominating the approach down the Ukhrul road on the right and the Iril valley on the left. The battalion had one company on the hill called 4057 (renamed 'Mound') and the remainder spread from there to the road. My company was tucked in behind the ridge in reserve, and with the greater part of the patrol responsibilities. This was no mean task, as about a third of the men were continually out on patrol up to distances of 12 to 15 miles in the very difficult country to the North East. The remainder had little rest as good positions had to be prepared, and there were frequent calls for strong patrols amounting to the remainder of the company, to carry out reconnaissance in strength near the battalion position. On two occasions we went out with tanks near the villages of Lamyenching and Sachungkhok to examine particular features, and in both cases were glad to find them unoccupied. On the first occasion I had to call down artillery fire on some unidentified troops who were shooting us up at long range, but they made off very quickly. I later established that they were Indian troops of another formation, and they can consider themselves very lucky that I didn't let the tank loose on them. Only one was wounded slightly.[3]

Within a fortnight of their arrival on the Imphal Front, the S.E.A.C. communication machine was finally getting into gear distributing the first public information of their actions in the Far East. To many at home who had only read brief passages in their local newspapers that hinted at a loved one's service on the Burma Front, this was the first official news in print that told them that the Battalion had been in action against the Japanese, even though the facts were not 100 per cent accurate:

> Wednesday April 5 1944. The Suffolk Regiment is among the troops fighting in Burma where it has been in action in the Imphal area, north of the Kabaw Valley. Here the Suffolks have been engaged in the recent operations following the infiltration of Japanese forces into Manipur State. Among the heavily wooded heights, the Suffolks helped to defend

the principal pass from Burma into India and denied to the enemy the opportunity of descending into the Manipur lowlands. The Suffolks are fighting over terrain which is among the most difficult in all our fighting fronts. The country is mountainous and densely wooded. In tropical conditions in which the British soldier now has an opportunity to display the result of his long training in jungle warfare tactics, the Suffolks are holding their own and heavily punishing the enemy. The regiment has a long experience of campaigning in Burma, for over a year ago it was in action against the Japanese in the Maungdaw area, among other places. The Suffolks have also served in Malaya, and in France and Flanders during the present war.[4]

On the afternoon of 6 April Lieutenant Duncan prepared to take an ambush party to Sejang, 12½ miles up the road towards Ukhrul. This patrol was out all night, during which time rain fell heavily. They were replaced in their positions by a relief patrol of 'C' Company under Sergeant Steward. When Lieutenant Duncan's patrol returned to the Battalion lines the following morning they reported 'N.E.S.' (No Enemy Sighted), but during the day there was much Allied air activity in the direction of the Nungshigum feature.

Later that afternoon, much small arms fire could be heard on the Battalion's left flank, where a gallant attempt was being made by 3/9 Jats to retake Nungshigum.

This feature was of crucial importance to both the Allies and the Japanese. The highest available vantage point between the already captured hill positions in the east and Imphal itself, it commanded an unrivalled view over the hills to the north, the direction that all future Allied assaults must now take.

The feature had been in Allied hands until 7 April, when the Japanese, attacking from the north, evicted the Jats after a fierce battle. The feature had to be retaken, and the following day the Jats went back and retook it with surprisingly few casualties; but over the next forty-eight hours the Japanese attacked again and again, forcing them to retire.

The following morning, 8 April, Sergeant Bunce took a relief patrol of 'D' Company out to relieve Sergeant Steward. It was drizzling and the roads were now becoming so bad that they were impassable to the Battalion's vehicles. The constant traffic moving along them to support efforts to retake the Nungshigum feature had churned the roadway to a muddy slush. Now movement could be made only on foot along the verges, which soon became worn away.

With the move from their previous position still ongoing, the Battalion were now running short of food. The CO therefore ordered Captain Anslow, who commanded HQ Company, to venture up the road towards Sejang village in order to obtain supplies of rice.

Whilst further actions were being mounted against the Nungshigum feature, the Battalion now received orders that they were to evict the Japanese from the Pimple and occupy the position as soon as possible.

At dawn on 9 April – Easter Day – Captains Forrest and Coward took the first patrols out to a position between the Mound and another hill that sat astride a rocky tentacle to the north, known as 'Ring III'. From here, they were to reconnoitre the Pimple from the north-east to see if an attack from that direction was feasible.

In their absence, the Japanese launched the first of several attacks on the Battalion from the Pimple along the rocky ridge that joined it to the Mound. In the first engagement, men from 'B' Company repulsed the attack, but two men were killed in the firefight and a further three were wounded and had to be evacuated back to the Regimental Aid Post.

Private Denis Haynes, who was killed that day, came from the tiny Cambridgeshire village of Foxton. His mother received the tragic news in April 1944 that she had lost both her sons in enemy action: her elder son, Arthur, to the Germans whilst serving on operations as a Flight Sergeant in the Royal Air Force, and then a week later, her younger son to the Japanese in India.

Private William 'Bill' Wigger, who was also killed that day, had served in the 70th (Young Soldiers) Battalion of the Royal Norfolk Regiment before being drafted to join Second Suffolk. Like his comrade James 'Tich' Hunter, who was to win the Distinguished Conduct Medal on D-Day, he came from East London, 'Tich' from Barking and Bill from Plaistow. Both were drafted to 1 Suffolk at Folkestone in December 1942, 'Tich' remaining with them, whilst Bill moved on to Second Suffolk in Burma.

The enemy dead of that first attack were later identified as being a Lieutenant, a Sergeant, a Lance Corporal and two Superior Privates. Information in the form of a diary was also recovered, and this led the Intelligence Officer, Captain Arrindell, to conclude that the dead Japanese all belonged to 1st Company, 51st Regiment.

At 1430 the Padre held an Easter service in the area of Battalion HQ, now situated just down a path from the Mound. It was no coincidence that such a service was being conducted on the eve of an action against the Pimple, for it was twenty-seven years to the day that the then Padre of Second Suffolk, Revd G. C. Danvers, had held a similar service in the chalk caves under the French town of Arras in 1917, before they advanced into battle the following day.

The Padre later recalled the event and his 'flock's' dedication in attending the service, even though they were in a highly exposed position:

> Services were held wherever possible in the front line. Often we were so close to the enemy that we could not sing the hymns in case our voices were

heard. Some services stand out more than others, but I always think of one communion service on the top of a very steep hill. The position had been attacked several times, and with the long elephant grass and thick bushes, it was difficult to spot the enemy. On this occasion two ammunition boxes acted as a Holy table. The men had their rifles beside them as they knelt and joined in the service. On the outskirts others stood in trenches with machine guns in front of them ready to ward off any attack by the enemy. Could the presence of God have been any nearer in cathedral or church as He was in that service? It reminded one so vividly of Psalm 23, verse 5 'Thou preparest a table before me in the presence of mine enemies.'[5]

Later that afternoon, he officiated at the funeral service for Privates Haynes and Wigger in Imphal Cemetery, whilst Lieutenant Duncan took a fighting patrol out from the Mound to the north-west. This time he moved around to the north of Ring III and returned to base some four hours later. He reported that he had accounted for nineteen enemy dead, one probable and six wounded.

They had, however, been spotted on their return to the Mound by a Japanese machine-gun crew, who now opened fire on them. This crew, who manned a gun mounted on a wheeled carriage, fired at Lieutenant Duncan's patrol, before disappearing into the undergrowth dragging their weapon behind them.

Major Hill recalled the positions his Company manned at that time:

Just beyond the 'Mound' lay the 'Pimple,' a small excrescence joined to the 'Mound' by a saddle of about 50 yards. The Company was too weak in numbers to include this important sub-feature in the perimeter defences. On Easter Sunday, preceding the attack, patrols had been pushed forward, but brought back no information. No movement had been seen on the hills beyond the position; countryside appeared completely deserted. In the plain below the villages lay quiet in the evening sun. It was hard to believe that the blue tinted hills hid a Japanese division poised for a decisive assault on Imphal.[6]

In the early evening, 'B' Company on the Mound observed a party of Japanese massing on a hill feature some 200 yards beyond the Pimple to the north-east. Standing by to repulse what they believed would be a large-scale attack, they waited in eerie silence, knowing that the enemy was on their way. But for all the tranquillity of the night, a vigilant watch was maintained:

The Company 'stood to' at seven o'clock that evening as usual. There was no wind and near-full moon was just rising above the dark line of hills.

The bark of distant pie-dogs emphasised the almost unnatural silence as men stood in their defences peering into the twilight. Then the normal sentries, two or three to a Section, according to strength, were posted and the remainder of the Company lay down to sleep, dressed and with their weapons beside them.[7]

In the eerie silence, apart from the usual rustling of the foliage in the wind, the sentries scoured the hills in front of them. The anticipated Japanese attack now came on but was repulsed:

About 8.30 [p.m.] a grenade booby trap on the 'Pimple' went off with a startling roar – it might only be a jackal or it might be the Japs. Within ten seconds, the company was in position. Then came the throb of the forward sections LMG. Two more LMGs opened up almost immediately after. At the same time the Japs appeared over and round the sides of the 'Pimple', an officer in front brandishing his sword; the latter was distinctly visible in the bright moonlight gesticulating and waving his men on. The enemy attack was covered by fire from Jap grenade dischargers; but when our men started to throw grenades among the attacking line the enemy faded away, melting into the shadows. There was silence and the night closed in again. But in the grass and on our wire there were bodies gleaming whitely. After a little time the Japs could be heard digging on the reverse slope of the 'Pimple'; but the Battalion's 3″ Mortar bombs effectually found this range. Next morning, extensive patrolling found one dead Jap officer and six dead other ranks, while there were signs of many wounded having been moved.[8]

It was clear, however, that for all their noise and bravado, the Japanese had not made any serious reconnaissance of the Mound or its defences prior to their attack:

Without warning a Jap company attacked strongly from the direction of the Pimple. They can have made no previous recce and were completely surprised by the thick belts of wire concealed in the grass. 'B' Company's first warning was the sound of the Japs tumbling and tripping into the wire. They were immediately engaged by heavy fire from the Battalion Brens and the attack was broken.[9]

Amid the confusion of that first battle around the Mound, Second Lieutenant Gilbert took the opportunity of the near-full moon and the enemy's distraction to take a reconnaissance patrol towards the village of Yaingangpokpi astride the Imphal-Ukhrul road.

As the patrol set off, a thunderstorm blew up with great ferocity and dark clouds obscured the moon. Using this to their advantage, the Japanese now switched their attacks to a hilltop position held by the Jats in the north, and as the rain poured down, those who could, sheltered in their cubbyholes or under their monsoon capes.

In the now pitch-black night, with the din of the rain beating down on their slouch hats, those in the forward defence lines waited again for the enemy. The men of 'B' Company, the majority of whom were veterans of Arakan, knew the drill. They kept their calm and remained quiet. More attacks came on and 2″ illuminating mortar bombs were now fired that fell attached to small parachutes, silhouetting the enemy as he advanced. Fire was brought upon them and many were seen to fall before the light burned out.

More attacks would follow in the hours of darkness: 'That night the Japs made several other attempts from other directions, only to meet the same fate, and in the morning a number of dead were picked up in the wire including an officer whose magnificent sword was taken and later presented to Lieutenant-Colonel H. R. Hopking.'

As daylight came, the enemy were conspicuous by their absence, and parties cautiously ventured out from the Mound to bury the enemy dead that remained from the previous night's attack.

The Padre also remembered the sword:

The first Jap sword was obtained by 'B' Company. The Japs put in a night attack on a hill feature which 'B' Company were holding. It was met by a hail of bullets and they had to withdraw, taking their killed and wounded with them. An officer's sword was found the next morning. Major Peter Hill, on behalf of the Company presented it to the C.O. as a souvenir.[10]

As clearance and intelligence-gathering continued, two men of 152 Parachute Battalion, who had escaped from Japanese captivity, came up to Battalion HQ from Brigade:

They stated that the Jap Coy which attacked B Coy on night 8/9 and the enemy which were shot up on the 9th by Lt. Duncan's patrol were the same Coy – which had originally started the attack with 150 men and was now 20 fighting men in strength, they stated that there were 80 casualties in area 5074 [the Nungshigum feature] guarded by 14 sentries with 1 M.M.G.[11]

Lieutenant-Colonel Hopking ensured that this morale-boosting information was distributed to all Companies on their various hilltop positions, and in the early afternoon he took these two men from the Parachute Battalion, together with Captain Arrindell, out in a Battalion carrier towards the village of Yaingangpokpi, where they pointed out to him the enemy dispositions on their various hilltops at the rear of the Pimple and beyond in the direction of 'Sausage' Hill.

Also that afternoon, Corporal Wheeler took a reconnaissance patrol out towards another hill feature, 'Point 4997', passing Second Lieutenant Gauld's fighting patrol returning to the Battalion area. Lieutenant Gauld relayed to Corporal Wheeler that the enemy were in strength on another small hill to the extreme north, close to Sausage Hill. Corporal Wheeler now moved forward to an area close to the hamlet of Lamboida Khul, where they encountered a party of twenty to thirty Japanese. Bringing fire upon them, he claimed at least two casualties before retiring.

Following these reconnaissance patrols, the Intelligence Section were now feverishly collating all available information about the enemy on his various hills in preparation for the Battalion's impending attack upon the Pimple itself.

Private Leslie Whetnell of the Intelligence Section worked all the available information he had been given into a sketch to be distributed to the attacking platoons. This showed the route of advance from the Mound onto the Pimple, with all known enemy positions, their probable arcs of fire and any ground that could be used for cover. It was clear from the intelligence that the gully from the north end of the Mound that joined the ridge up to the summit of the Pimple would afford them only limited cover.

Lieutenant Watt now took a platoon out to harass the enemy in the area of Corporal Wheeler's earlier patrol, but in retaliation, at 1845, the Japanese brought down a heavy barrage of discharger shells onto 'B' Company's positions on the Mound in advance of what was anticipated to be another infantry assault.

At 1832 'B' Company HQ made wireless contact with the Guerrilla Platoon, who were out in the valley to the east of the Pimple. They reported to Major Hill that there was much enemy activity on a small spur to the south of the Pimple itself, south-east of his positions on the Mound. Artillery was now requested to pound the area, and after a lull no further activity was spotted. However, the Guerrilla Platoon came through again to report that the Japanese were moving round to the east of the Pimple and were also now occupying a small hillock in the north-east beyond 'Ring I'.

Then, further alarming reports came from the Guerrilla Platoon that more Japanese were infiltrating round the south-eastern side of the Mound, crossing their lines of communication with the remainder of the Battalion in positions

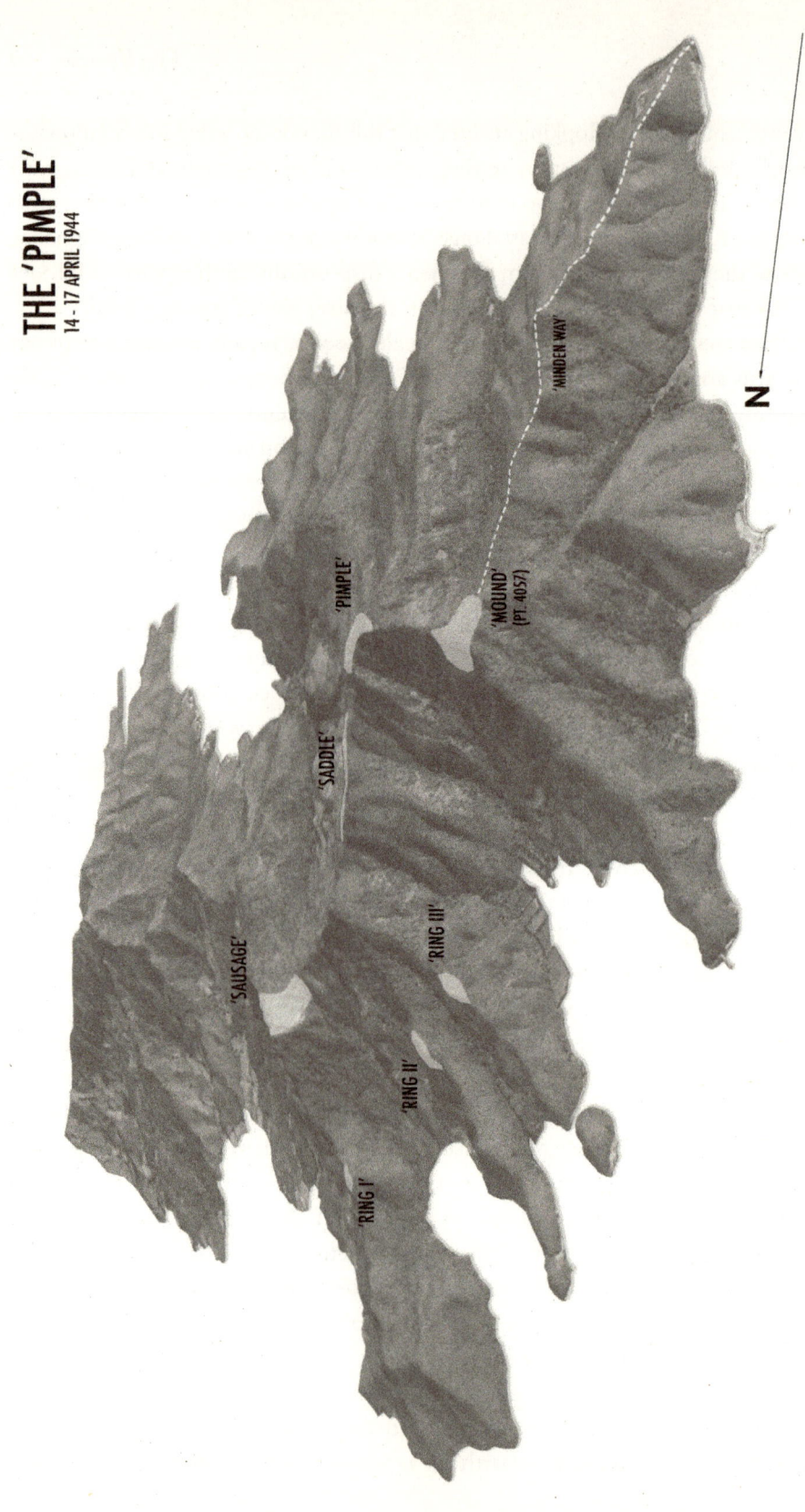

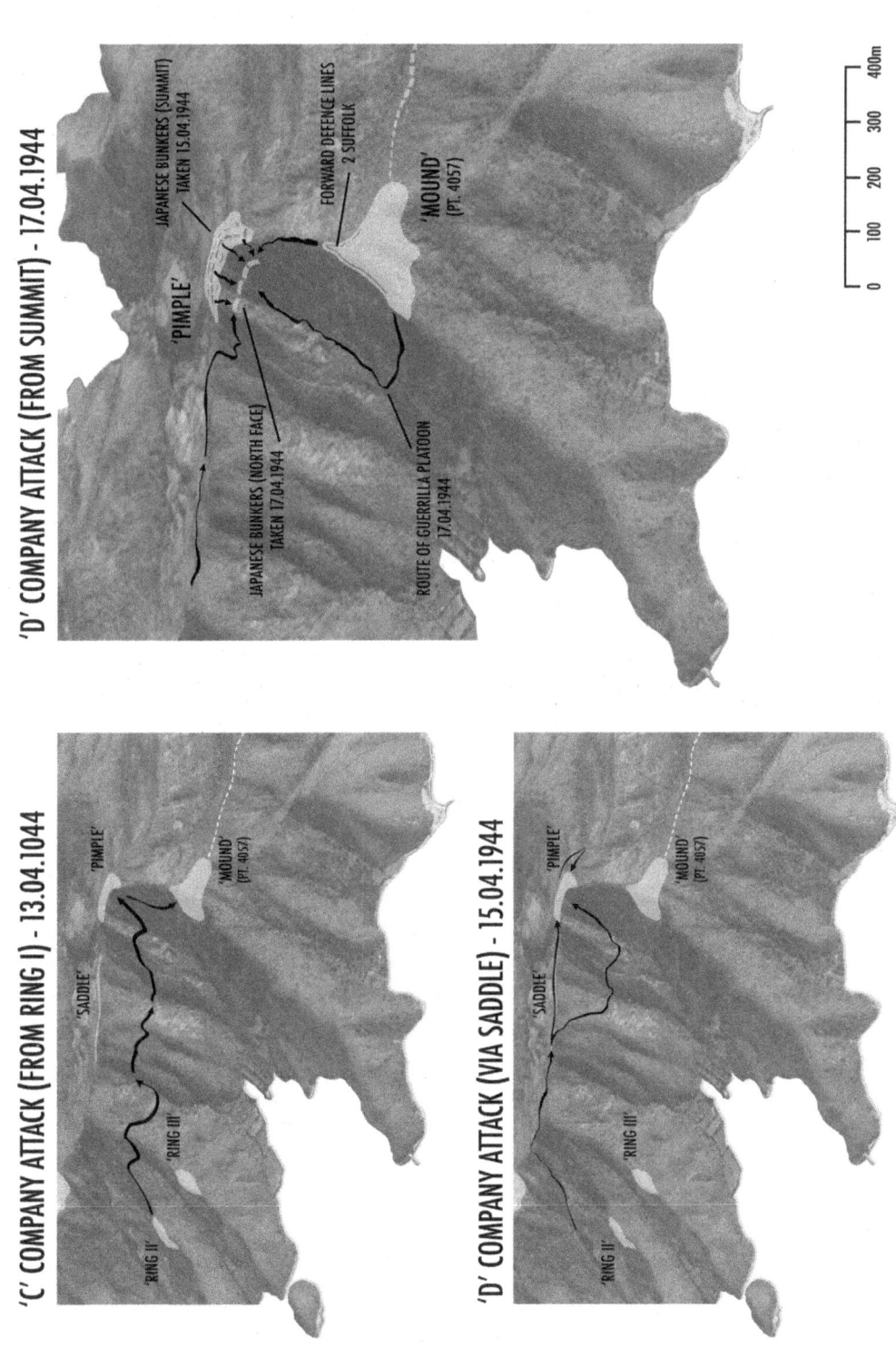

on the valley floor. 'B' Company now engaged them, but at 2028 telephone communications between Battalion HQ and the Mound were severed.

Unable to ascertain what was happening on the Mound, and concerned that the enemy were now encircling 'B' Company, Lieutenant Colonel Hopking was preparing to go forward immediately. He had heard the firing, but just as he was preparing to leave, a Royal Artillery unit reported from an observation post to the west that 'B' Company were holding back the Japanese on two fronts and looked to have the 'situation in hand'.

At 2104, the CO received a message via a 'B' Company runner who had dashed down from Major Hill's HQ to report that their positions were now 'much quieter'. Lieutenant Colonel Hopking therefore decided to remain at Battalion HQ and, at first light, to send out a party from the Signal Platoon to find the break in the line and restore telephone communications with the Mound. However, in the early hours, his communications with the Artillery were also severed. Now cut off from information, Lieutenant Colonel Hopking could hear firing again and could only hope that all was well with 'B' Company and that Major Hill was still holding off the Japanese in the darkness.

At first light on 11 April, a 'Line Party' left Battalion HQ and set off to find the break in the telephone wire to 'B' Company's positions. Accompanying them was a fighting patrol of 'A' Company, who followed them through 'D' Company's area in the foothills and up towards the Mound. Within ninety minutes the party had found the first break in the wire and were busy repairing it, whilst the remainder of the patrol formed a defensive ring around the men at work, keeping a lookout for the enemy. By 0830 they had found the second break, and soon communications between Battalion HQ and the Artillery were restored.

Whilst the line party concluded their work, Second Lieutenant Bradley of 'D' Company took out a fighting patrol to a small hill to the north-west of the Pimple. From here they moved further north towards Sausage Hill, before dropping down into the Iril River valley and moving south-westwards behind Rings I, II and III on the valley floor.

The CO now sent Sergeant Bunce out with three carriers to see if any intelligence could be gathered from the enemy dead known to have fallen to fire from Corporal Wheeler's patrol the day before. Only one enemy body was found, but not long afterwards Lieutenant Watt came up to Battalion HQ to report that his men had successfully taken Point 4241 without opposition. Keen to consolidate this gain, the CO was just about to order a platoon out to strengthen the position when reports started to come in from 'B' Company on the Mound that Second Lieutenant Bradley's patrol, which was then down in the *nullah* (ravine) between them and Ring III, was now engaging the enemy in positions just north of the Pimple.

It transpired that as Second Lieutenant Bradley's patrol had left Ring III for their final leg to return to the Mound they had spotted an enemy position to the north of the Pimple and decided to attack it from their current position. However, it soon became clear that this was not an isolated position but a cluster of well-camouflaged machine-gun posts.

In a bitter firefight against these well-concealed positions, three men were wounded, and Second Lieutenant Bradley decided that they should retire to the Mound as soon as possible. Upon reaching its forward defence lines, Privates Ward, Sinclair and Carr received treatment, but it was discovered that another man, Private Blake, was missing. Lieutenant Bradley reported that 'they had killed some Japs near Lamyenching on the way to the Battalion', but it was hoped that the missing man would appear soon.

Private George Blake never did return. George was a Barnardo's boy who joined the Suffolk Regiment in 1938 and was transferred to Second Suffolk in early 1939. He received regular letters from his foster family which he shared with his comrade Private Ernie Bates:

> It was in the latter part of 1943, prior to the Battalion moving to the Arakan. The letter had been sent to my friend George Blake, wanting me to share the news from England, he tore the top off the letter, and gave the remainder to me. I put it in my ration tin where it has remained ever since.[12]

The section that Bates retained concluded:

> Old England will never go under, God is protecting us on every side. It's glorious here today, George, so quiet and sunny, one would wonder why war should be. Mr Churchill has been very ill, hope he will live to see victory, you are old enough to look after yourself, and you only have yourself.[13]

At dawn on 12 April, two platoons of 'A' Company moved off towards Lamyenching to meet a possible force of thirty-five to forty Japanese who were advancing from that direction. The night before, a patrol of 2/1 Punjab had reported a strong concentration of enemy in that area, and because of this, one troop of Lee tanks accompanied the advance.

Whilst the enemy's attention, it was hoped, would be drawn away to the left flank, where a renewed attack was going in against the Nungshigum feature, Sergeant Steele of 'C' Company, took a patrol of twelve men north from 'B' Company's positions to reconnoitre the Pimple from that direction. The plan was that if opportunity presented itself, they would attack the Pimple from that direction using the 'Saddle' – a sharp, rocky ridge that connected the position to Sausage Hill. An NCO from 'D' Company and six men were to form a small fighting patrol to harass the enemy if required and to act as a diversion from Sergeant Steele's activities.

Meanwhile, Sergeant Bates, who was then commanding a platoon of 'A' Company, was taking out another patrol to positions north-east of the Pimple. Having worked up to the Pimple from the east, they were fired upon by Japanese light machine guns on its northern side. Sergeant Bates worked his platoon round and brought down fire upon the Japanese positions: 'Without regard to his personal safety and by his courage and leadership, he succeeded in silencing the enemy, but in the crossfire several casualties were incurred, including Sergeant Bates himself who was shot in the chest.'[14]

Despite the Sergeant's gallantry, their position on the lower northern slope of the Pimple was untenable. With fire being brought upon them from above, and now out of the range of covering fire from 'B' Company on the Mound, an enforced retirement was necessary. Making it back to the Mound, carried by his men, Sergeant Bates was transferred by stretcher down the precipitous path to the Regimental Aid Post, but his condition deteriorated and he died of his wounds early the following day.

James Bates had been a regular soldier with the Royal Norfolk Regiment before joining Second Suffolk earlier in the war. An old soldier who had served on the North West Frontier, he had been introduced to Lord Mountbatten six months before when he came to visit the Battalion in Arakan. For his actions against the Pimple he was Mentioned in Dispatches. His mention noted that: 'Sgt. Bates directed his platoon's fire without regard to his personal safety and by his courage and leadership, although wounded, inspired his men.'[15]

Corporals Finch and Stewart were also wounded in the action, and a further three men were missing.

At 1545, 'C' Company moved off to attack a feature to the west of Ring I. Their attack coincided with an airstrike by Hurri-bombers that were heading towards the Nungshigum feature on the Battalion's left flank. As this aerial attack went in, 'C' Company saw an opportunity to take the Pimple whilst the enemy's attention was diverted, and just after 1600, one platoon of 'C' Company moved off towards the Pimple from the north. Reaching a position some 400 yards from the feature to the right of the Saddle, they halted for the night and put out sentries.

During the night, the Guerrilla Platoon came up to their positions and harassed the enemy together with a Troop of Lee tanks far off to the east, but no enemy were sighted. Just after midnight, four 'stragglers', three of whom had been reported missing following the previous day's actions, crawled in through the forward defence lines; after a mug of tea, they were taken on to the Intelligence Officer and then to Brigade, who were keen to gather as much intelligence about the area as possible.

One of these stragglers was Private James 'Jim' Worlledge. He had been hit in the shoulder by a Japanese sniper and had lain low in great pain, hoping that someone would come back for him. He was reported missing earlier that evening, but as soon as it was dark he made his way back through the Battalion lines to the Regimental Aid Post, where his wounds were dressed.

Jim had been called up in 1940, serving first in the 8th Battalion, before being transferred to the 4th Battalion bound for Singapore. Luckily, his ship was diverted and he missed being captured, joining Second Suffolk in India in mid-1942. After he recovered from his wounds in 38th British General Hospital in Assam, he returned to the Battalion for some months, but he then suffered dysentery and malaria and was invalided home later in 1944, just before the Battalion left the Imphal front.

One man of 'C' Company who did not return that night was Private William Fallowfield from Southend-on-Sea. He was called up the previous year and posted to join Second Suffolk in Burma. His brother, Alfred, was a Lance Corporal in the Royal Norfolk Regiment and had been taken prisoner at Singapore. The Japanese transport he was travelling on was torpedoed, and the survivors, including Alfred, were picked up and taken to Australia, but he died there in April 1945.

At 0900 on 13 April news came that 'C' Company had successfully occupied Ring I in the north without opposition. Now, in an attempt to consolidate, two platoons remained on the hill, with the other down in the valley below, pushing south along a spur and trying to link up with 'B' Company on the Mound.

As they moved off, a flight of Vengeance dive-bombers passed over them on their way to again attack the Nungshigum feature. Following their airstrike, the artillery opened up on Nungshigum, followed by more airstrikes – this time by Hurri-bombers. From their positions, the Battalion watched as the Dogras, supported by a troop of tanks, advanced up its slopes to take the summit. Lieutenant Duncan recalled the attack on Nungshigum which he could hear from Battalion HQ,

One hill dominated the northern part and it was called Nungshigum. Not actually a hill but a four-mile-long ridge, several peaks rising to thirty-seven hundred [feet]. Now remember the base of that peak would be about 2,600 above sea level. So up to thirty-seven hundred and very steep near the summit. The Japs took it but couldn't be allowed to stay on it and, after a couple of failed attempts, a full-scale attack was planned. Now, the Suffolks and I were about 4 miles away across the paddy fields and we heard, we didn't see, we heard an awful lot. First the Vengeance dive-bombers came along, and then machine-gunning, Hurri-bombers and then the mass artillery of 5th Indian Division all softened the Japs up. Then our Dogras, climbing up behind tanks, although with the steepness, the tanks could only go in low gear at 1 mile an hour. But the hill was finally cleared although every tank commander, for they had to observe from their turrets, every tank commander and infantry officer was either killed or wounded in the taking of the hill. Overwhelming strength and firepower. But much earlier, the Japanese Chief-of-Staff decided no tank could climb such hills so they hadn't taken any anti-tank guns.[16]

Back in the north-east, the platoon of 'C' Company were now almost at the base of the Pimple, having crossed the 'Spur' where Lieutenant Bradley's patrol had been fired upon two days earlier. Under the command of Lieutenant Watt, they were making good progress and, seeing an opportunity to attempt an attack on the Pimple from that direction, they moved left and started climbing its slopes; but as they started their ascent they came under heavy fire from above.

In an attempt to outflank the position, Lieutenant Watt moved out into the open to draw the enemy's fire, whilst one of his Bren teams now engaged the position. Lieutenant Watt, using another Bren, now brought fire upon the Japanese positions and then, using grenades, accounted for at least four enemy dead.

However, seeing that there was little prospect of silencing the position, Lieutenant Watt now ordered his men to retire as quickly as possible and make for the Mound round to the south-west. They were almost back through the safety of 'B' Company's forward defence lines when Lieutenant Watt discovered that one man was missing.

Pushing his men through a gap in the wire into the safety of the Mound, he now went back alone to try and locate the missing man. Having backtracked along the route they had taken, he appeared a few minutes later, covered in blood and carrying the wounded man over his shoulder.

For his actions that day, Lieutenant 'Tommy' Watt was awarded the Military Cross. His citation noted that his 'Outstanding courage and devotion to duty were of the highest order and an inspiration to the whole Battalion'.[17] Thomas Watt had been commissioned into the Worcestershire Regiment but had served on detachment with Second Suffolk since October 1943.

Seeing that any further attack from the north would now be impossible, the other two platoons of 'C' Company, who were preparing to move forward to support Lieutenant Watt's advance to the Pimple, now decided to withdraw from their position on Ring I and moved down into the Iril valley to the west.

From here they started to move south back to the Mound. Despite the ferocity of the afternoon's actions, the War Diary recorded: 'Quiet night on Bn. front, though noisy from 1/17 Dogra area on Nungshigum'.

Taking advantage of this quiet, Lieutenant Colonel Hopking, who was puzzled as to why 'C' Company had decided to leave the safety of the unoccupied Ring I which commanded an excellent view over the route of any Japanese retreat from the Nungshigum feature, decided that he would send 'A' Company back immediately to reoccupy it. They set off on the night of 13/14 April, as Major Browne recalled:

> In the meantime the Japs had closed up to the hill 'Mound' and the company there was having quite a lively time. A platoon I lent them for a day had nasty casualties including the commander killed. The hill over to the left, Nungshigum, had been lost to the Japs and re-taken with the help of tanks, which climbed right to the top of the feature. Now came our turn. The company with two mortars, and two machine guns manned by Gurkha paratroops, moved out on the night of 13th April at about midnight. It was pitch dark and bullets were whining over from the area of brigade Head Quarters where they were having fun with a Jap patrol. We were laden with food, ammunition, and water for three days, which meant that each man was carrying about 80lbs – the hell of a weight. We were aiming to get into an unoccupied hill before the first light in the morning which was at about 0530 hours. This involved a march of about 4 miles, and a climb up an almost perpendicular slope of about 1,500 feet. The slope was jungle-covered, which meant that we had to move in single file, which is a frightful formation at the best of times. However, we made it – except for the mortars which arrived much later – though many of the men were literally on their hands and knees. The heavy weight was a great strain for so long. We dug in straight away like all wise men. Later in the morning another company came past us, and swung in to attack the Japs from behind, who were worrying our company on 'Mound' but failed.[18]

The amount of kit being carried was essential to establish a position and remain self-sufficient for a maximum of three days, during which time reinforcements and mules carrying supplies could be brought up to strengthen it.

In the early hours of 14 April it was confirmed that, with assistance from tanks, the Dogras had finally taken the Nungshigum feature the previous day, and it seemed likely that as the last salient of enemy resistance the Pimple would now be heavily reinforced by the Japanese; from Ring I, 'A' Company observed reinforcements being sent forward to the Pimple along the Saddle.

The Pimple was now the enemy's only remaining vantage point in the area, and it was anticipated that the Japanese defence would now stiffen. Lieutenant Colonel Hopking therefore moved Battalion HQ forward from the path up onto the rearward slopes of the spine that led to the Mound. He did not wish to be separated from his companies by any Japanese encircling moves.

It rained heavily for three hours in the early afternoon, which made the going slow for the mules that were transporting the various elements of Battalion HQ. The rains had made the track extremely slippery, and with only a narrow, sludgy path to keep to, the move took much longer than anticipated.

It was only the redoubtable mule that could take supplies forward over such terrain. The Padre recalled with affection, these loyal, strong animals and their worth to the Battalion:

> We are inclined to think of the mule as an animal which is stubborn and continually kicking, and biting, at all and sundry. We realised their worth again and again as they climbed the steepest of hills with a full load, or without a stumble they walked along a narrow twisting path with a thousand foot drop on one side. It was delightful to note the wonderful affection, too, which the drivers had for their mules – 'Lily, darling,' 'Come here, love', 'Sweetheart mine' etc. are only a few of the loving phrases that were used. I have known drivers refuse to go on leave because their mules would miss them. I have seen a man in hospital shed tears as he thought of his mules, who were certain to be neglected because he was not there to care for them. So, in future remember the mule is man's friend and burden-bearer.[19]

With his HQ in its new position by mid-afternoon, Lieutenant Colonel Hopking now called a conference at which he outlined a new plan to attack and take the Pimple. 'A' Company would harass the Pimple from their positions on Ring I, supported by medium machine guns, whilst 'D' Company would move up to their positions straight away and attack from the north.

Early on 15 April, Lieutenant Colonel Hopking opened up a forward 'Tac HQ' in 'B' Company's area on the Mound. By 0700 Royal Artillery observers reported that both 'A' and 'D' Companies were in position on a Ring feature just north of Ring I, and five minutes later 'D' Company reported that they were in position close to Ring II and were preparing to assault the Pimple from the north-east by crossing onto it via the Saddle.

Whilst one platoon of 'D' Company remained on their feature, at 0744 the fire platoon set off for the Pimple using the Saddle. At 0750, the distinctive sound of a burst of Japanese machine-gun fire came through the mist, indicating that 'D' Company must have come into contact with the enemy in the area of the Saddle. Immediately afterwards, a Bren opened up, and a period of silence suggested that it appeared to have silenced the enemy position.

Back on the Mound, which was still shrouded in mist, just after 0800, the CO, who could also hear the firing, asked by wireless for Major Leach, 'D' Company's commander, to report his progress. Soon afterwards came the reply, 'Nan Tar Roger' (Nothing to Report).

As the mist finally began to lift, 'A' Company, from their positions in the north, observed a Japanese soldier running into a bunker on the far end of the Saddle just below the Pimple itself, but they could not relay this information to the assaulting platoons as the latter were already close to this point and, despite continual calls, could not be contacted by radio. More firing was heard as the forward attacking platoon of 'D' Company dealt with this position, and at 0828 a mortar post in 'B' Company's positions on the Mound reported that 'D' Company were now well up on the Pimple itself.

There was now considerable enemy fire coming from the north around Sausage Hill, and one platoon of 'A' Company moved south off the Saddle and Ring III to protect the left flank from any enemy infiltration.

'D' Company were, however, making good progress on their ascent to the summit of the Pimple. From their vantage point on Ring III, a platoon of 'A' Company reported seeing 'D' Company moving round the western slopes of the Pimple with their fixed bayonets glimmering in the early morning sun. Private Ernie Bates remembered watching their advance:

> They seemed to move quite quickly, but we had difficulty in spotting them in the thick bracken. Occasionally, a glint of the sun would catch a bayonet or the edge of a tin hat, but they kept steadily plodding on up that hill. It looked as if they were almost going up it in a spiral as they moved sideways as well as upwards.[20]

Unlike for their counterparts in the Royal Norfolk Regiment, the wearing of steel helmets was not governed by brigade orders, and it was very much a personal choice what form of headdress one wore in action. The bush hat was practical since, as Bates observed, 'It was much better at keeping the sun from one's eyes.'[21]

At 0836 it was reported that 'D' Company were working round from the east, making for the northern face of the Pimple, where they were engaging Japanese positions with grenades. A bunker with a light machine gun was reported, and they were experiencing difficulty in silencing its fire. However, elements of 'D' Company had now reached the summit on the southern side and were finally occupying the complex of enemy trenches across the crest of the Pimple itself.

With the summit reached, 'D' Company now set about making a defensive position there. Whilst men dug frantically with their entrenching tools, the Japanese started to bombard the Pimple with their 75mm guns positioned on Sausage Hill. Enemy Zero fighters then swept in low overhead escorting a flight of bombers destined for targets in the east. Thankfully, they ignored the battle raging below around the Pimple and flew on. It was believed that they were heading to attack the airfield at Imphal.

At 0852 Major Leach himself appeared at Battalion HQ, exhausted. He had dashed down under fire from the Pimple along the track to the Mound to report the situation to the CO personally. Communications had been severed, and the radios were again not working, but he reported that he had two platoons of 'D' Company on the Pimple itself and one platoon on Ring II, between Ring I and Ring III on the left flank.

Major Leach went on to report that his men occupied the enemy trenches on the summit of the Pimple but that bunkers on its northern face about 30ft below him had not yet been silenced. However, before he set off back to his men, he watched with horror as the Japanese now shelled the summit of the Pimple in his absence.

Whether the Japanese knew the summit had been taken was then unclear, but their men remained there on the northern face as their own shells fell on them. They may have observed 'D' Company's advance to the summit and perhaps foreseen that the position was shortly to fall. Now, in an attempt to silence their fire, Major Browne and his men on Ring I brought fire upon them with the assistance of their machine guns:

> We had given what support we could with M.M.G.s and sniping and had a certain amount of stuff thrown back at us. One grenade discharger hit the tree under which I was sitting potting at the Japs and peppered a good many people, and one platoon commander had to be evacuated. A small bit hit my shoulder, but was nothing to worry about.[22]

Removing the grenade shard himself, Major Browne applied a field dressing and carried on sniping. He never reported his injuries to the Medical Officer.

Back on the Mound, a plan was now formulated between Lieutenant Colonel Hopking and Major Leach to allow 'D' Company to deal with the bunkers. The artillery would pound the Japanese positions on Sausage Hill, starting as soon as possible. With their fire temporarily silenced, Major Leach and his men would descend to deal with the bunkers and pave the way for 'B' Company to advance swiftly from the Mound up onto the Pimple itself.

As Major Leach made his way back to his men, the artillery strike on Sausage Hill began. In the lull, Lieutenant Gilbert's platoon had started to attack the bunkers with assistance from the Battalion's mortars located on the Mound.

Fire was brought upon the position for over twenty minutes before its occupants emerged and ran away north towards Sausage Hill over to the right side of the Saddle. Captain Forrest, Second-in-Command of 'B' Company, himself situated on Ring II, reported that he had seen them retreating at 0926, and 'D' Company later reported killing one Japanese soldier by Bren fire when he ran through their positions along the Saddle.

'D' Company's attack had successfully silenced one bunker, but there were at least another two that were yet to be put out of action, and it was thought that they might possibly be connected. Whilst the artillery continued to pound Sausage Hill, a platoon of 'A' Company now brought down fire upon the bunkers on the north side of the Pimple from their positions on Ring III and, as was hoped, the Japanese retaliated, drawing fire away from 'D' Company's efforts in dealing with the bunkers from above.

Back on the Pimple, Lieutenant Gilbert's platoon were making a slow right-flanking movement around the southern side of the feature, and at 1009 a flight of eighteen Vengeance dive-bombers flew across the Battalion area to attack the northern end of the Nungshigum feature just as Lieutenant Gilbert's platoon reached the summit.

Almost immediately, the platoon had fire brought upon it from the bunkers below and several casualties were sustained, including Lieutenant Gilbert, who now had to be helped down from the Pimple to a suitable spot from where the stretcher-bearers could convey him to the Regimental Aid Post. In the absence of their commander, his platoon now dug in on the summit, strengthening the enemy's abandoned positions there.

Viewing the unfolding situation from the Mound through his binoculars, the CO saw two men fall, and moments afterwards, the first 'walking wounded' of 'D' Company came through 'B' Company's forward lines for conveyance to the Regimental Aid Post. Private Clifford Price, then serving with the MT Section, recalled the trail of wounded who came down to the road to where carriers were waiting to take them to the Advanced Dressing Station:

> The 'Pimple' was a tough nut to crack, but I was not directly involved. I was part of a group from Battalion HQ who were looking after the two carriers we had been allocated. We knew there was a big battle going on, we could hear it, and soon, the wounded came down in ones and twos and we knew that we had to get them away to the dressing station about a mile away in the village of Kamlaga [Kameng]. We could see that they had had

a time as the bearers struggled to get down to us with their stretchers. We had to load them on and get away and back before the next ones came down to us. I seem to recall that we made many trips that day.[23]

As the battle on the Pimple continued, about twenty minutes later, another flight of Hurri-bombers flew over to attack Sausage Hill, and under cover of this diversion in the north, Captain Forrest now prepared to make an attack on the bunkers from the Mound.

Back on Ring III, one platoon of 'D' Company were holding on. A section of eight men, including Private Cyril Wilkinson and his 'Number Two' armed with a 2″ mortar, remained dug in observing the action to the south-east. Their Sergeant ordered the pair to stay put whilst he took the remainder of the section forward to help Captain Forrest attack the bunkers on the Pimple. Wilkinson recalled:

They disappeared quickly into the dip to attack a Japanese-held bunker on a pimple, we fired a number of rounds of smoke off when a shell landed nearby and, looking round, my number two had disappeared never to be seen again. Two men, one from Birmingham and one from Norfolk, from the attacking party appeared ahead both wounded. They said [Private] Narduzzo had been killed, shot twice through the neck and cheek.[24]

Another platoon of 'B' Company under the command of Lieutenant Duncan, had in parallel to these actions now moved forward from the Mound, in anticipation that the Pimple would soon be taken. Accompanied by another section of Gurkha paratroopers, they had successfully edged forward, crossed down into the *nullah* on the south-eastern side of the Pimple and were now digging in on a small hillock to the east. Suddenly, however, they were spotted, and the Japanese brought down a mortar barrage upon them:

I was ordered to take over a completely new position on a rounded mole, topped with some trees. So, we had to start digging in again and it was practically solid rock. I had some Gurkhas with me, I don't know why, but they were soon burrowing down with their entrenching tools. I did what I could and got down maybe twelve or fifteen inches, with one or two rests I admit, and sat in my new slit trench trying it out. Very comfortable, I was in a bath, I could rest elbows and forearms on the level ground, so I sat there looking round. Gurkhas still burrowing away, some other Suffolks doing what they could, some had given up, one soldier obviously writing a letter, and of course there had been no firing of any sort from either side. It was peaceful. So, I turned around as best I could, sat down facing the other way, looking in that direction, when BANG! a mortar bomb hit the tree above me and I felt my left leg go. What excitement and what digging thereafter![25]

A runner was sent back to get aid, and in a great physical feat, the Company stretcher-bearers now came forward onto the hill to collect the wounded:

The stretcher-bearers, excited as well, had to treat a casualty, not too messy a casualty at that, although no real need for me to point out that that mortar had come just seconds, say fifteen seconds earlier, the piece of metal would have come down somewhere around my right ribs. One of the stretcher-bearers asked me if I could waggle my toes, and I could, and he said, 'Well, so your leg isn't broken anyway.' My tibia was smashed. After a bit of an argument, because I didn't think it would hinder me too much, I handed over the platoon, said cheerio to the chaps and then began a very painful descent of the hill on my bottom holding my gammy leg up as best I could. And down there, an even more painful journey standing on the back of a truck while it belted across the dried paddy fields and associated *bunds* [embankments] to the casualty clearing station. From there, perhaps three days to when I was comfortably in a hospital in India and subsequently downgraded from A1, and that was the end of my active service in the Burma War.[26]

Despite the efforts of both 'B' and 'D' Companies, the attack had temporarily ground to a halt, and at 1413 Captain Forrest reported to Battalion HQ that he had called off any further assault upon the bunkers. His Company had suffered three men killed, two wounded and two missing.

Captain Forrest informed Lieutenant Colonel Hopking that he and his men had managed to get to within 50 yards of the bunkers before they came under machine-gun fire from at least three positions. Forced to go to ground, they had had to retreat back the way they had come, using what cover they could.

Now under pressure from his superiors to press on and take the whole position, Lieutenant Colonel Hopking decided he would not attack the bunkers in such a way again and ordered Captain Forrest to take a message to Major Leach that 'D' Company should now withdraw all its men back to the summit of the Pimple.

The CO wished Major Leach to assist in reinforcing 'A' Company's positions on Ring II and III by sending a platoon to be split between the two hilltops. He would leave the other two platoons of 'D' Company dug in on the summit of the Pimple.

The remainder of the afternoon was relatively quiet, but at 1950 machine-gun fire and grenade explosions were heard by a listening post of 'A' Company on Ring I, and later, a party of 'A' Company who had proceeded south to lay booby-traps between their hill and the Pimple were intercepted by a Japanese patrol of about eight men trying to break through towards Sausage Hill.

It was clear that these Japanese were coming from the direction of the Pimple and they gave chase to the Suffolk party, who ran all the way back through 'A' Company's forward defences on Ring I. The Japanese patrol followed, running straight into 'A' Company's Brens, whereupon many were seen to fall:

> As it was getting dark one platoon of the attacking company came into our company area for the night, and were in the uncomfortable position of not being dug in for the night. We stood to. 'Stood down' when it was dark, and almost immediately there was a loud bang – a booby trap we had put out – followed by wild yelling and shouting as Japs charged up the slope from the direction of 'Sausage'. There weren't very many and they met an extremely warm reception, particularly as they arrived in the exact spot they had been expected. Hell was let loose and shot and shell was flying all over the place for a few minutes. Then silence, and we could hear the Japs dragging dead or wounded away, and also certain rather vulgar remarks directed at us in English![27]

However, the battle discipline of some 'A' Company's men was not all it should have been. Newly arrived reinforcements, some coming from the Royal Scots and the Royal Berkshire Regiments, were a little 'careless' in their movements:

> Some of the men who were not dug in started moving about during the battle and one nearly got the Sgt. Major's bayonet into him and another was on the end of my pistol: but we saw the silhouette of their hats against the sky during the rest of the night. Only one grenade was thrown which was a compliment to the state of nerves of the men. The gunners were always ready to give us very accurate support if we needed it, and our mortars were also in action by now.[28]

Beaten, the Japanese withdrew, and afterwards 'slithering noises' were heard 'as though bodies were being dragged away'; then for a couple of hours all was quiet, until the Japanese on Sausage Hill were spotted firing grenades off the southern end of the feature down its western slopes towards Rings I and II. As was their custom, this was accompanied by much shouting.

The situation was precarious, however. The Battalion occupied the summit of the Pimple and three of its sides, but the northern face that contained the troublesome bunkers remained in enemy hands. Though there was less than 20 yards between the two sides, the night was quiet. However, with renewed pressure from Brigade HQ to take the entire position, Lieutenant Colonel Hopking now had to make a concerted effort at dawn.

The following morning, 16 April, 'A' Company on Ring I sent one platoon north-east towards Sausage Hill. Their advance was part of a larger 'deception' to assist the Punjabis, who were attacking the hill from the north-west. The remainder of the morning was spent establishing Battalion HQ in a new position, that of the previous 'Tac HQ' on the Mound, and then strengthening its perimeter with additional wire and slit trenches.

After an early morning visit from the Brigadier at which Lieutenant Colonel Hopking was again pressed to take the Pimple as soon as possible, at 1100 a rainstorm broke and continued for two hours, during which the CO and the Adjutant worked out a fire programme with their colleagues in the artillery to finally dislodge the Japanese from the north face of the Pimple.

The Brigadier was adamant that the position had to be taken that day, and this left Lieutenant Colonel Hopking little choice but to mount another attack, even though his men were exhausted. He and his Second-in-Command made a new plan to deal with the bunkers on the north face.

The agreed plan was that for fifteen minutes a 3.7in. gun on the plain to the east of the Pimple would pound the bunkers, assisted by one section of medium machine guns and mortars from the Battalion now dug in on Ring I. Then, for ten more minutes the 3.7in. would continue to fire but would switch slightly left to avoid hitting those dug in on the crest of the Pimple itself. Finally, from the crest, the Pioneer Platoon would, with the assistance of 'D' Company, roll down from the summit, improvised 'Molotov Cocktails' made from oil drums and tins filled with petrol but with the stoppers removed. Their trails would then be ignited by grenades, and rapid fire would follow onto the bunkers for five minutes before the infantry went in. 'D' Company on the summit would position two Brens to catch any enemy escaping eastwards along the Saddle.

It was a risky plan and one that carried a strong possibility of injury to men of the Battalion by friendly fire. Lieutenant Colonel Hopking was not keen on the plan and suggested that he would try a final infantry assault that afternoon, using one platoon from 'D' Company heading down from the summit towards the bunkers.

That final assault was fixed to start at 1655. The platoon from 'D' Company moved down from their positions on the summit to attack the bunkers, but they were beaten back by heavy and continuous fire. On returning fire from the summit, at least twelve Japanese were seen to abandon the position and make off in the direction of the Saddle. However, despite their retreat, machine-gun fire from the bunkers had not slackened and, seeing that it would not yet be possible to assault the position from that direction, Major Leach called off the attack.

Fortunately, no casualties had been incurred and all managed to get back to the safety of their foxholes on the summit. No further offensive action was undertaken that night, but grenade explosions were heard just after 2100, and 'D' Company on the summit later reported hearing enemy movement in the area around the bunkers.

Just after midnight on 17 April a heavy rainstorm started which lasted for just over an hour. Using this to cover their movements, the Pioneer Platoon now rolled their huge Molotov cocktails up the rocky path from the Mound and into position on the summit of the Pimple.

At 1100 that morning, Captain Lee Hunter set off with some of the Guerrilla Platoon to find a suitable spot from which to fire up at the bunkers from the base of the Pimple.

In parallel to this, the Pioneers now enacted their plan. Their Molotov cocktails were pushed down from the summit towards the Japanese positions on the north face. Two larger drums which had been fitted with crude fuses ignited just before they hit the position, and as the fireball erupted, phase two came, with the Pioneers lobbing six tins of petrol down behind them with the stoppers removed. The flammable spirit splashed out over the hillside, and the final phase now came as No. 36 grenades were lobbed down to create the desired effect. When the Pioneers had thrown all forty-eight bombs from the four boxes that they had taken to the summit, they retired over to the south face and back round to the safety of the Mound.

When a member of the Guerrilla Platoon fired across into the bunkers using a 'Springfield Rifle' fitted with a telescopic sight, no return fire came. Confused, Captain Lee Hunter took two men cautiously forward up the hill under the crest of the Saddle to investigate. Passing a number of enemy dead and much strewn equipment, upon investigation he found the positions silenced.

The very last of its defenders lay dead in their foxholes, their bodies charred by the explosion. The movement that had been heard the previous night was evidently the majority of the defenders retreating along the Saddle:

> On 17th April there was intermittent firing from the north face of the 'Pimple' by the enemy until approx. 1200 hrs. At 1400 hrs a fighting patrol from the north came southwards and found the enemy positions unoccupied – many bodies of our own and of the enemy's lay around – with an assortment of kit including abandoned 4 LMGs which the enemy had

taken from the bodies of our own men – one foxhole contained many .303 empty cases where an automatic weapon had obviously been. Many bodies of our own men lay 20–30 yards off the enemy positions.[29]

The Japanese had evidently been running short on weaponry and had pressed into service several captured Bren guns together with their own light machine guns. An after-action report noted the effectiveness of the explosive devices that had been used against the position:

The 'Molotov Cocktail' and the 3″ mortar fire had definitely caused most of the damage – many of the Jap bodies lay charred near their positions. The fact that the enemy had occupied single foxholes had obviously cut down his casualties where nothing but direct hits would have damaged him.[30]

Moving forward onto the Pimple that afternoon, Lieutenant Colonel Hopking, with his Second-in-Command, Major Menneer and the Intelligence Officer, Captain Arrindell, held a small conference and examined the enemy dead and their positions.

Contrary to their previous belief, the enemy's positions were not interconnected and their foxholes were for one, or at a push two, men; they had left behind a vast amount of equipment and, more crucially, intelligence, which was key to ascertaining who opposed the Battalion. Any snippets of information that could be gleaned from the enemy dead were most helpful. Major Browne recalled that 'Corpses were valuable just now for identification purposes.'[31]

At 1930 the first of three Japanese patrols attempted to penetrate 'A' Company's positions on Ring I. They were repulsed by accurate Bren and rifle fire and withdrew. They tried again at 0230 in the morning, and later at 0430. Both further attempts were also unsuccessful.

Early on 18 April, a concerted effort was made by the artillery against Sausage Hill. Tragically, one gun fired accidentally onto Ring I, killing four men in 'A' Company's area and wounding seven more. Privates Doyle and Young were killed when shells landed on their slit trenches, and Privates Pittard and Reeve were a stretcher-bearer team caught going to their aid.

CSM Tommy Warren recalled the horror of witnessing the event: 'The long, painful journey down the hill to evacuate the wounded; one of our own 4.5 shells landing in the trees shading Company HQ. Neither shall I forget watching, helplessly, A Company being shelled by our own artillery'.[32]

Lance Corporal James 'Ginger' Doyle had been a pre-war Territorial soldier with the Derbyshire Yeomanry. He had suffered an accident just prior to his unit being sent to North Africa and had remained at home in hospital; after his recovery he was transferred to Second Suffolk in December 1943. His father, also a Territorial, had served during the Great War and had been evacuated through Dunkirk.

Corporal Wheeler, Lance Corporal Presland and Privates Cannell, Hart, Last, Perkins and Sayfritz were all evacuated for treatment. One of these men, Private Leslie 'Jim' Hart, was called up on the same day as his brother, William, in June 1940, the pair being given consecutive service numbers in the Regiment (5833011 and 5833012). Both men were sent to join Second Suffolk in India, with Leslie joining HQ Company and William joining 'C' Company. Later, as the Battalion was reshuffled prior to their departure to Burma, Leslie joined the Medical Platoon, and William joined the Transport Platoon. William had been wounded three months earlier on 24 January, when 'A' Company made their initial advance onto Bamboo Hill.

The brothers were later sent home on repatriation at the same time, spending twenty-eight days' leave with their mother at the family home in Stanground, near Peterborough. Their local newspaper, the *Peterborough Standard*, noted in March 1945: 'Pte. W. Hart has had malaria and was wounded by a Japanese hand grenade. His brother has had malaria twice, was wounded by our own shell fire, and came home straight from convalescence after typhoid fever.'[33] Their father, Robert, had been killed on the Somme in September 1916 whilst serving with the Bedfordshire Regiment.

Angered by these events and by what he saw as the needless death of his men, Lieutenant Colonel Hopking requested an urgent meeting with the Brigadier, and just after noon, Brigadier Evans arrived at Battalion HQ on the Mound, where the two men were in conference all afternoon.

Sadly, Private Harry Perkins never recovered from the wounds he received and died three months later in hospital in Madras. He had originally been a member of the Wiltshire Regiment, joining the Battalion in Arakan.

The bombardment of Sausage Hill earlier that morning was to pave the way for another attack by the Punjabis, and shortly before 1000, 'A' Company on Ring Hill reported that they had taken the feature. It was an important moment, for now the Japanese had been pushed back on both sides of the Iril River, at Nungshigum, the 'Pimple' and now Sausage Hill; but sadly, as was often the case in the jungle war, it was not to last, and later that afternoon, the Punjabis were thrown back off the peak by a determined Japanese counter-attack. However, they retained a foothold on its slopes and dug in for the night, in preparation for a renewed attack the following morning.

Major Browne recalled the shelling of Sausage which cleared off the vegetation to expose the enemy's positions. He also recalled that unfortunate artillery fire that killed his own men:

By now our troops were on top of 'Pimple' and had burned out the Japs by rolling down petrol drums. There was also a 'build up' going on below us in the valley for an attack on 'Sausage' by another battalion. We had cleared out a good deal of the cover on 'Sausage' by setting fire to the vegetation with mortar smoke bombs. Eventually we were relieved by this battalion and moved on but not before being shelled by our own medium guns by mistake with considerable casualties.[34]

Another one of those caught in this bout of friendly fire was Lieutenant Pat Thursby, when his temporary positions took a near-hit. Rising from his scrape, he looked none the worse for the experience, but behind him, his batman, Private Johnson, came into the light looking somewhat dishevelled, having taken the force of their collapsed foxhole.

Sid Johnson was a Battalion footballer, having played before the war for Abbey United (later to become Cambridge United), before he was called up in December 1942. His experience did not affect his footballing skills – he returned to play for Abbey in the 1946/47 season, having been demobbed just a few weeks earlier. A teammate in his first match back was a former Far East prisoner of war, Private Ernest 'Ed' Bruce, who had served with 5 Suffolk and had been captured at Singapore five years previously.

Patrick 'Paddy' Thursby had been born into the Regiment in 1922 when his father, Francis, a veteran of Great War service with Second Suffolk, was stationed in Ireland. After being called up he served first with the Royal Corps of Signals before obtaining a commission in the Royal Engineers. His unit was close to the Battalion in Arakan, and he managed to request a transfer to join his father's old battalion at the end of January 1944.

That afternoon, Captain Lee Hunter took the Guerrilla Platoon out to what was suspected to be the last enemy-held position in the Battalion's area – 'Point 4066'. This hill was of comparable height to the Pimple and lay off to the north-east. His orders were to ascertain whether the hill was still in enemy hands, and if not, to hold it for 24 hours.

With the enemy gone from the Pimple, the task of collecting and burying the dead of the Battalion began. It was a grim business, but it had to be done as swiftly as possible, before the jungle creatures came to feed upon the remains. Corporal Cyril Dell recalled: 'If you do not bury the dead quickly the wild beasts get them and just leave their bones, although that is what the Japs deserve, but we have to bury them because they stink so much.'[35] Major Hill, 'B' Company's commander, also recalled the aftermath of the battle:

Later during the fighting on and around the 'Pimple' several more dead were found, the result of this action. How coarse and brutal their dead looked, scarcely human. The pile of captured equipment was an impressive sight. There were further sleepless nights, but though the Japs fired into our lines they attempted no more attacks.[36]

If enemy activity in the area permitted, most of the dead were conveyed to cemeteries that were being created away from the main battle areas.

The wounded fared much better at Imphal than at any previous time in the Burma campaign. The airstrip was a lifeline to India, and wounded left daily for treatment, whilst in return, supplies and reinforcements came to bolster the men in the front line. It was, however, the initial journey from the Regimental Aid Post down to the Advanced Dressing Station that was the most difficult and the most crucial, to ensure that wounds were properly treated as swiftly as possible. Christened 'Minden Way', the route from the Mound was little more than a precipitous dirt track leading to the foothills. It was often muddy, and a slip by a stretcher-bearer could send a wounded man tobogganing down into the undergrowth.

Once stretchers reached the roadside, carriers or ambulances would arrive to convey the wounded to hospital for treatment or, in the more serious cases, straight to the airstrip for evacuation to hospitals in central India.

After calling the roll, it was now clear that losses had been higher than had been first thought. From the initial attacks of 11 April, Sergeant Steele, Corporal James and Privates Blake, Dowell, Ebbage, Pigden and Torrence were still unaccounted for from 'C' Company, whilst Corporal Goudie along with Privates Bennett, DuFue, Mott, Narduzzo and Tod, were missing from 'D' Company's actions on 15 April. Private Mace of 'A' Company was also unaccounted for from their attack on 13 April.

However, as the action moved away, the Pimple continued to give up its dead. As the Pioneers started to dig a grave some yards off, the bodies of sixteen men were discovered and subsequently buried.

From 'A' Company, Private Mace's body was recovered; he had been killed in their first attack on 13 April. From 'C' Company, Private Blake's body was recovered from their attack on 11 April, together with those of Sergeant Steele, Corporal James and Privates Dowell, Ebbage, Pidgeon and Torrance. From 'D' Company, the bodies of Corporal Goudie and Privates Bennett, DuFeu, Knox, Mott, Narduzzo, Savage and Tod, were recovered from their attack on 15 April.

Nineteen-year-old Private Robert Savage, who fell that day, was a recent reinforcement from the Royal Scots; he had been employed at Bathgate Public Baths in West Lothian before he was called up.

Another former member of the Royal Scots who died in the final attack on the Pimple was Private David Tod. He had previously been employed as a foreman by a local firm of joiners in Midlothian and left behind a wife in Gewskill.

Private Arthur Reeve, the stretcher-bearer killed on Ring I, came from the village of West Bergholt and had originally enlisted into the Essex Regiment.

Descended from Italian immigrants, Private Serafino Narduzzo was born in St Pancras, London, where his parents ran a delicatessen. He had arrived in early 1944 as a reinforcement from the Oxfordshire and Buckinghamshire Light Infantry.

Private Cyril 'Sonny' Mott, who fell in the final assault by 'D' Company, was a Suffolk man. He had been called up in 1943 and had lived before the war in the village of Long Melford, where he had previously been a member of his local Home Guard unit.

Private Leonard Ebbage, who was killed on 13 April, came from the South Norfolk town of Diss. He had written home just three weeks earlier to tell his mother that he had seen two old friends from the area who were also serving with the Battalion in India: Private Cotton from Billingford and Private Youngman from Heywood. Private Youngman would be wounded just weeks later in another major attack north of Imphal.

Private Forrest Knox, another man lost attacking the Pimple, also came to the Battalion from the Royal Scots. Aged nineteen, he had been called up the previous summer. His parents lived in Armadale, West Lothian.

Sergeant David 'Herbie' Steele of 'C' Company was a pre-war regular who joined the Regiment in 1933 as a boy soldier aged fifteen. Promoted to Lance Corporal in 1941, he had been Provost Sergeant of the Battalion before he was posted away to serve with another unit in early 1943, but he was then posted back to the Battalion, joining them in Arakan on 11 March, when he was sent to 'D' Company. Steele had been born in the East Suffolk town of Leiston where, upon leaving school, he enlisted into the Regiment. Overcome with grief at his loss, his parents moved away from Leiston to Anerley, near Crystal Palace in London. After a campaign of many years, in 2003 his niece finally obtained permission to have his name added to the Leiston War Memorial.

Two officers, Lieutenant Duncan and Second Lieutenant Gilbert, were wounded, along with nine other ranks, but by far the highest proportion of losses attacking the Pimple was suffered by the newly arrived reinforcements who had joined the Battalion in the weeks before. A draft of six men from the Royal Warwickshire Regiment, together with fifteen men from the Royal Scots, arrived in late March, along with a host of individual private soldiers from the Black Watch (Royal Highlanders), the East Surreys, the Bedfordshire and Hertfordshires and the King's Regiment (Liverpool).

At that time, the Battalion was 713 men-strong, all ranks, with 674 men (94 per cent) being Suffolk Regiment men and the remaining thirty-nine coming from these other units who had joined since their arrival from the Arakan front. RSM George Jasper wrote home of the Battalion and its spirit:

> At the present moment I'm afraid that many of the men of this Battalion are far from 'Suffolk' in respect of birth, but all are working as we have always done, as one happy family, and the newcomers are quick to take to the ways of the old time 'Suffolk'; which as you I'm sure are well aware, has a peculiarity of its own.[37]

On the morning of the 19 April, news came to the CO that the Battalion were to be relieved from their positions and be allowed to rest for a few days in the valley below. The past week had exerted great strain on the Battalion, and in the past few days valuable supplies had been redeployed to needier sectors of the front line. Basic essentials such as clean drinking water had now been almost completely depleted, and the normal requirement to shave daily was now reduced to every third day:

> Those were strenuous days both for officers and men, rations had been cut, water was scarce, cigarettes had been drastically reduced, amenities were nil and yet the morale kept up. Officers and men shared the same hardships, the same dug-outs, the same bed on mother earth. No one was put on a charge for failing to shave as there was only sufficient water to give each man half-a-mug of tea, and that had to be brought up the mountain-side on the backs of mules. When one position was cleared, those in command could always find another hill feature which was still in the hands of the Japs and had to be cleared.[38]

Major Browne also recalled those strained days and the water shortage: 'We were very, very tired, having been weary when we started, and having had little sleep for over a week. There had only been just enough water to drink, so we were disgusting and had beards. Mine was rather a handsome auburn!'[39]

As the Battalion packed up their kit and prepared to vacate their hard-won positions for a well-earned rest, one man would not be going with them. The CO had that morning relinquished his command of the Battalion.

Lieutenant Colonel Hopking had protested strongly to his superiors the previous day that during the attacks on the Pimple he had not been given sufficient time to reconnoitre the position he was being asked to take, and that it was due to the hurried nature of the initial attacks and his Brigadier's continual insistence to attack the feature, that so many casualties had been incurred. The Regimental History recorded his standpoint:

> Lieutenant-Colonel Hopking considered that insufficient time was given to him to reconnoitre by patrols the enemy's positions which he had been ordered to attack, that in consequence men's lives were being needlessly lost. As a protest he asked to be relieved of the command of the Battalion.[40]

Lieutenant Colonel Henry Richard Hopking, who had taken command of Second Suffolk seven months before, was described as a man of 'delightful personality' who had during his tenure of command 'set the Battalion back on its feet'. He was a Battalion Commander who was held in much affection by his men and he had always seen to it that they were as well cared-for as possible: 'He took it [the Battalion] into battle, and both his Brigade and Divisional Commander paid a tribute to his unfailing courage in action.'[41]

The Padre, too, recalled the affection he had for his men: 'With great regret, we said "good-bye" to Lieut.-Colonel H. R. Hopking. Like a true soldier, he put his men first and always had the greatest consideration for them.'[42]

Lieutenant Gray, who was then the Battalion Signals Officer, recalled the situation that Lieutenant Colonel Hopking faced when his men were attacking the Pimple: 'I remember that my CO was told to keep attacking this position. I heard all the radio signals coming in. The Japanese were in bunkers, and very difficult to dislodge. He refused and resigned. I admired him for this.'[43]

Now 'Huffy' Hopking quietly made his exit, taking with him as a souvenir the Japanese sword that 'B' Company had retrieved from the attackers of the Mound. Later, he would become the Regimental Secretary looking after, amongst other regimental matters, the Old Comrades Association, to which he devoted the remainder of his life. His son, who completed his National Service with the Regiment in the 1950s, would later present the sword to the Regimental Museum. A fellow officer paid him an affectionate tribute in the *Suffolk Regimental Gazette*:

> It is impossible to express adequately how terribly sorry every officer and man was to lose him. During the seven months he commanded us we can honestly say we learnt to love and respect him and were an extraordinarily happy Battalion – often under very adverse conditions. We wish you the best of luck, 'Huffy', and thank you for all you did for us.[44]

In his place, Major Menneer now assumed command of the Battalion. Kenneth Menneer had been a pre-war officer of the 4th Battalion and had briefly commanded 7 Suffolk in 1941. He later also commanded 1 Suffolk in England prior to his departure to join Second Suffolk in India. He was later known affectionately, though of course not publicly, in the ranks as 'Colonel Manure'.

Major Menneer had been Second-in-Command since joining the Battalion in January 1944 and came 'straight from 1st Dozen'. The *Suffolk Regimental Gazette* noted: 'We apologise most humbly to him for the amazing and fantastic type of warfare he has been suddenly pushed into, but we feel we must point out that we didn't start this one – we are just here to finish it off!'[45]

Leaving his foxhole on the Pimple, Private Jim Smith was carrying off the ultimate piece of war booty in the form of a tattered Japanese flag. Smith had previously been a member of the 70th (Young Soldiers) Battalion, before he was transferred briefly to the 8th Battalion at Epping in 1942. Shortly before they moved to Spilsby in Lincolnshire, he joined a draft for Second Suffolk in Burma:

> The first attack I did was with the 2nd Battalion Suffolks and it was rough seeing my mates going down. It was in April 1944 while on an early morning patrol that I got the Jap flag. Two weeks later while attacking a Japanese hill position, I was badly wounded in the right shoulder and was flown out of India along with some of my wounded mates.[46]

The Regiment's ancient watchword '*Stabilis*', meaning 'Steady', had held firm once again and been displayed by all those men who fought tenaciously to take the Pimple. Now they marched off that hill proud that theirs was a job well done, but sad that their commander had gone.

The happiness that he had fostered now seemed gone, perhaps never to return. Their dead now lay some yards off, watching over the position they had fought so hard to take. Those graves were testament to the ruthlessness and determination of their enemy, an enemy who would rather die than surrender his positions. They had done what their Brigadier asked of them, yet their actions would go virtually unmentioned in the records of the day. The 'Battalion in the East' had earned their rest.

A piquet of Second Suffolk up above Razmak Camp, 1940. The men wear rolled-up balaclavas and leather jerkins against the cold. The man second right trains his Vickers-Berthier light machine gun on the hills opposite, whilst his comrade views the enemy through binoculars. The 'VB' gun would be carried by Second Suffolk until the end of 1941, when it was replaced by the Bren.

A lonely pair of stone *sangars* in the snow on the North-West Frontier, 1940. In the one nearest the camera, a 'VB' team is keeping watch. In the centre is Bandsman Dennis 'Arab' Chaplin. Behind is 'Holly' Piquet and some yards beyond is 'Toady' Piquet.

A Vickers machine gun team on exercise in the Tochi Valley, 1942. Seated behind the weapon is Lance Corporal Ernie Fountain, who would serve with Second Suffolk in Burma before being repatriated to join First Suffolk in Europe. He was tragically the last man of First Suffolk to be killed, on 4 May 1945, when his Sten gun was accidentally knocked off a chair in a café in Bremen. The men wear the flat-topped *topees* with the Regimental device of a yellow castle affixed to the left hand side.

A patrol from the Guerrilla Platoon wade along a *chaung* for the benefit of the cameraman. The man in front carries the EY rifle, a standard .303 that was reinforced to take the velocity of a ballistite cartridge which propelled a grenade from the cup fixed to the end of the muzzle. The corporal behind is armed with a .45 Thompson sub-machine gun, and the penultimate man carries an American 1903 Springfield rifle with a telescopic sight attached.

A reverse shot, with the order now mixed. The corporal takes the lead, with a Bren gunner and 2″ mortar man further down the line. The corporal looks to be wearing a pair of rubber overboots tied around the ankle.

On the eve of their moving into the front line in Arakan, the Commander of 5th (Indian) Division, Major General H.R. Briggs, addresses men of the Battalion.

In a jungle clearing the Supreme Commander inspects men of the Battalion. Various types of weaponry can be seen, including the Thompson sub-machine gun, and the special pouch for its straight magazines being worn by the man closest to the camera. Standing second left is the Battalion Commander, Lieutenant Colonel H. R. Hopking.

Lord Louis Mountbatten speaks with Sergeant Bates of 'A' Company. To Bates' left, closest to the camera, is Corporal J. Steward, and to his right, Privates Cunnington, Baker, Crossland, Gant and Brighty. The muzzle of a newly arrived No. 4 rifle can be seen being held by Private Cunnington. The small brass numeral 'XII' can be seen on the upturned brim of Bates' slouch hat. He wears a universal pouch on one side of his belt and a binoculars pouch on the other. Private Crossland carries a .38 revolver in addition to his SMLE rifle.

Elements of 'C' Company scale the impressively steep slopes of 'Wrencat' in support of 1/17 Dogras' attack that successfully captured the hill on 14 March 1944. Two members of the Dogras, one of whom is wearing their distinctive native cotton hat, are standing right. The Dogras were often seen in this headdress, preferring it to the steel helmet.

As many men as could be spared front-line duty crowd around to hear a speech by the Supreme Commander. Some are wearing steel helmets, others slouch hats.

Viewed obliquely from the vicinity of 'Hook' Hill, 'Bamboo' Hill can be seen on the right with its plateau leading up to the summit. Beyond to the left are the group of hills known as the 'Wrens' consisting of 'Wrencat' in front, with 'Middle Wrencat' beyond. Out of shot to the left would have been 'Long Hill'.

'By letter, months-old newspaper or magazine, and above all in thought, the link with far-off England is strong.' At the entrance to his dug-out, with cigarette in hand, Major 'Ossy' Leach, commanding 'D' Company, reads a recently arrived copy of the *Suffolk Regimental Gazette*. To his left on the rear of the trench his revolver can be seen in its holster, whilst to his right is what looks to be a brazier made from an old petrol tin. His paludrin tablets to ward off malaria can be seen in a small glass bottle beyond.

Men gather around the cookhouse for their midday meal looking a little dishevelled. Various styles of uniform are seen. None of those seen here wear webbing anklets, but they appear to be wearing boots or canvas and rubber plimsolls. The shirts worn were made of grey flannel and came from depots in India. Their hair looks to be a little long and in need of a cut, and they eat from plates rather than out of their mess-tins. The young soldier standing centre right is Private Norman Rolfe of 'C' Company.

In a captured Japanese position, two men of the Battalion, one glum, one cheerful, take advantage of the cool interior of a cave hollowed out of the muddy Arakan hillside. The soldier on the left is armed with an American .45 Thompson sub-machine gun.

'Men of "The Old Dozen" ready to take over forward positions. Life in the Arakan is harder than in the Western Desert worse dust, same heat, flooding rain.' The two men in the centre wear a drill version of the standard woollen battledress, whilst the others wear the more commonly seen aertex battledress blouse in cellular cotton. The lack of equipment, apart from weapons, belts and a bandolier, suggest that these men could just have returned from patrol.

The Battalion's precious Vickers machine gun set up in a captured jungle cave and trained on the enemy-occupied hill opposite. Crouched left is Private Dicky Horsecroft, some of whose 'famous' tattoos can just be seen.

'Men of a South Country Regiment on the Arakan Front.' Standing third left, Sergeant F. Wilson from Bristol stares at the photographer smoking a home-made bamboo pipe. The soldier standing left is the same man seen in the photograph at the bottom of the page. Here the height of the tall grass can be seen. It was crucial to retain as much of this vegetation as possible, to hide movements between positions.

'Mortar men – one from Suffolk, the other from London – at the entrance to a position.' Standing right is Corporal Robert Lambert, who had served in First Suffolk before being transferred to Second Suffolk in 1942. This photograph later appeared on the front cover of the 3 September 1945 edition of *Victory* – the weekly magazine for India Command. It is unclear what is hanging above the entrance to their dug-out – possibly a shaving mirror.

'In the jungle, the slouch hat replaces the forage cap.' The felt hat was by far the most comfortable and practical form of headdress in the jungle, with its wide brim which kept the piercing sun out of the wearer's eyes.

'Sergeant Parr with his 8¾ inch moustache. The largest in the British Army?' Charlie Parr, photographed at Arakan with his splendid waxed moustache. Pinned to his aertex battledress blouse is the ribbon of the India General Service Medal. Men serving at Razmak would earn it with the accompanying clasp 'North West Frontier 1937–39'.

A virtually identical photograph taken at the same time that later graced the front cover of *Parade* magazine in April 1944.

The Battalion Cookhouse in Arakan. Its location is well concealed within the tall Arakan undergrowth. 'Dixies' look to be heating on a petrol burner on the left, whilst the man in the centre looks to be engaged in the ancient art of 'spud bashing'. Water tins lie close by, with a steel helmet covered in a net. This may possibly be the reverse shot of the previous image of the cookhouse.

Private Arthur Partington cuts the hair of a comrade whose Thompson sub-machine gun lies beside him. Before being called up, Partington was a barber in Welwyn Garden City. He had served first in the 8th Battalion in Essex, before joining Second Suffolk in India. Trained as a bugler, upon the Battalion's move to Arakan, Arthur reverted to his active service role as a stretcher-bearer. The boxes of mortar bombs in the background are covered with branches so as to not be seen from the air. The rolls of coconut matting were placed in areas such as Battalion HQ where the muddy pathways were soon worn away.

On an Arakan hillside at the grave of their fallen comrades, the Battalion's buglers sound the last post. An assortment of kit is worn, including shorts, khaki drill slacks and woollen jerseys. The padre, Revd Brown-Moffet, always ensured that men were buried as soon as possible and saw to it that their makeshift 'XII Military Cemetery' was well looked after.

Regimental Police photographed in Arakan. Standing right is No. 5826106 Corporal 'Wally' Reynolds, who joined the Regiment in 1932 and served through until 1948. The armband worn by the man on the left bears the letter 'C' and may have been to denote to which company he belonged.

One of 'The New Suffolk', as CSM Tommy Warren referred to them. Here, after just ten months of active service, Corporal 'Alf' Woollard of 'HQ' Company has changed from a fit, youthful soldier, to a worn and tired veteran. The jungle wore down men's resolve and sapped their strength. Young men became haggard and old-looking in weeks.

The Imphal-Ukhrul road looking south-west towards Imphal snakes its way through the hills. On the peaks beyond those seen here was Point 4057, known to the Battalion as the 'Mound'.

After his departure as Commanding Officer, Lieutenant Colonel H. R. Hopking is photographed in India with the sword captured by 'B' Company after the Japanese attack on the 'Mound'. 'Huffy' was a commander held in great affection by his men. He never lost contact with the Regiment, serving in his retirement as both Regimental Secretary and Secretary of the Old Comrades Association until his death in 1965.

Battered, faded and pock-marked by jungle mites, this small, blurred photograph was carried by Lance Corporal Lionel Ruffles throughout his life. Ruffles, left, is seen in the jungle with three comrades of Second Suffolk.

A view of the Imphal-Kohima road past the village of Kangpoki. The Battalion never got as far north as this, their advance halting close to Milestone 17 before they were sent to positions south of Imphal. It shows, however, similar country to that found around the positions of both 'Pyramid' and 'Isaac'.

Private Fred Hulse photographed at the end of the campaign at Imphal. Hulse had served first in the South Staffordshire Regiment, before being transferred to Second Suffolk. The ubiquitous slouch hat was later to be a symbol of service in Burma. It was known by many veterans as the 'IWT hat' – 'I was there!'

Officers of the Battalion photographed upon their return to India in 1945, with the Commanding Officer, Lieutenant Colonel K. C. Menneer. Left to right, rear row: Lieutenants Ellis, Haygarth, Trollope, Morgan, Theobald, Gunton, Tomkinson, Kinghorn and Thomas. Middle row: Captains Gould (RAMC) and Wilenitz, Lieutenant Robin, Captains Ellis and Woodward, Lieutenants Jackson and Baldwin, Captains Gray and Watt. Front row: Captain White, Majors Ennion and Cooper, the CO, Captain Thursby, Majors Gurney and Hudson, Captain Squirrell.

Taken at the same time, 'A' Company photographed at Muree in 1945 with their commander, Major Gurney. Upon arrival, they numbered just 108 all ranks.

'B' Company with its commander, Major Hill, who had been wounded in the attack upon 'Pyramid'. They numbered 141 all ranks.

HQ Company taken at the same time with its commander, Captain White. They numbered 138 all ranks upon their return to India, which included men of the Mortar Platoon, the Medical Section, the Signallers and the Machine Gunners.

In Lahore in 1945, officers of the Battalion are photographed with a drink in hand. Left to right, rear: Lieutenant Robin, unknown, Captain Gray, Major Ennion, unknown, Lieutenant Tomkinson, Captain Watt, unknown. Front: unknown, Captain Squirrell, Lieutenant Gunton, Captain Baldwin, Lieutenant Jackson. The ribbon of the Military Cross can be seen on the jacket of Captain 'Tommy' Watt. He won the award for his actions in attacking the 'Pimple'. It is not known why Lieutenant Jackson has a bandaged head!

Minden Day 1945. The retrieval of the Battalion Colours from Lahore Cathedral, where they had been deposited for safekeeping two years earlier. They had been presented to the Battalion in March 1935 by the Governor of Madras, Lord Erskine.

The Colour Party under the command of Captain P. H. Jackson forms up outside the Officers' Mess. The King's Colour, left, was carried by Lieutenant G. W. P. Baker, and the Regimental Colour, right, by Lieutenant K. M. Gauld. The brief return of the solar topee can be seen here together with the Regiment's distinctive three-point *pugaree*. It would be a further twelve years before the Regiment finally decided to add the Battle Honours of 'Burma 1943-45', 'North Arakan' and 'Imphal' to the 1st Battalion's Colours.

The Staff of the orderly Room upon arrival back in India. Standing: Privates 'Tojo' Evans and Petfield, Lance Corporal Woodhouse, Privates Edwards and Talbot. Seated: unknown, Captain Hudson, Corporal 'Wally' Reynolds.

The final farewell parade of the Battalion at Gibraltar Barracks, Bury St Edmunds, before the cadre went to join the 1st Battalion in Greece in 1948. The CO, Lieutenant Colonel H.W. 'Sweat' Dean, had brought the Battalion home from India prior to Independence for it to be placed in 'suspended animation'.

Reggie Leeke, the man who saved Mountbatten. Prior to joining Second Suffolk in Arakan, Leeke had served with the Chindits. He met a slightly inebriated Lord Louis dressed in his white naval uniform when he visited the Chindits on a riverside jetty. Unbeknown to Mountbatten, a Japanese sniper was close by, but Leeke got him first. Mountbatten promised Leeke a 'Mention in Dispatches', but he never received it!

Cyril Wilkinson of 17 Platoon, 'D' Company presents a battered Japanese flag to the Regimental museum in 1985. To the right is Lieutenant General Sir Richard Goodwin KCB, CBE, DSO, who commanded the 1st Battalion in North-West Europe. Mrs Anstice Gilson-Taylor looks on, as does Major 'Tommy' Warren standing behind Wilkinson. Warren served with Second Suffolk in the Burma Campaign and was, together with Wilkinson, a chronicler of the Battalion's actions there.

Corporal Ernie Bates visits the Regimental Chapel to view his old Battalion Colours. Bates was a keen poet and enjoyed corresponding with other Second Suffolk veterans in his retirement. He wrote once: 'I get pleasure putting my thoughts on paper. I suppose it is a kind of ego trip!'

Minden Day 1996. Veterans of Second Suffolk chat before the march-past of the Old Comrades Association. Soldiers scanned the boards to see who had signed in, but most looked around for another man who wore the famous 'Burma Star'.

On Minden Day 2002, ex-sergeant Charlie Parr watches the march-past of Suffolk Regiment veterans. He still sported his resplendent waxed moustache and proudly wore the blazer badge won for being a champion shot on the Short Siberia Range at Bisley.

'Tell them of us and say.' VJ Day Parade, London, 2010. A tearful Norman Rolfe recalls those with whom he served who made the ultimate sacrifice. (*Photo courtesy of N. Rolfe*)

Chapter Eight

Guerrilla Raids

'The silence was changed to a wild din'

Retiring from their various hills, the Battalion were now withdrawn south-west down onto the plains around the village of Pungdonbam, having been relieved by 4/5 Mahratta Regiment in 37 Brigade. Taking over positions from the Dogras in the village, the Battalion was now allowed a brief respite.

Whilst six replacement officers arrived and were posted off to their new platoons, a slaughtering party went out to kill four cattle for the Battalion cookhouse. After weeks on a bland diet of bully beef and biscuits, interspersed with occasional vegetables and rice, the men's health had suffered; and whilst they spent the afternoon bathing, Cook Sergeant Cropley and the Battalion Cookhouse got to work to prepare a decent meal.

As the new CO, Major Menneer, held a conference with all Company Commanders, news was received that Private Charles Davidson of 'A' Company had died of wounds received on 15 April near Ring III. He had lived in the village of Fressingfield near Diss and had originally enlisted into the Royal Norfolk Regiment.

Early on 21 April, 'B' and 'D' Companies left the village and proceeded north-west over the Iril River towards the Nungshigum feature. Intelligence had been received that a battalion from the 138th Japanese Infantry Regiment were approaching the feature from the north, with a view to retaking it. As Zero fighters now came in low, heading again for Imphal, fresh orders were received for the remainder of the Battalion to move on to Nungshigum. Their much-anticipated period of rest had lasted just short of twenty hours.

Upon arrival on the feature, the Battalion dug in and strengthened the positions they had taken over. 'A' and 'C' Companies' journey forward was accomplished more quickly by travelling on the back of two troops of Stuart and Lee tanks.

On 24 April, a patrol of 'C' Company went north to Wakhong (Wakhan) to see if the enemy remained there. Finding no one, they turned right and followed the Iril River south between Nungshigum and the Mound to the village of Nungoi, then back onto the feature. The remainder of the day was 'quiet', except that a patrol of 'B' Company under Lance Sergeant Good 'bumped' a party of Japanese to the north of the Mound. Killing one of the enemy, they beat a hasty retreat, leaving their radio behind. The men were badly bruised, having slid over the edge of the feature on which they were spotted, and later that day, Private Idris Jones was detailed out with a party of men to recover the abandoned equipment and make a return to base via a newly erected 'Bailey' bridge to the east. It did not go well:

> We re-climbed the hill to retrieve some important equipment. Unfortunately after descending once again, we discovered that the Bailey bridge was impassable. We couldn't get to the road after all and were therefore stuck on the wrong side of the river – without food. By the following morning, though, the flooding had eased and we managed to wade across the bridge and re-join the battalion.[1]

The following day, whilst the CO was away at a brigade conference, the Guerrilla Platoon went out to raid the village of Uyumpok. A patrol under Sergeant Izzard had been to the village earlier that morning, but the inhabitants reported that a party of fourteen Japanese had raided the village the previous day, carrying off rice and other foodstuffs. Later that evening, the CO gave orders for the Battalion's move the following day to the village of Haraorou, west of the Nungshigum feature. Upon arrival there, Major Menneer undertook a thorough reorganization of his Company and Platoon commanders.

On 27 April, another sizeable draft of men left the Battalion for repatriation to the UK. Among these were more of the longest-serving senior NCOs who had been with the Battalion since the late 1930s in India and had served throughout the campaign thus far.

It was another bitter blow to morale, since these 'old sweats' did much to instil confidence and regimental pride in the younger members of the Battalion. Private Cyril Wilkinson recalled these men and their worth to the Battalion, even though they had their 'own' way of doing things:

> We listened to the time expired men of the regular 2 Suffolk. Those of us that were conscripts and Deolali B.B.R.C. [British Base Reinforcement Camp] of the many various infantry regiments that helped make up the strength of 2 Suffolk, and we the conscripts (civilians in uniform) listened to the old soldiers, many with twelve, fifteen, twenty and more years service, talking of the good times they had had and they would conceal their intentions to stay in India and as they reached the Arakan, they would put in for their rights and go home on repat. We of the civilian conscripts

straight from the barracks were told that the first stoppage on the Bren gun is 'feel for the cocking handle' – the NCOs of the regular Suffolk having trained on the Vickers machine gun, but we knew that when a Bren gun stops, first immediate action 'mag off, new mag on!'[2]

Among the departures were CSM Warren and Sergeant Parr. 'Tommy' Warren had joined the Regiment in 1933 and went with 1 Suffolk to Malta in 1937. He joined Second Suffolk in 1940, bringing out a draft of Militiamen from the Depot. He would continue to serve with the Regiment, later being commissioned in 1956 as Captain and Quartermaster of the 1st Battalion at Colchester. He finally retired from the Army in 1966 on what he described as his 'black day'.

Charlie Parr later joined the Royal Military Police and was an undefeated champion pistol shot in the British Army, retaining the title when the competition was abolished. Parr, who came from the village of Snailwell, was a pre-war Territorial with the Cambridgeshire Regiment, before he signed on for regular service with the Suffolk Regiment in 1938. He later served in the Korean War. Well into his nineties he attended Regimental Reunions, still resplendent with his waxed moustache. Private Cyril Wilkinson remembered him with much affection as an exceptional NCO noting that 'he deserved the VC'.[3]

Two other old soldiers who were also going home on that draft were Privates Ted 'Jack' Dash and Jim 'Fitz' Fyson. They enlisted together into the Regiment in 1937, being issued consecutive service numbers (5826834 and 5826835). They trained together in 'Gibraltar' Squad before they were both posted to join 1 Suffolk in Malta in 1939. They both came home just before war was declared and were posted onwards to Second Suffolk at Razmak in 1940, training as Signallers. When they were repatriated, Jack joined 1 Suffolk in Holland, fighting through with them until the end of the war. Fitz was posted to join 4 Welch and died of wounds on 11 April 1945 at Stedorf, when his carrier patrol was attacked by Germans armed with Panzerfausts. He is buried in Becklingen Cemetery beside many men of 1 Suffolk who fell in their final major battle of their war at Hallen-Seckenhausen.

Also heading home was Private Stanley 'Maxie' Mattin of the Signal Platoon. Maxie had enlisted in the Regiment in November 1935 aged nineteen and served in India since 1936. Following his discharge from the Regiment in 1948, he never missed the annual Minden Day reunion, except the one the day before he died in 1988. Private Ernie Bates later recalled: 'Maxie was a tough character, clashed with some, looked up to by others, but he will always be remembered by all who served with him.'[4]

Particularly sad to be departing, CSM Tommy Warren recalled later with much affection that 'happy cheerfulness' of the Battalion, fostered by the previous CO, that he now had to leave behind:

> Imphal will always mean those dirty, youthful faces that smile a cheerful 'Good morning, Sergeant Major' when I visited platoons after stand down. It will mean cursing our tanks for, in attempting to dislodge the enemy from our Company front, firing up the wrong re-entrant and blowing up our precious wire; and it will mean those grenades with the sharp metal ridge in the detonator sleeve. But strangely, I most remember the liquid bully beef; the weevil-infested biscuits; the brilliant moonlit nights; and, last of all, that rancid, nauseating smell of unwashed bodies.[5]

Lance Corporal Lionel Ruffles also recalled the bully beef: 'We had bully beef every way you can think of – fried, as fritters, as stew – you name it!'[6]

The Burma Campaign, perhaps unlike any other, forged a close bond between comrades. With no escape from your front-line positions, a sort of intimacy with the enemy was in some ways unique to the campaign:

> The enemy being dug in 50 yards away for the next two weeks; the continual rain of shells, probably the equivalent of our 2 inch mortar, hundreds of which were fired during the night attacks; our own faulty 2 inch mortar illuminating flares that exploded about 10 feet above the firer and, sadly, I remember the brave young soldier who, after a shell had exploded on his steel helmet and wounded the remainder of his section, fought for his life throughout the night only to expire in the morning.[7]

It was Private Wallace Pittard that CSM Tommy Warren recalled above, who after a brave fight died of his wounds following the accidental shelling of Ring I.

Back at Haraorou village, patrols now ventured west towards Sengmai, about twelve miles up the Imphal-Kohima road, whilst others ventured back to Wakhong in the north. The following morning, as the drill parades and kit inspections continued in the relative safety of their new positions, Lieutenant Yonge was warned by Brigade HQ to prepare for a special patrol to take various elements of the Division out towards the Imphal-Kohima road, with a view to attacking northwards along it.

The last day of the month started with rain that would continue spasmodically all day, but fresh orders were received that evening for another move to new positions in the north-west, where they would be responsible for pushing the enemy back in a wider area along the Imphal-Kohima road close to the hilltop village of Motbung.

As the Battalion moved off, with mules carrying the bulk of their heavy equipment, each man carried two days' 'K' rations in his small pack. Apart from cardigans and monsoon capes, all other equipment remained in the Company areas to be brought up later, when they reached their objective. Major Henderson recalled that time and the optimism of a fresh offensive:

> The monsoon arrived at this time and we were living under constant rain, sometimes under canvas sometimes in the open, with mud everywhere. Eventually the attacks weakened and we then went on the offensive forcing the Japanese back down all the roads (such as they were) by which they had arrived.[8]

May opened with a dull, cloudy day, as the Battalion established their new positions. Lieutenant Yonge returned off patrol reporting that the enemy were in occupation near Ithol Lok and also around the village of Safarmaina in the north.

The following morning, after a postponement, a patrol went out to 'Point 4428', known on some maps as 'Runaway' Hill. Here they observed movement which they thought to be Japanese, but upon returning to the Battalion area it was confirmed that the men they had observed there were elements of the West Yorks from 9 Brigade. At 1430, the CO, the Intelligence Officer and the Signals Officer set off with the advance party for the new area.

The advance party also contained the Quartermaster and the Battalion Cookhouse, who were to set up their kitchen and be ready to provide a hot meal at a prearranged spot en route for the infantry companies following behind. In case the column met any difficulties and were unable to make the rendezvous, Field Service rations – more monotonous tinned bully beef – had already been issued to the men. If not consumed, however, these were to be 'handed back complete to the QM on his instruction to do so'.[9]

At 0930 on 3 May, 'A' and 'B' Companies set off for these new positions, with 'C' Company moving off to occupy a hill feature in the north-west, whilst 'D' Company headed for the village of Purum. Both 'A' and 'B' Companies arrived in the new area later that afternoon, reporting that no enemy had been sighted, and that evening, one platoon of 'D' Company left the village to mount a night ambush near the village of Wakhong.

The Japanese were known to be still located to the west, and early on 4 May an airstrike commenced, followed by an artillery barrage. From their new locations, the Battalion had a 'ringside' seat to watch their counterparts, 3/14 Punjab, attack the 'Hump' feature to the west. The Punjabis were, however, unsuccessful in their endeavours, being beaten back by heavy enemy machine-gun fire.

As Second Lieutenant Tomkinson, who had been wounded attacking Bamboo Hill, returned from hospital bringing some twenty reinforcements now passed fit for duty, another old soldier was being dispatched home on repatriation.

A space had become available and suddenly the CO was looking for a time-served man who was eligible for 'repat'. Corporal E. A. 'Charlie' Howlett was swiftly packed up to a chorus of cheers. He had joined the Regiment in 1938 from the Royal Artillery and rose in 1955 to be Orderly Room Quartermaster Sergeant with the 1st Battalion at Wuppertal in Germany. By May 1956 he was, along with Captain Tommy Warren, one of just eight men still serving with the Regiment who had been present on the NW Frontier in 1939.

On 5 May, the Battalion watched to the north as 3/9 Jats attacked 'Point 5521', known as 'Everest' – on account of its great height – but they were unsuccessful. Artillery had pounded the position throughout the day and Hurri-bombers strafed it later that afternoon, but all to no avail. The Japanese resolve appeared to be stiffening once again.

Captain Lee Hunter now set off with a Guerrilla patrol to the south to lay an ambush in the village of Mapeo Khunou, but returned the following afternoon reporting only that they had spotted a small party of Japanese near Sedang. Rain fell throughout the night, thoroughly drenching a platoon of 'D' Company who had set off in the darkness to occupy an area near the village of Pukhao.

On the afternoon of 7 May the Guerrilla Platoon returned to patrol to the village of Sedang, and by midnight they had reached it unobserved:

> There was considerable enemy movement there and Lee Hunter manoeuvred his patrol so that by midnight they had reached the outskirts of the village of 20 native huts or 'bashas'. They were not challenged, so crept up to a basha where a light was seen. Inside were several sleeping figures wrapped in blankets on the floor; these were sprayed with tommy gun bullets and three hand grenades thrown in for good measure, The silence was changed to a wild din, the sound of a wooden clapper spreading the alarm. The patrol quickly withdrew and slipped quietly out of the village.[10]

Having rested up in the hills above the village for the night, in the morning Captain Lee Hunter decided to split his force and make another attack on the village. One Bren group would remain up high to give covering fire, whilst a 'raiding party' entered the village. This group would be led by Captain Lee

Hunter, who was accompanied by his senior NCO, Lance Corporal Peck, and another Bren group:

> A number of Japs were seen digging, and a party of over a dozen sitting around a board playing some kind of game. Both Bren guns and a tommy gun were fired into the party at the board, who were all killed or wounded. The diggers ran off into the jungle. An enemy MMG engaged the Bren group.[11]

Spotting a Japanese machine gun firing from a hillock to their right, Lance Corporal Peck seized the initiative and led his section forward together with the Bren team to assault the position. Forced to go to ground due to its fire, Lance Corporal Peck returned fire, and his expert shooting quickly silenced the enemy machine gun.

Advancing cautiously forward to collect intelligence from the enemy dead, his section were within yards of the corpses when a hail of fire came upon them from three more Japanese machine guns firing from their left. They were forced to retire, and Captain Lee Hunter was also now in the thick of it:

> The raiding party approached the village where they engaged eight Japs who scattered at once. The raiding party entered the village and ran through it, firing into 'bashas' as they went. A party of eight Japs ran out of one; but as soon as they were engaged with tommy guns, ran in again, leaving several casualties behind. The raiding party left the village and returned to their previous rendezvous. From here a party of five Japs under a Warrant Officer with binoculars was seen; when they came within point blank range fire was opened and all were killed. More Japs ran out and there was some pretty wild firing during which the Guerrillas withdrew to their rendezvous.[12]

At the fall-back rendezvous, Captain Lee Hunter was becoming concerned that Lance Corporal Peck and the Bren group had not arrived. Unbeknown to him, Lance Corporal Peck's group had returned to the original rendezvous, where they found three other members of the patrol. They all decided to stay put for the present, in the expectation that Captain Lee Hunter would soon arrive with his group.

Captain Lee Hunter, believing that the original rendezvous had been overrun, had proceeded straight to the fall-back rendezvous. When Lance Corporal Peck did not arrive, he decided that he must return to the original rendezvous to try and locate them. However, just as he was about to set off, Lance Corporal Peck appeared along the track with some of his men.

Deciding to fall back, Lance Corporal Peck reported to him that he found his section alone and the Bren team missing. Captain Lee Hunter now ordered Lance Corporal Peck to remain in case the missing men came through. Meanwhile, he took the remainder of the party back to Battalion HQ and, once he had seen his men safely through the Battalion lines with a message for the CO that he was returning, set off alone to the rendezvous to see if any of the missing men had made their way there. Upon arrival there, he found two waiting for him along with Lance Corporal Peck, but two other men were still missing.

The following morning, as the Battalion were preparing to move to a new area, Captain Lee Hunter requested permission to move out ahead of the main party to try and locate his missing men. Lance Corporal Peck volunteered to accompany him, and the pair set off once again for Sedang.

Approaching the village, they came under fire, and Lance Corporal Peck moved round to outflank the enemy position, killing one Japanese officer and five other ranks at point blank range. One wounded member of the previous day's patrol was found around midday, but the final man, Private Foster, could not be located.

For their actions on that patrol and during the previous days, Captain Lee Hunter was awarded a Bar to his Military Cross, and Lance Corporal Peck, the Military Medal.

Captain Douglas Lee Hunter was an incisive commander, quick in thought and action. Before joining the Royal Norfolk Regiment he had lived in north London. His local newspaper recorded his award under the title 'Thunderstorm Attack Caught Japs Napping – How Paddington Captain Won M.C.'[13] The Regimental History paid tribute to him:

> No better choice could have been made for a Guerrilla Platoon commander. Lee Hunter, a young officer of the Royal Norfolk Regiment, had an instinctive grasp of this type of warfare. It is estimated that he led at least fifty long distance patrols; these he handled with great boldness and skill; the results were markedly successful, very heavy casualties were inflicted on the enemy while his own losses were negligible.[14]

The citation for Lance Corporal Jack 'Tiny' Peck's award noted:

> In spite of the fact that this N.C.O. had been on patrol for 48 hours over extremely heavy and difficult country, under the worst of weather conditions, he volunteered to return to locate the missing men who were believed to

have become casualties. L/Cpl Peck's enthusiasm, his able leading of his group and his outstanding offensive spirit against greater odds, were not only an example to his men, but caused considerable casualties to the enemy.[15]

The newspaper for Allied forces in the East, 'SEAC', also wrote an appreciation of his actions:

> L/Cpl. Jack Richmond Peck, Suffolk Regiment, of Brookfield Road, Ipswich, during an attack on an enemy occupied village, led his section which was fired by enthusiasm and keenness to collect identifications from casualties. When searching for a missing machine gun group, he helped to kill or wound six Japs with Tommy gun fire and grenades.[16]

Jack Peck was called up for service in 1941 and served briefly with the 8th Battalion before being posted with a draft for Second Suffolk in India. He died in Ipswich in 1987, having owned a shop in the town for many years. Along with another Suffolk Regiment Military Medallist, Bill Linge, the story of his actions later graced the front cover of the *Victor* comic in 1971 under the unusual title of 'The Fighting Nurse-Maids'. Ten years later, Captain Douglas Lee Hunter was given the same 'honour' on the front cover of that same comic.

A scribe for the *Suffolk Regimental Gazette* heaped praise on the gallantry of the men of the Guerrilla Platoon:

> Captain Lee Hunter, Sgt. Brown, and Cpl. Peck were all members of the Battalion Guerrilla Platoon, an unorthodox body whose deeds have received all too little publicity in past news, probably owing to an ability to handle the Tommy-gun more readily than the pen, as a considerable number of Japs have found to their cost during many long-range patrols carried out by the Platoon.[17]

As the patrol returned to base on 9 May, the Battalion were preparing to move north-west towards the Imphal-Kohima road. Intelligence suggested that the Guerrilla Platoon's actions at Sedang had claimed over thirty enemy dead, and had forced the Japanese to withdraw to the west near the village of Sengmai.

Despite passing back over the same ground towards their new positions, the missing man, Private Foster, could still not be located, and the following day he was officially declared 'missing believed killed'. Donald Foster was a founder member of the Guerrilla Platoon, joining it in early September 1943 when it was formed in India. He had originally been a member of 'A' Company and transferred to the new platoon on the same day as Corporal Richard Brown, who would win the Military Medal in Arakan.

The Battalion now moved off towards Sengmai. Moving south of the village of Mapao, they crossed the Imphal Turel (river) and the main Imphal-Kohima road, just south of the village of Sengmai, and then moved north up the road.

The Japanese were still in occupation of the next village along the road at Kanglatongbi, and that afternoon, Lieutenant Yonge crossed the road and moved north along the west side with a view to finding a 'covered route' which the Battalion could use to advance northwards to attack positions beyond Kanglatongbi.

He returned reporting that no enemy were sighted, but the following day, their Brigadier ordered further patrols north to confirm the enemy's dispositions. Using both sides of the road, Captain Anslow and Second Lieutenant Stephens set off at 0800. Moving widely around the village of Kanglatongbi and the recently overrun position of 'Lion Box' – close to an old British ordnance depot – they made it as far north as Milestone 17, close to a position known as 'Pyramid'. They returned to the Battalion area later that night reporting that the Japanese were still in occupation along the road.

In view of this revised intelligence, Major Menneer decided he would send another patrol north, again using Lieutenant Yonge's route. This patrol also returned reporting that no enemy were in occupation of the hills on the left hand side of the road, and so now Major Menneer made plans to advance northwards using that route.

On 13 May, Lieutenant Thursby, who had by now been placed in command of the Battalion's 'Porters' – on account of some slight knowledge of Urdu – moved the heavy equipment of the Battalion up by mule to join the advance elements around Sengmai.

At first light on 14 May, Captain Ennion and Second Lieutenant Gauld moved off with three men to confirm that Lieutenant Yonge's route north towards Pyramid was still clear of the enemy. While they were out, intelligence was received from a Dogra patrol, who had the previous day observed the Japanese on the high ground to the left around a hill called 'Point 4743' north of Pyramid and close to a small hilltop settlement called Makhan.

The Dogras confirmed that although not in occupation here, the Japanese did conduct regular patrols from Kanglatongbi over this area, and they had spotted them on more than one occasion; but at 0100 on 15 May the route party set off from the Battalion area and crossed the Imphal-Kohima road just north of Sengmai.

They followed a fast-flowing stream up into the hills east of Makhan, but from here they could not now find the track that Lieutenant Yonge had used in the previous days. Heavy rain had obliterated it.

With a thunderstorm gathering and the night being 'intensely black', the route party halted. However, hard on their heels, the remainder of the column had moved up swiftly behind them. Their advance had not been without incident:

> A bullock dislodged some boulders on the high southern bank of the *chaung* causing the animal to stampede into the Bn. Column. A few porters dropped their loads but were controlled almost instantly – this noise of falling boulders and running feet caused a bit of commotion in the column but silence was restored after a few minutes and not a single shot was fired.[18]

Major Browne of 'A' Company also recalled the commotion:

> The first operation was a left hook with the whole battalion at night to cut the road about 5 miles behind the Japs. The move out was disrupted by some bullocks which charged the column and scattered the native porters, and by a torrential storm with vivid lightning which made movement quite impossible for many hours. We eventually arrived some place and it soon became clear that we were lost. It took us most of the day to decide where we were – and we were still wrong.[19]

The Padre also recalled the advance:

> The Battalion was given the task of infiltrating through the enemy lines and harassing them from the rear. Shall we ever forget that march which began at sunset and finished at noon the next day? In single file we moved out, each man with three days 'K' rations in his pack. Scouts were sent ahead to mark the path and to warn us of approaching Japs. When we had crossed about two miles of paddy fields we followed a wild animal track up into the hills and, by making a wide detour, we hoped to get behind the Japs.[20]

As the storm that had raged overhead dissipated at around 0500, 'C' Company at the head of the column now recommenced the march. Lieutenant Yonge met Captain Ennion, who guided the column to a spot close to Pyramid.

'A' Company spotted two unarmed Japanese fleeing from a hill position near Kanglatongbi further up into the hills, but despite having brought fire upon them, they failed to bring either of them down. No doubt they were heading off to warn their comrades that the Battalion were trying to outflank them through the hills to the left of the road.

Upon arrival at the new location, Major Menneer decided that this position was unsuitable owing to its being overlooked, and he moved the column back a few hundred yards to the south, to a small plateau overlooking the main road.

Major Menneer now ordered Major Browne and 'A' Company to move to the east and establish a roadblock around Milestone 17 east of the Pyramid feature. Not long after moving off, the leading section were ambushed by the Japanese in well-concealed positions as they reached a junction in the track they were following:

> My company were sent off to block the road, which was supposed to be within a couple of hundred yards, and meet some Indian troops. We moved off down a jungle track, and after going about four hundred yards came to a track junction. I went up to have a look at it, and was standing looking at my map when I saw a bush move about ten yards away. My mind immediately went to the Indian troops, but then I saw a Jap helmet. I shouted, and at the same moment dived into the undergrowth as a grenade landed where I had been. Every man got his muzzle pointing somewhere and a good deal of stuff started flying around. We were scoring hits, but weren't very well placed. I was lying on a red ants' nest while one Jap appeared to be potting at my nose and another was shivering the leaves near my heels with a tommy gun. My batman had a bullet through his pack, cape, and slit his trousers! One platoon tried to get round the Japs' flank, but met too much fire. By now I had reached my company Head Quarters, darkness was not far off, we were out of water, and had not found the road; so I decided to return to the battalion base. We could not afford heavy casualties on this operation as the only method of evacuating wounded was a six-hour journey by porter.[21]

During the action Private Hook was killed and Privates Coleman and Tuffield were wounded. Later, on getting back to the Company area, it was discovered that Private Buck was missing, and Private Coleman could now not be located.

With Major Browne being unable to make it to the road, Major Forrest was ordered to take a patrol of 'C' Company out and now head for Milestone 17, which they reached by mid-afternoon. They found an abandoned roadblock made of tar barrels, but not long after their arrival they heard firing in the south between them and the village of Kanglatongbi. It was later reported that this was a patrol of 3/2 Punjab who were attacking another roadblock, and later that afternoon, news was received that Kanglatongbi was now free of the enemy and that half of 'Point 3813' to the east of the 'Kanglatongbi Spur' had been taken by the King's Own Scottish Borderers (K.O.S.B.).

In the early hours of 16 May another thunderstorm arrived, with accompanying heavy rain beating down for a couple of hours. During the downpour, news came that the Dogras were working up the western side of the Imphal-Kohima road towards the area of Pyramid, supported by tanks.

On their journey forward, the Dogras had captured two 'Jiffs' who had previously served with the British. One was a Sikh who had been taken prisoner at Singapore. The other came from 50 Parachute Brigade and had only been captured recently from a position east of the Pimple.

As enemy artillery and mortar fire increased on the area of Milestone 16, a patrol under Corporal Davies of 'B' Company set off in search of water, whilst Lieutenant Hastie went out with a party of Indian Engineers to find a suitable route to bring forward the Battalion's mules with their heavy stores.

When Corporal Davies returned a couple of hours later he reported that his patrol had crossed the main road between Milestones 16 and 17 and had explored positions to the east of Kanglatongbi, but surprisingly, they had not seen any enemy.

However, the enemy had seen them, and soon their artillery began to shell the area of Battalion HQ. The Battalion War Diary now coined a new term, 'overs', to describe this form of barrage. Major Browne, a keen cricketer who had played for the Regiment, also used the term:

> The next day we moved off for our original objective, having established exactly where we were on the ground. The country was very difficult indeed and very careful recce should have been carried out. It wasn't, and the leading company walked straight into the hell of a packet. I was working around a flank and getting the full benefit of the overs from the Japs. We had no artillery or mortar support and it was obvious that we must cut our losses, so retired and just got into a harbour area as darkness came down.[22]

That evening, Lieutenant Hastie arrived with his mule column, carrying the Battalion's heavy equipment and some much-needed drinking water. One mule had been struck in the neck by a shell splinter as the column crossed the paddy fields along the Imphal Turel, north of Sengmai, but its kit was unloaded and it was sent back for treatment.

The following day, 17 May, as a party of Indian Engineers now constructed a special stretcher to evacuate Private Tuffield, who had been badly wounded in the thigh two days before, the mules were returned to Sengmai with the Dogras along with their two Jiff prisoners.

'A' Company had now advanced eastwards towards the road just below Pyramid, where enemy activity had been previously reported. Upon reaching their destination they reported hearing much firing from positions in the south-west along the road near Milestone 16, where the Punjabis were thought to be in action.

'B' Company returned to the Battalion area having patrolled to a position on the main road below 'A' Company, between them and the Punjabis. They reported that in the darkness of the night before they had heard much chopping of wood and what sounded like sandbags being filled. It appeared that the Japanese were strengthening a substantial barricade somewhere near the road. It was this barricade that the Punjabis had attacked earlier that morning.

In the afternoon, Lieutenant Yonge returned with a fighting patrol reporting that they had come upon a lone Japanese soldier and were about to take him prisoner when the man sensed danger and ran. He was shot by one of Lieutenant Yonge's men and was later identified as a First Class Private, but no other information was found upon his body.

As their comrades 1/11 Sikh in 89 Brigade put in a determined attack upon the hilltop village of Ekban/Ekwan to the south-east, a patrol went forward onto the main road just north of the Punjabis' positions, reporting back that no enemy had been sighted and that only a single coil of enemy wire lay parallel to the road, not across it.

Now with intelligence collated on the land around three sides of the feature, Major Menneer prepared a plan to attack Pyramid as soon as possible.

Chapter Nine

Pyramid

'I was shot in an awkward place – the bum!'

With the planned 'left hook' now completed, the Battalion found themselves in a position south of Pyramid. In the past few days they had been moved 'lock, stock and barrel' by porters and mules over some of the highest features in the locality to reach their new position.

The Allies had been forced south from this area in early April when the Japanese had overrun the Ordnance Depot north of Kanglatongbi, forcing its occupants to regroup and reform in a defensive position further south known as the 'Lion Box', which was itself, evacuated on 7 April. With a large force of Japanese still known to be located in and around Kanglantongbi, this sweeping move around their left flank was designed to encircle them; they could then be dealt with, making it possible for a second major force to advance north over the hills either side of the road and effect a link-up with the forces driving south from Kohima:

> The operation entailed an encircling move through thick jungle to seize the high ground covering the first defile north of Imphal and to establish a roadblock near the 17 M.S. [milestone] on the Imphal-Kohima road on a precipitous and jungle-clad spur. A study of air photos of the area showed the terrain densely wooded with many cliffs and ravines. Officers' patrols were sent out to select a route, and an unused track was discovered which it was hoped would lead unseen to the objective which had been called 'Pyramid'.[1]

Pyramid was a pair of hill features which, although relatively low compared to the Pimple, were strongly defended and commanded an uninterrupted view into the valley to the south towards the Ordnance Depot, and to the north up the road to Kohima.

The feature had a deep valley, or re-entrant, between its two small peaks, with dense scrub up its sides. On account of its appearance from their positions to the south, the men of the Battalion christened this part of the feature the 'Baby's Bottom'.

On 18 May, a patrol under Lieutenant Watt of 'C' Company left to patrol towards Pyramid. Taking a northern route to the left of the feature, they turned east along a track that ran around its northern edge and rejoined the main road. When they crossed the northern fringe of the feature they were spotted by an unarmed Japanese soldier on Pyramid who made a dash for cover. Despite this, the patrol continued along the track until they were out of sight of the hill. Now, making their way back to the Battalion area by a track to the south, they heard further movement on Pyramid itself, but saw no enemy,

In parallel with Lieutenant Watt's patrol to the north, a second patrol under Sergeant Cunliffe moved off to the south of the feature. They set off early and returned later that afternoon. They had ventured further north to the small village of Saitu, and from there, they advanced towards the lower feature of Pyramid, following a small *chaung*. They met no enemy, only two natives from the village who seemed most surprised to see them.

Whilst these patrols were out, a mule convoy under Lieutenant Gray had arrived in the Battalion area bringing up rations and new orders for Major Menneer to move to another new position later that day. This new position was closer to Pyramid at the northern end of the old Ordnance Depot, and Battalion HQ was to be established on a track that ran north-west below the southern side of Pyramid. Major Menneer now altered his plans accordingly.

The Mule Convoy set off again at 1100 to return to Sengmai and by 1500 had arrived there. Back at Battalion HQ, Major Menneer received a wireless message from Brigade HQ that he was to immediately place a roadblock across the main road to the east, but he replied that he was unable to move because he still had several patrols out around Pyramid.

Later that evening, he received revised orders to move out at first light and occupy Pyramid as soon as possible, and also to establish the requested roadblock astride the main road around Milestone 17 – where 'A' Company had encountered the enemy two days earlier.

A patrol of 'A' Company now returned to the area of their action, ensuring that there were no enemy there who might impede the advance north to take Pyramid. They returned to the Battalion area reporting that they discovered the remains of Privates Buck and Coleman, who had both been reported missing on 15 May. The locations were marked for future removal of their bodies.

At 0515 on 19 May, 'B' Company moved off to attack Pyramid, heading for the northern part of the feature. Given the intelligence that Lieutenant Watt had brought back from his patrol the previous afternoon, they strongly suspected that at least one enemy company were dug in on Pyramid in very well concealed positions. The plan was now to dislodge them and establish a firm base on the feature. 'A' Company would then pass through, swing right and establish their roadblock in the area of Milestone 17, just south of another enemy-held hill feature in the north known as 'Zebra'.

Following in the wake of 'B' Company's initial advance, 'C' Company were to follow, with Tac HQ following them. 'D' Company were to be in reserve. In parallel to the main advance to Pyramid, Second Lieutenant Gunton was to lead a patrol out to the hill feature known as 'Mouse', approximately 150 yards to the west of Pyramid, that was later to be attacked by tanks.

At 0930 the airstrike started, and Vengeance and Hurri-bombers attacked the rear of Pyramid. It was hoped that this would briefly suppress any resistance there as 'B' Company set off to advance onto the northern side. As soon as the aerial bombardment ceased, a barrage by 3" Mortars from the 28th (Jungle) Field Regiment, Royal Artillery was brought down upon the northern part of Pyramid. Just before it ceased at 0955, Stuart tanks were heard advancing from the south towards Mouse.

'B' Company's advance was steady, and within two hours they were up and onto Pyramid, moving across its southern feature. Although they did not know it, they had already passed through the cleverly camouflaged Japanese forward defences. Their advance of almost a half a mile had been closely monitored by the enemy, and at 1445 a Japanese machine gun crew brought fire upon them: 'The leading platoon of 'B' Company had reached "Pyramid" and was inside the Japanese defences, pinned to the ground. The leading unit was in a trap anchored by cross-fire of automatic [weapons]. Their commander, Lieut. C. W. Stephens, was killed, and his platoon had suffered many casualties.'[2]

The Japanese had let them come on far enough to trap them within their inner defensive perimeter. Now, seeing the danger of being caught in the dead ground between the northern and southern features of Pyramid, Tac HQ retired swiftly back to the shelter of a *chaung* on the southern side of the southern feature. Out in front, 'B' Company, now alone, held on and went to ground in whatever cover they could find in the scrub. Entrenching tools were rapidly employed to dig shallow scrapes among the dense undergrowth.

Lieutenant Cyril Stephens, who had been killed, had been commissioned from the ranks of the Wiltshire Regiment into the Royal Berkshire Regiment in October 1943 and joined Second Suffolk in Arakan on 31 January. Before the war he had been articled to his father's firm of solicitors in Great Yarmouth. He left behind a wife in the adjoining town of Gorleston.

Unable to advance, 'B' Company were now in a dangerously exposed position atop of the northern feature; and to make matters worse, the Japanese were now climbing the trees in the *nullah* of the Baby's Bottom to fire at them from the rear. Seeing their predicament, a quick-thinking Major Hill took a section of 'C' Company to the north, skirting around the cleft of the Baby's Bottom onto the northern side of Pyramid. From here, they fired down on the Japanese in the trees, allowing 'B' Company to withdraw successfully from their exposed positions with their casualties into the Baby's Bottom and then back over onto the southern side of the feature.

Now 'C' Company moved up on the right flank, closer to the road. Major Hill moved his section further up the slopes of the northern side of Pyramid as best he could, before he received a painful glancing wound to the buttock. As a corporal assumed command of the section, he allowed himself, in great pain and, it was said, a tirade of bad language, to be evacuated back for treatment.

With the wounding of Major Hill, Captain Forrest now came forward to assume command of the elements of 'C' Company that Major Hill had taken forward, and with them he pressed on to attack the summit of the northern feature. In parallel to their advance, another platoon of 'B' Company under Captain Anslow now left the Baby's Bottom and proceeded north once more. Advancing, Captain Forrest saw Captain Anslow on his left shot in the head by a Japanese sniper. Grounding his men, Captain Forrest crawled over to him but could see at once that he was dead.

Captain Denis Anslow was a regular officer of the East Surrey Regiment, his father having served with its 9th Battalion during the Great War alongside the playwright R.C. Sherriff, of *Journey's End* fame. He joined the Battalion on 24 January 1944 as a reinforcement and was shortly to be given temporary command of 'A' Company following the death of Captain Gray, who had been killed attacking Bamboo Hill.

To the left of where the Japanese had taken to the trees, one of their machine guns now barked into life deep in the Baby's Bottom, raking the slopes of both sides of the feature. Surprisingly, they had missed Major Hill's advance to their rear, but now the men trapped in the open on the southern side of the feature were taking fire and were unable to advance or retire until the machine gun could be silenced. The situation was looking critical, but a retirement would be right across its field of fire:

> Meanwhile, 'B' Company was badly placed; parties of Japs endeavouring to get between them and the remainder of the battalion. This enemy encircling move was nipped in the bud by 'C' Company from an adjoining ridge where they were able to shoot down the Japs who had climbed up in the trees in the *nullah* between the two companies.[3]

At 1618, 'B' Company now used its 2" mortars to lay down fire on the northern feature of Pyramid, trying to knock out a Japanese 50mm discharger whose firing position had been identified. Its fire was now causing many casualties,

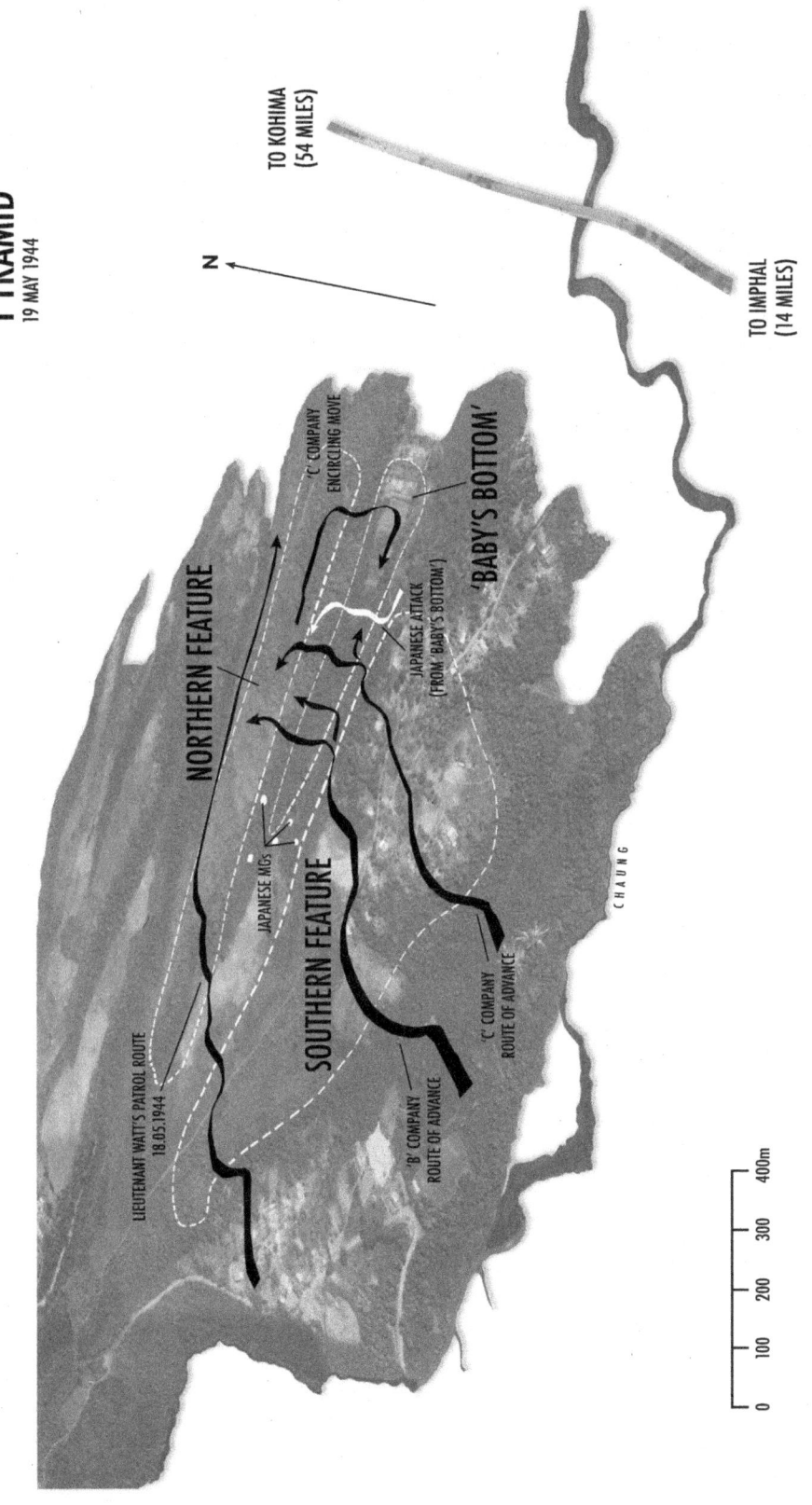

and both it and the machine gun in the Baby's Bottom had to be silenced if the advance was to continue, or if the forward companies pinned down in the open were to be able to conduct an ordered withdrawal.

Many other Japanese positions had been identified and were still known to be active on the forward slopes of the northern feature, but being close to elements of 'C' Company, these could not be dealt with by artillery or mortar fire, and had instead to be silenced, if possible, one-by-one, by the men on the ground.

Moving forward onto the southern feature, Major Menneer could better assess the situation that confronted his men. Though supplies were coming forward to assist those in the frontal positions, they could not be sent over to the men on the northern feature until the machine gun in the Baby's Bottom had been put out of action. Private Clifford Price, who had latterly been serving with 'C' Company, recalled that afternoon:

> 'Pyramid' was a battle in which I got too close, but thankfully I was not injured. An advance had gone in to take two hills linked together at the top. We had moved forward with Battalion HQ in anticipation that it would soon be occupied, but they had a tough job taking it and eventually retired. I had been asked to bring forward some small arms ammunition and we were dumping the boxes in a pile where they were being ferried forward to the men. I heard a loud crack and we threw ourselves to the ground. When I looked up, a tree beside us had taken the full force of a shell. A few feet to the right and myself and the ammunition would have all gone up. Major Menneer was beside us when it happened. A tall man with a huge 'Colonel Blimp' moustache, he seemed unbothered by it all and just smiled as we picked ourselves up. We brought up more ammunition and supplies, but later we heard that the battalion had withdrawn from the position.[4]

Private Richard 'Dicky' Moss of the Mortar Platoon, who was attached to 'B' Company for the advance that day, recalled how the machine gun in the Baby's Bottom was finally silenced: 'The position was a machine-gun post dug in at the base of the hill, impossible to reach with mortar fire from above, finally destroyed by using high-octane fuel and mortars to ignite it.'[5] Now, just as at the Pimple, tins of petrol were brought up to the southern feature to be 'lobbed' into the *nullah*, and 2″ mortars from 'B' Company were then used to ignite the fuel, firing bombs directly at the tins.

These petrol bombs had the desired effect, but the Japanese, having spotted their enemy, brought down another barrage of discharger shells onto 'B' Company and they were forced to withdraw from their positions back onto the southern feature. As they retired, Private Moss was wounded in the right arm by grenade shards.

Any further progress over the northern feature was now halted. Major Menneer spoke by radio with Brigade HQ to advise them of the situation. He was ordered to cease the attack on Pyramid and shortly afterwards he sent runners with messages to what elements of 'B' Company remained there, to withdraw through 'C' Company's positions on the south-eastern edge of the southern feature and back to Battalion HQ in the *chaung* on its southern side.

'B' Company had suffered many casualties, but the walking wounded were trickling in, and by late afternoon the majority were back in the area of Battalion HQ. As platoon commanders checked their ranks, however, it was soon established that several men were missing.

A few scattered elements remained on Pyramid, but with the onset of evening, the position of the Battalion looked precarious. The Punjabis were still fighting in the south at the northern end of Kanglatongbi, and 'A' Company were still away to the north manning their roadblock alone:

> The situation this late afternoon was not easy. The battalion was many miles – jungle miles – forward of their own troops and had a number of wounded. Rations and ammunition were limited. With C Company as their rear guard, they moved back to the south side of the ravine which they had crossed early that morning. With the burden of wounded men retirement was painfully slow and laborious, but the Japs made no serious attempt to follow.[6]

The failure of the Battalion to take Pyramid was in part due to the overstretching of their lines of supply, coupled with their being too widely dispersed upon their objective. Had a concerted effort been made by three companies, together with a further company and artillery in support, success might have been possible.

Throughout the action, the Regimental stretcher-bearers carried out their crucial work. As one of the last casualties was being conveyed away, a Japanese mortar barrage came down upon a pair of 'SBs' from 'B' Company. The barrage wounded Lance Corporal Lockey, who was carrying one end of the stretcher, and badly dazed Private White, who was carrying the other.

Having checked on Lance Corporal Lockey, who was badly wounded but still conscious, Private White slung the wounded man they were carrying over his shoulder and set off back to the Regimental Aid Post. He was about to return for his mate when a fellow 'SB', seeing that he was exhausted, went out alone and brought Lance Corporal Lockey back for treatment.

Sadly, the following morning, Lance Corporal Roy Lockey died of his wounds. He had been employed as a Regimental stretcher-bearer attached to 'B' Company from HQ Company and had done sterling work running the gauntlet of Japanese snipers on the Pimple and on Pyramid. It was a sad twist of fate that in the weeks before his death he had written home to his local newspaper in Bedfordshire stating that after the war he wished to take up market gardening, and could anyone send his mother any unwanted books on the subject. Tragically, by the time the newspaper had printed his letter he had died.

His fellow 'SB', Private Graham White, had been called up in July 1940 and had spent two years with the 8th Battalion, during which he had trained as a stretcher-bearer, being part of a team that won several shields for their efficiency. In July 1943 he was drafted to join Second Suffolk in India, just prior to their leaving for Burma.

Looking back some thirty years later, Regimental Stretcher Bearer Gordon Scriven, who had served first in 8th Battalion with Privates Lockey and White and who went on to serve with 1 Suffolk in NW Europe, recalled Roy with much affection:

> As I look back over the years I often think of men I called my friends who died in active service. There was Roy Lockey (who often expressed himself when we were on training in England that he was so hungry he could eat a horse sandwiched between two haystacks!). There was Larry Makepeace, and both of these died whilst serving as stretcher bearers in Burma.[7]

Lawrence Makepeace was killed with 1 Royal Berks at Kohima in July 1944.

Back on Pyramid, the Japanese now turned their attention to Tac HQ, which was still in the process of retiring from its forward positions. As the enemy sent over several more barrages of discharger shells, Major Menneer made plans for a final withdrawal. A couple of minutes later, 'C' Company arrived at Tac HQ reporting that they had killed seven Japanese snipers in the trees in the Baby's Bottom who had been active all that afternoon.

Enemy activity now switched to the right flank on the Imphal-Kohima road, where heavy firing was reported around Milestone 16. Soon, a message was received from the Brigadier that the Battalion were to prepare to move to an area close to this action at a spot known as 'Charing X', and at 1718 the order came through for Major Menneer to move off immediately in that direction. Major Henderson now took the lead with 'D' Company.

Whilst two Companies moved off, the Intelligence Officer, Captain Arrindell, took a party of wounded back to the Regimental Aid Post. Crossing the flooded *chaung* on the southern side of Pyramid, they scrambled across to meet Captain

Lee Hunter on the other side. Here they were fired at by a Japanese machine gun on the north-eastern side of Pyramid that was shooting over the Baby's Bottom. Luckily, no one was wounded.

By dusk all forward elements of the Battalion were harboured at Charing X, and although harassing fire was brought down on Pyramid throughout the night by both the artillery and the Battalion's mortars, all was quiet on the Battalion front.

Losses to the Battalion had been heavy in this nine-hour pitched battle. Together with Lieutenant Stephens, 'B' Company had lost Privates Collison and Whitehand killed, with Major Hill and Privates Fletcher, Green, Hawkins, Leech, Long, Moss, Shafaron, Sherman and Stutters wounded.

'C' Company suffered Privates Keelan and Twite wounded, whilst in 'D' Company Captain Anslow was 'missing believed killed' and Private Aldren was wounded. Later, Captain Forrest would confirm the death in action of Captain Anslow.

Major Peter Hill later recalled the intimate nature of the wound he received at Pyramid: 'I was shot in an awkward place – the bum! Though luckily it missed the bone and so with a bit of help, I was able to hobble down to the Regimental Aid Post, and then onwards to hospital where I was cared for by some lovely British nurses.'[8]

A fellow officer also noted the unfortunate, though amusing placement of his wound after he returned to service a few weeks later: 'Peter Hill finds it a bit hard to sit down as he was "caught bending" but, fortunately, it didn't get him to Kashmir and he is back with 'B' Company.'[9] It was in Kashmir that Peter had met the nurse who was later to become his wife.

However, despite their losses, Major Hill recalled that his men were still in good form: 'Morale, however, was high amongst the men. Most were good old ordinary Norfolk and Suffolk boys who now found themselves thousands of miles from home, fighting in a foreign land.'[10] But it was 'B' Company that bore the brunt of the 'missing believed killed' casualties of the action. That night, they had reported ten men missing, but by dawn the number had risen to thirteen, with Sergeant Studd, Lance Corporal Pettit and Privates Anderson, Hewat, Lucas, Mynott, Neighbour, Page, Parker, Robinson, Stanton, Terry and Thould still unaccounted for.

One man of 'B' Company killed on Pyramid was Private George Parker. He was the George referred to by Private Leslie Whetnall in his letter home about the action at Bamboo Hill. George was killed by shrapnel fire, as Leslie reported in another letter home.

Already exhausted, George and his comrades had trudged forward to get into position for the assault: 'A dangerous two-and-a-half hour climb lay before

George, and as he rose wearily to his feet – his face dirty and streaked with sweat with four days' growth of beard on his chin – he said, "Les, I'm tired out. I feel like a long, long rest."[11]

Leaving George in his foxhole, Private Whetnall returned later that day with a carrying party, bringing up ammunition for those fighting on Pyramid. It was then that he learned that George had been killed within 200 yards of the southern feature, when two salvos of Japanese shells came over, hitting the crest of the hill. Private Whetnall discovered from a comrade of George's that he had been reading a newspaper in his foxhole, awaiting the order to move forward, when shrapnel hit him in the back of the neck and killed him instantly:

> I never heard a wrong word from George all the time I knew him and I often wonder if he had some kind of premonition the last time he spoke with me. I wish I had found George's address and had written to his wife, but things happened too fast at that particular time … and there were many besides George.[12]

Despite being just thirty when he was killed, George Parker was affectionately known as 'Dad' within his platoon. Like his chum Whetnall, he had been transferred from the Royal Warwickshire Regiment to the Battalion when they were stationed at Deolali. He left behind a wife in London.

Together with Privates Anderson, Collinson, Neighbour and Whitehand, Parker was originally buried on a small plateau on the northern feature of Pyramid about 400 yards from the main Imphal-Kohima road. When their bodies were recovered for interment in a larger cemetery in December 1944, the jungle had already reclaimed their graves; the original crosses could not be located for Privates Collinson or Parker, but they were recognized by their identity discs.

However, Corporal Jack Dash, a pre-war signaller with the Battalion, recalled later that it was the expectation that if you were killed in the jungle you would be buried where you fell and your body would never be recovered. For this reason, he and others seldom wore their identity discs, and it was often only the sketches drawn by the Intelligence Section of the original locations of numerous jungle graves that allowed bodies to be found and reinterred in larger cemeteries.

Returning some days later, the bodies of fourteen men were found lying in two separate concentrations on the northern feature of Pyramid, with a further two being found in the Baby's Bottom. These were all moved off Pyramid to a temporary grave beside the main road, from where, six months later, they were moved again to the larger concentration cemetery in Imphal.

The location of these concentrations of dead from 'B' Company, showed just how close Major Hill and his men had been to the summit of the northern feature, and had it not been for the enfilading fire from the Baby's Bottom, just how close they were to taking the position. These concentrations also showed how fierce the enemy's fire had been.

The actions of the Battalion against Pyramid and the raids by the Guerrilla Platoon around Sedang were tough for the Battalion, especially when they were already exhausted after their attacks on the Pimple. However, these two major actions received nothing but the briefest of mentions in their Divisional History:

> 2nd Suffolks would send patrols to Nurathen and Modbung, always on the alert for any change in the enemy's dispositions, constantly seeking to disrupt his lines of supply by ambushing a mule convoy and destroying a stores dump or attacking a group of enemy soldiers. Villages where the Japanese habitually obtained food were raided. A basha in which some enemy soldiers were sleeping was shot up, and heavy casualties inflicted. In the course of these small raids and pinprick tactics, our troops inflicted upon the enemy more loss than we ourselves incurred.[13]

But for those 'pinprick tactics' the Battalion had suffered greatly.

On the morning of 20 May, Battalion HQ reverted to its original position south of Pyramid, where the Regimental Aid Post had remained. It was here that Lance Corporal Lockey was originally buried, but sadly, as the Battalion moved on, his original grave was lost and his body was never recovered.

Within the relative safety of their old positions, Major Menneer organized the hasty digging of a line of trenches along the northern border of the Battalion area facing the southern feature of Pyramid. Whilst the already exhausted men dug, he was conducting another reorganization of his platoon and company commanders, following the losses of the previous day.

Captain Coward was now given command of 'D' Company, whilst Captain Ennion was given 'B' Company following the wounding of Major Hill. Tony Ennion had only just returned from hospital, having 'got too near to a Jap mortar bomb', and was still 'a bit deaf'.[14] As Lieutenant Gray arrived bringing mules from Sengmai for the wounded, 'C' Company moved off to secure a position on the western edge of the old Ordnance Depot, where the Battalion would make its new base. As the wounded departed, 'A' Company left once again to try to form their roadblock. The move was completed in just over an hour, and for the rest of that day all was quiet on the Battalion front.

The following day was spent making good these positions and allowing the Battalion a brief period of rest. Indian Engineers cleared the road to the east of the Ordnance Depot, and now the Battalion made a cautious advance towards the site to see what enemy remained there.

The Guerrilla Platoon moved off first in the darkness of 21/22 May to explore the Depot. They found various huts full of abandoned British equipment and clothing, some of which the Japanese had made no attempt to destroy before retreating; some stores were still sealed in bales. The Guerrilla Platoon seized the opportunity to re-equip themselves with whatever they could find:

> The Guerrilla Platoon, which had done a grand job of work right from the start, were first in the area and re-clothed themselves from head to foot (except socks). They also found a dump of blankets which was to them of more value than gold. Orders were given to move and the Guerrillas loaded their blankets on to a mule cart. Ropes were attached and they pulled and pushed that cart up hill and down dale. The sweat poured off them, but those blankets were too precious to leave behind. We were given new positions near the main road, but still in the Depot. The Guerrillas hauled their cart to their area and, much to their disgust but to everybody else's amusement, they found themselves beside a hut which was packed with blankets, even better than those they had sweated so much to retain![15]

Everyone looked to get hold of a new pair of socks, but where were they? The answer soon became apparent:

> I should think the morale of the men went up 30 per cent when they were permitted to re-clothe themselves with what was absolutely essential. I can still see men sitting on top of hundreds of pairs of boots trying one after the other until they got the right fitting. Where were the socks? We discovered later that the Japs had used the socks to carry their rice in. The socks were filled, tied together and slung over the shoulder or over a pole.[16]

Returning from their roadblock, Major Browne and his men also recalled the treasure trove of kit that was found there: 'We were in an old ordnance depot and were all able to re-equip ourselves with battle-dress and boots which were badly needed.' The War Diary, however, took an 'official' line, in case of any future accusations that the Battalion might have misappropriated stores:

> There were cases of clothing and equipment lying strewn about everywhere, where the enemy had opened and pilfered. The Commanding Officer allowed organised parties from Coys to go and obtain the necessary clothing and equipment needed by their Coys. The articles included:- blankets,

boots, bush hats, underclothes, cookhouse burners and dixies, drill battle dresses etc., though Regimental Police were posted around the area to stop 'indiscriminate looting' by individuals.[17]

As morale soared within the Battalion with the issue of new kit, crushing news came that their comrades, the Dogras, had taken Pyramid just after lunch, without opposition. It was a bitter blow to the Battalion that their losses, which had been so high, had paved the way for an occupation of the feature with complete ease by others; but it was clear that their actions had broken the resolve of the Japanese and convinced them to abandon the position.

However, the Dogras reported that the position, which had only recently been evacuated, had been built for at least 200 men, and that the enemy had, it was thought, retired on the evening of 19 May after the Battalion had inflicted very heavy losses upon them. They had fallen back across the road to now form a defensive stronghold around the hilltop village of Motbung in the east.

The following morning, a party from the Pioneer Platoon under Lieutenant Thursby went back to Pyramid, and soon the dead of the Battalion began to be discovered. Graves were rapidly dug for them and their locations recorded.

It was the Padre who found the body of Private Lucas on 26 May when he returned to Pyramid, though he noted nothing about the body of Private Mynott which was lying beside him. Private Whetnell had sketched the location of their graves on 31 May as being beside one another in the Baby's Bottom, but later only Lucas's original grave marker and body could be found. The pair were almost certainly killed by the fire of the Japanese machine gun positioned there.

Private Paul Lucas had originally been a member of the Royal Norfolk Regiment, joining Second Suffolk at the end of August 1943 whilst they were in India. His mother, a Norwegian, requested that the epitaph on his headstone be inscribed in her native language: '*Sovi I Jesu Navn*' (Sleep in Jesus's Name).

Private Frederick Stanton, who had been killed with 'B' Company, hailed from Coventry and before joining the Army had worked for the Standard Motor Car Company. Another 'B' Company man, Private Leonard Collison, came from Coggeshall in Essex. He had been a farm worker and a Co-op bakery roundsman before being called up in 1943. He had joined Second Suffolk just before they left India for Arakan.

As more bodies were found, the men became appalled at what they saw. The bodies of several members of the Battalion were found gagged and bayoneted, implying that they had been wounded and captured but that the Japanese had had no intention of treating them. Major Browne recalled the high cost of the action for Pyramid and the discovery of the bodies of the fallen:

Casualties in the battalion had been rather heavy, and it was the only occasion on which all the wounded were not recovered. One man was found some days later gagged and bound, and with his own bayonet stuck in him. There were never any prisoners. We continued operations, and eventually my company put a block on the road in an alternative place, but the Japs retired by another route.[18]

The sight of their comrades' abused bodies angered those who saw them and only stiffened the resolve of the Battalion. Sergeant Bill Watts recalled his hatred for the Japanese, a feeling which was widely shared amongst the Battalion, especially by those who already had friends and relatives in Japanese captivity:

Bastards. Quite frankly they are the most unruly, uneducated people in the world, and although they are now well educated, and we're dealing with them, I shall never like the Japanese, because I saw things there that they done to our blokes in the jungle that I can't describe even now, and I won't, and it's just sad, too horrible and believe me, the world doesn't know what they're like, and they never can realise what it's like, unless it happens to them.[19]

On 24 May the Battalion were on the move again, this time to a position on the eastern edge of the Ordnance Depot by the main road. Whilst 'A' Company remained in their previous positions, the rest of the Battalion spent the rest of the day digging in and make suitable shelters against the now continual rain.

It was monsoon season, and the weather had returned with a vengeance. In their positions in the valley north of Kanglatongbi the sheer volume of rainfall now overwhelmed the men's positions: 'The monsoon came down in all its fury; tracks that had been inches deep in dust, became mud, slush and waterways. Digging was an impossibility, for holes became sump pits; it was only the thickness of the jungle that afforded cover from the enemy as well as the weather.'[20]

Over the din of the falling rain, shots could be heard in the north-east beyond the Dogras' positions as harassing fire was being brought down upon the village of Motbung. The following day, Major Vallance arrived as the Battalion's new Second-in-Command.

Major Guy Richardson Aymer Vallance was a pre-war professional soldier who had been commissioned into the King's Own Yorkshire Light Infantry (K.O.Y.L.I.) in August 1931. A keen sportsman, fine athlete and horseman, he had represented both his Regiment and the Army at polo, and he had already served with 2 K.O.Y.L.I. in Burma and later commanded 4 Burma Rifles. He retired as a Lieutenant Colonel and took up breeding racehorses, sometimes falling foul of the authorities. He was known on the turf as 'Ricky', and it was said that David Spencer, a Welsh pop star of the 1960s, chose 'Ricky Valance' as his stage name when he saw 'Ricky Vallance' as a trainer's name on the card at Chepstow races.

On 28 May an unfortunate accident occurred in forward positions when men of 'A' Company were cleaning and priming a box of No. 36 grenades. One exploded, killing Private Sewell and mortally wounding Corporal Salter, who was overseeing the working detail. Corporal Salter was quickly conveyed to the Regimental Aid Post but died soon afterwards.

Private Charles Valentine Sewell was just twenty years old. A native of Ipswich, he had been called up in 1942, having worked before the war in his uncle's garage. Corporal Frederick Salter had only recently learnt that he had been gazetted with the Military Medal for his actions at Bamboo Hill, and with it had been promoted to full Corporal. The two men were buried side by side in Imphal Cemetery later that afternoon.

The following day, as Japanese planes circled overhead, Captain Arrindell and Lieutenant Box left to take up their temporary positions as Brigade Intelligence Officer and Battalion Liaison Officer, roles that they had been understudying in the previous days. Lieutenant Gray now returned to the Battalion and resumed his previous role as the Battalion Signals Officer.

As the month drew to a close, the Battalion continued to make good their positions along the roadside. On 29 May, 'D' Company, with two anti-tank guns, were detailed to assist the Dogras in their advance to take Zebra.

The Dogras' plan involved getting one platoon of 'D' Company onto a spur to the west of the road below the feature so that they could fire north onto it. In parallel, the other two platoons of 'D' Company would advance up the road. One platoon would remain at a bridge that crossed the Imphal Turel, whilst the other platoon would advance further and 'simulate an attack' from the east as a diversion to the main attack being put in by the Dogras.

By 0905 on 30 May all elements of 'D' Company were in position. The forward platoons moved back to the bridge shortly afterwards, as the agreed airstrike against Zebra began. The simulated attack then went in as planned, and the men withdrew. However, the follow-on wave of artillery came down too soon, wounding three men who had to be evacuated to the Regimental Aid Post.

Privates Anderson, Dearsley and Gray were all hit by shrapnel that day, and Private Henry Dearsley would later die of his wounds. All these men had joined the Battalion since their arrival on the Imphal Front as reinforcements from other units.

As the anti-tank gun crews knocked out several Japanese bunkers, 10 Platoon, 'B' Company were called forward to support the Dogras' advance by bringing Bren fire upon Japanese positions at the base of a track that led from the main road up to Zebra in the west.

Major Menneer, who had been observing their actions from a hill to the east side of the road called 'Wigan', saw the Dogras' attack falter in the face of heavy fire from bunkers on Zebra, and by 1800 he was ordered to withdraw 'D' Company back to the Battalion area.

The month concluded with an unfortunate accident to a member of a patrol led by Sergeant Izzard. Upon returning to their foxholes, one of his fellow NCOs, Lance Corporal Nick Carter, jumped back into his own hole and accidentally shot himself in the foot with his Thompson sub-machine gun. To a chorus of roars, and many ribald remarks, he hobbled alone to the Regimental Aid Post for treatment. It was perhaps an act of providence for the recently demoted Lance Corporal Carter, retribution for having kicked 'D' Company's Christmas Dinner over the parapet of their trenches six months earlier.

Sergeant Sidney Izzard, who joined the Battalion in early 1944 as a reinforcement from the Royal Berkshire Regiment, had not long left its 70th (Young Soldiers) Battalion before he was posted to India. In the days following their actions at Pyramid he had seen three of his closest chums, Lance Corporals Carter and Pooley and Private Green, with whom who he shared a jungle scrape, all wounded:

> I was shipped on the *Athlone Castle* to Bombay. In early 1944, as acting Sergeant I took a reinforcement draft to join 2nd Bn Suffolk Regt – 5th Indian Division. With the Suffolks I saw action on the Arakan Front (at that time we were led by Lt. Stephens) and heavy fighting along the Imphal to Kohima road, just north of Kanglatongbi, and this was the last time I saw my friends as they were on stretchers having been wounded. A few days later, I too was wounded by a 10" mortar [Type 10] and hospitalised.[21]

Chapter Ten

Isaac

*'Here stood the new Suffolk, the rather grubby,
slightly tattered product of one year's living in the jungle'*

The month of June began with a complete move of the Battalion up into an area previously occupied by 4/8 Gurkha Rifles on the hills to the east of Pyramid across the Imphal-Kohima road.

The monsoon season continued and rain fell heavily, turning the tracks and paths into muddy streams. The lack of fresh food was now causing illness in the ranks and beginning to impair the fighting efficiency of the Battalion:

> The physical condition of the men was now beginning to deteriorate badly. Continual wettings, combined with hard work and poor rations, were pushing up the sick rate to a very high percentage. A large number of the men had a form of chronic diarrhoea, and there were not enough suitable drugs to cope with the situation. We were drawing a very much reduced scale of rations for only six days a week, and there was no fresh food at all, not even potatoes. Fit men were always hungry, and sick men couldn't stomach the food.[1]

The Battalion now established itself on two hilltop positions. 'A' Company occupied a position known as 'George', whilst 'D' Company occupied a similar one to the north known as 'Harry'.

By 2 June the Battalion had relieved all elements of the Gurkhas on their respective peaks, including 'Adam' and 'Eve' to the south. Battalion HQ was in the valley below, situated upon a spur that rose up to George at its summit. Their new positions commanded an enviable view over to the village of Motbung in the north and the Imphal-Kohima road to the west. From here they could observe Zebra to the north-west and the villages of Ekban/Ekwan and Kanglantongbi in the south.

Harry – the most northern hill in the range then in Allied hands – had been the limit of advance for the Gurkhas, who on 31 May had been successful in overcoming a Japanese bunker on the very north of the feature. Beyond lay another hill, 'Isaac', and beyond this yet another, 'James' – close to the hilltop village of Motbung. On the northern side of Harry was a small feature known as 'Twin Pimples'. These, like the towers of a bridge, led onto the 'Saddle' – a sharp, steep-sided ridge that linked Harry to Isaac. Isaac had now been allotted to the Battalion as its next objective.

Isaac was a plateau that encompassed three separately defended but interconnected features. First, heading north from the Saddle, was the 'Platform', a large central area that continued to the north-west. Here, well-concealed 75mm gun emplacements were positioned to fire onto the hills around, whilst in between them ran trenches around numerous weapon pits, each containing light machine guns and mortars.

Next, to the extreme right of the Saddle, was the 'East End' – a small island outcrop that contained several light machine gun positions which acted as watchtowers onto Isaac from the south. Finally, to the rear of the Platform was the 'Centre Bump' – two smaller interconnected hills that housed more bunkers and the sleeping quarters for the occupants of the entire complex. The whole feature was, from the end of the Saddle to the rear of the Centre Bump, about 1,200ft in length by at most 150ft wide.

When Major Menneer was ordered to take over the Gurkhas' positions, his immediate priority was to gather as much intelligence as possible on the Japanese positions that confronted him. He now used the Guerrilla Platoon as a reconnaissance unit to establish the enemy's dispositions and, with the assistance of the Intelligence Section, recorded the location of all the known enemy bunkers and their possible arcs of fire.

The Japanese soldier was, as had been established, a master of camouflage, and Major Menneer now placed an observation post on the northern edge of Harry and a listening post on the Twin Pimples to watch for any signs of movement.

The following day, Private Batten, a Battalion sniper, killed a Japanese soldier on Isaac from a concealed position on Harry. Observing the position through his telescopic sight, he noted the construction of the bunkers that now faced the Battalion and the general layout of Isaac:

> Bunker positions on 'East End' [right], 'Platform' [centre], and Isaacs Nose' [left] were pinpointed. These bunkers were on the crest and a few feet below it, and were seen to be made of logs, covered with turf and dead branches; at a distance they appeared like piles of brushwood, and were quite obvious as the loopholes were clearly visible with the naked eye. Some of them may have been dummies, but movement was observed in others.[2]

Early on 4 June, a fighting patrol working round to the east of Isaac reported that they had not encountered any enemy in this area, and later that day, a reconnaissance patrol went forward to investigate the possibility of establishing a 'Forming Up Place'(F.U.P.) in this area, from where a possible advance onto Isaac could be mounted.

A suitable F.U.P. was found, but this involved a journey down the steep sides of the Saddle and then back up the even steeper eastern slopes of Isaac itself. From here it was thought that they could assault the East End, but after careful deliberation, this route was abandoned as it was felt that the troops would be too fatigued by their climb and would not be 'sufficiently fresh' to then continue with an advance to their objectives of the guns and the bunkers.

This patrol made good progress in advancing unobserved to the area between the East End and the Platform, where they discovered one unoccupied bunker surrounded by wire; beyond it, a dead Japanese soldier lay about 30 yards away. Unbeknown to them at the time, this section of Isaac's defences was unmanned, with the Japanese only in occupation of the Centre Bump. Had this patrol remained here and consolidated the position, the battles of the forthcoming days would have been quite different.

In parallel to this patrol, another was being sent further round on the right flank, but at a lower level across the feature. Following the first patrol's journey, they moved off the Saddle and dropped down much lower, skirting below the other patrol to move around the East End and right around to view the rear of Isaac from the north. They halted at a position to the north-west of the Centre Bump.

Their advance had, however, not gone unnoticed. They had crossed a Japanese line of communication and killed two Japanese who were coming down the reverse slope from Isaac. With their whereabouts now known, they now beat a hasty retreat back round towards the Saddle. They managed to slip away without the Japanese bringing fire upon them, and it was thought that an attack from this direction might be possible, but the Japanese had now been alerted to the Battalion's activities.

More reconnaissance patrols now left the following morning before sunrise to explore the rear area of Isaac and the small ridge that ran out to a crest on the north-west of the feature known as 'Isaac's Nose'. Beyond this was the Centre Bump, though it could only be seen obliquely from the Battalion's forward positions on Harry.

One patrol moved right around the rear of the feature, passing around the East End and the Platform onwards to the Centre Bump. Another patrol struck west, dropping down to the left hand side of the Saddle into the valley and up again towards Isaac's Nose.

Here they met thick country and found the going tough. It took some hours to get into position, but by midday they were past Isaac's Nose and in position on another spur to its north. Here, to their left, they could observe Centre Bump, whilst in front they could see Isaac's Nose. To their right, they could see down into the valley below, and behind them a spur that eventually led to another hilltop peak, Wigan, where Major Menneer had observed the Dogras' attack on Zebra a week before.

The patrol stayed there for the remainder of the afternoon, observing the enemy coming and going to the Centre Bump carrying up ammunition and coils of barbed wire to strengthen their position. They were now able to observe that the main accommodation and stores area for the entire position was beyond Isaac's Nose, and it was worryingly clear that in the short time that they had been observing the position the Japanese had heavily fortified it with more wire entanglements and several newly-dug bunkers made with logs.

They sketched what they had observed from their spur and waited until dusk, when they observed that, just like the Battalion, the Japanese 'stood to' in anticipation of an attack. Waiting until it was pitch dark, they then made their way round to the Saddle and crossed back over onto Harry.

The other patrol was also now returning to Harry. As they skirted round below the East End, it is likely that the Japanese spotted them, for shortly afterwards 'A' Company in their positions on George were subjected to a heavy enemy barrage for over twenty minutes from the mortars on Isaac. Later, the patrol from the spur near Isaac's Nose confirmed that they had seen the flashes of mortars being fired off the reverse slopes of Isaac as they retired. The enemy's artillery, it was believed, had already been put out of action as a result of previous raids by the Gurkhas.

As preparations continued for the impending assault, artillery was being brought up to assist the Battalion. A 6-pdr gun was being hauled up onto George by a team of almost thirty men from 'B' Company. The work was tiring, and they could not complete the climb in one go. The gun had instead to be kept in their Company area halfway up George, to be hauled up again the following day to the top. It had to be staked into position that night, as it was feared that in the soft soil any more rainfall might cause it to slide back down the hill.

That day, too, 221 Anti-Tank Battery, Royal Artillery started to move one of their larger 25-pdr guns gingerly up onto the rear spur of George. The steep climb to the top again passed through 'B' Company's positions, and the unstable ground and further rainfall meant that the gun could only be moved a few feet at a time before its wheels had to be chocked. As it neared the summit of George, men of the Signals Platoon, who had their temporary Signals Office in a small *basha* near its summit, came out to assist in the final haul to the summit. Private Ernie Bates recalled that day:

I recall the episode well. Lance Corporal Mortlock had poked his head under our tarpaulin and said, 'You're all wanted to help get a gun up to the top.' 3 or 4 of us volunteered! I recall the little R.A. chap hanging on the barrel. The gun had been passed thru' Coy's up the fairly steep, narrow track, each group doing a stint of 20–30 yards. Us few signal types were HQ pool, therefore near the crest, where the C.O. was. We handed over to another group – it could have been stretcher-bearers? It was intended to soften up the bunkers at Isaac. I did not hear the 25-pdr fire, for one thing, I did not see any ammo follow the gun up the hill.[3]

Although this 25-pdr was intended to be used to 'soften up' targets in advance of the infantry attack on Isaac, no one, as Bates noted, recalled that it was actually fired. During the haul Private Roome of 'D' Company was seriously injured and had to be evacuated by air to hospital.

Private David Roome had previously served with 2 Royal Norfolk before he was posted to Second Suffolk, and had only just escaped from Kohima on one of the last trucks before the Japanese cut the road. Evacuated from Imphal airstrip, he was sent directly to a military hospital in Karachi, but within two hours he was loaded onto another plane and after a total of thirty hours in the air he arrived home in the UK. After his recuperation, he was interviewed by a reporter and described the Japanese as 'more brutally treacherous than the Germans'.[4] He later recovered and returned to his old job in a hosiery factory in Nottingham.

In parallel to these efforts, attempts were also being made to get tanks up the spur onto Harry. The success of tanks six weeks before when taking the Nungshigum feature had proved that, when used effectively in co-operation with supporting infantry, armour could have a devastating effect on Japanese positions.

3 Dragoon Guards (3.D.G.) were now called forward to bring one tank up across the spur between George and Harry. The track was certainly wide enough to take such a vehicle, but the camber, combined with the unevenness of the ground, made it a risky proposition.

However, confident of success, 3.D.G. decided that they would have a go; but soon after starting out, the tank was lost, careering over the *khudside* [edge of the ravine] into the deep jungle below. It had to be left there until it could be safely recovered. Major Browne recalled the event and the overall plan of attack:

> The next operation was to clear the Japs from a very dominating hill feature about three quarters of a mile to the East of the main road. As a preliminary we took over a hill about 1,000 feet high from Indian troops, as a base for operations and recce, and had a certain amount of mortar and M.G. fire

directed onto us, usually when we were all in our holes 'standing-to'. The general idea of the plan was that 'C' company would attack only along the ridge and get a foot-hold, with three tanks in support moving along the very narrow ridge in single file. Getting the tanks up the mountain was an incredible achievement, as was the hauling of a 6-pounder anti-tank gun onto the 'C' company position. The latter took 48 hours hard work. Heavy rain interfered with preparations.[5]

At first light on 6 June, as their colleagues in 1 Suffolk were travelling in their landing craft towards the French coast on D-Day, another patrol of Second Suffolk was advancing from Harry across the Saddle onto Isaac.

The usual early morning mist helped to conceal their advance onto the Saddle, but as they cleared the dead ground in the dip of the Saddle and came back up in front of Isaac, they were fired upon by Japanese positions to the left at Isaac's Nose. Diving off the Saddle and into the cover of the jungle on either side, the now divided patrol retired, both groups making it back to Harry without suffering any casualties.

In parallel to this, another patrol went forward to try and find another F.U.P. to the north-east, somewhere in the vicinity of the East End. Moving off the Saddle soon after leaving Harry, they dropped down to the right and found a suitable spot from where they felt they could launch an attack up onto the East End:

> At the same time a further recce was made from the east of the Saddle and a shorter and easier route to a F.U.P. under East End was found; on this route it was estimated that the assaulting troops could be in position and ready to assault within 50 minutes of leaving Harry. The first stages of this route were, however, under observation from Isaac and artillery or smoke was required to take them over the first 10 minutes.[6]

At Battalion HQ on George, the newly promoted Lieutenant Colonel Menneer now finalized his plans for an attack the following day. He requested air support to pound Isaac before the infantry attack went in, and seeing that his advance was to be in full view of the enemy, he brought up more anti-tank guns onto Harry to provide a barrage of smoke to cover the initial waves of infantry as they crossed over the Saddle towards Isaac.

These guns would all have to be hauled up the precipitous route through 'B' Company's area and onwards to Harry, which would take some time. The Support Platoon, with whatever other men could be found, started work straight away to assist in getting the guns into position.

The use of armour to support the taking of the position by the infantry would still go ahead, despite the failure to get the first tank up to their positions. Therefore, in parallel to bringing up the anti-tank guns, a party of Sappers from 74 Field Company, Royal Engineers were called upon to lay logs across the crest from George to Harry, to give the tanks a stable surface for their journey across and then onwards onto Isaac.

By 0800 on 7 June the tanks were up and in position on Harry, and half an hour later, Major Forrest moved 'C' Company, less one platoon and Tac HQ, onto Harry ready to advance via the Saddle onto Isaac. The Sappers now came forward, ready to check that the Saddle was free from mines, although the infantry had crossed it several times in the previous forty-eight hours and had reported none.

The usual thick morning mist again covered their movements, and at 0930 the first tank moved forward. Stopping at the Twin Pimples, it waited, whilst out in front the Sappers continued their crucial work. Once the 'all clear' was given, it rumbled forwards onto the Saddle. The track was barely wide enough for it, and only a few inches were left on either side for single column of infantry to pass.

Major Forrest, who had gone forward with his men, was now climbing up the eastern slopes of Isaac, having left the tank on the Saddle. As he climbed he observed anxiously the advance of the tank to his left. It rumbled onwards and after some minutes was close to the far end of the Saddle that connected to Isaac. The infantry had by now left its sides and were moving off down into the undergrowth on either side of the Saddle.

They were making good progress in their ascent of Isaac, and Major Forrest and his men were about fifteen feet from being level with the tank on the Saddle, when suddenly the Japanese opened fire. To his right, on the East End, they opened up with medium machine guns positioned in the bunker that had been reported as abandoned four days earlier.

In the centre of Isaac around the Platform a light machine gun in a bunker now burst into life. The heat of the action had caused the mist to dissipate, and the tank was now able to see to fire upon both these positions. With supporting fire from Harry and from the Twin Pimples, the tank was close to overcoming the enemy bunkers. From Major Forrest's positions, it looked as if all was going to plan:

> The leading tank continued to climb the slope to the East End blasting out bunkers with 75mm shells and silencing with Browning fire positions covering the line of advance, the infantry meanwhile working forward with great spirit towards the crest. As the leading tank climbed the final steep slope up to the right mound of East End it ran up against an anti-

tank ditch, in the form of a 3ft step in the side of the slope with loose earth thrown forward. In spite of many attempts, the tank was unable to negotiate this obstacle, nor could it engage the positions behind the large bunker covering the top of the ditch which had already been knocked out.[7]

Seeing that the tank had now floundered, and that the attack was in danger of grinding to a halt, Major Forrest beckoned over the third platoon of 'C' Company from their holding positions on Harry. They crossed over, using the Saddle, and passed the stricken tank, heading for the Platform.

Anticipating an imminent link-up, Major Forrest now pushed his men up the last few feet of the slope; having broken out onto the level plateau, they now made for the Platform to link up with the opposite platoon, who had worked up the western side of the Saddle, and the third platoon, who had just crossed over:

> Meanwhile, the infantry had worked forward ahead of the tank and the leading section under the Company Commander, Major Forrest and Lieut. Yonge got into position behind a knocked-out bunker. While this was going on the platoon on the right had reached the top of the east of the right mound [East End]. Lance Corporal Shanks working with great dash knocked out one bunker by throwing a grenade inside, but they were unable to make any further progress.[8]

Lance Corporal Lionel Ruffles of 'C' Company recalled his advance onto Isaac:

> To get to Isaac we had to cross over to it using an exposed track which they called the saddle. It really wasn't much more than a muddy path. The grass grew tall in the centre with tracks either side from where a tank had crossed over in the previous attacks. We were on the path when the Japs opened fire on us. It came from bunkers straight ahead and instinctively we broke right and left into the *nullah* on either side. I found myself beside Dennis Ireland and together we crawled up the sides of the hill towards the Jap positions. We found ourselves soon with several others and we waited lying almost upright in the grass and bracken as the hill was so steep.[9]

He now waited for the advance to continue:

> The firing died down suddenly and someone shouted, 'On!', we all scrambled up as best we could and saw that the Jap position had been overrun and that men out in front of us who must have crossed from the Saddle were already firing into the Jap positions further ahead.[10]

With assistance from Lieutenant Yonge, Lance Corporal Shanks' section, which had advanced along the left hand side of the tank, now reached the crest of the Platform, where they came under heavy fire from a light machine gun situated in a bunker there. His men went to ground and returned fire, wounding at least six of the enemy, whose groans could be heard.

To his left, another section under the command of Sergeant Barnes was now leaderless. Barnes had been wounded by a discharger shell just a few minutes earlier and had passed command to Corporal Toms, who was himself wounded shortly afterwards. Now Lance Corporal Shanks took overall command and ordered everyone to remain in their present positions, which were coming under increasingly heavy enemy grenade and discharger fire.

Sensing that the advance could only continue if the bunkers in front were silenced, Lance Corporal Shanks now went forward alone and through a hail of fire threw a grenade between the logs of the nearest bunker which exploded and successfully silenced it.

Just a few yards away, Lieutenant Yonge was about to do the same to another bunker that confronted his advance. He had been lobbing bombs from a distance of some ten yards from the enemy's forward positions, and like Lance Corporal Shanks, he knew that no further advance onto the Platform would be possible until it was silenced. These Japanese bunkers were constructed of thick wooden logs driven vertically into the ground for the sides, with further logs laid over them as a roof. They were impervious to grenades exploding above; only a grenade through the front opening would silence them.

As Lieutenant Yonge straightened up to throw another bomb from the cover of his scrape he was mortally wounded by another Japanese machine gun firing ahead of him on the Platform:

> By this time, the leading sections of both platoons were under fire from the automatic weapons on the left, and the Japs, realising that the tanks were having difficulty, started throwing hand grenades and grenade discharger bombs. 'C' Company was beginning to suffer serious casualties, Lieut. Yonge being killed by a burst of L.M.G. fire through the head. In order to shelter from small arms fire, the leading men dropped back under the crest.[11]

As the action in front of it continued, the tank was still stuck fast. It had struck the simplest of defences; a shallow ditch dug some ten feet off the end of the 'Saddle' pointing towards the East End. 'Nose-in' and unable to extract itself, it remained like an immovable blockhouse and could not even back out the way it had gone in. The status of its crew was unknown, for the fire had become so intense that no one dared venture out to bang on its hull and enquire.

'ISAAC'
6-9 JUNE 1944

'JAMES'
'ISAAC'
'HARRY'
'EAST END'
'GEORGE'
'EVE'
'ADAM'

IMPHAL TUREL (RIVER)

N

'C' COMPANY INITIAL ATTACK (VIA SADDLE) AROUND BEACHED TANKS - 07.06.1944

2 SUFFOLK POSITIONS, NIGHTFALL 07.06.1944

FINAL ADVANCE - 09.06.1944

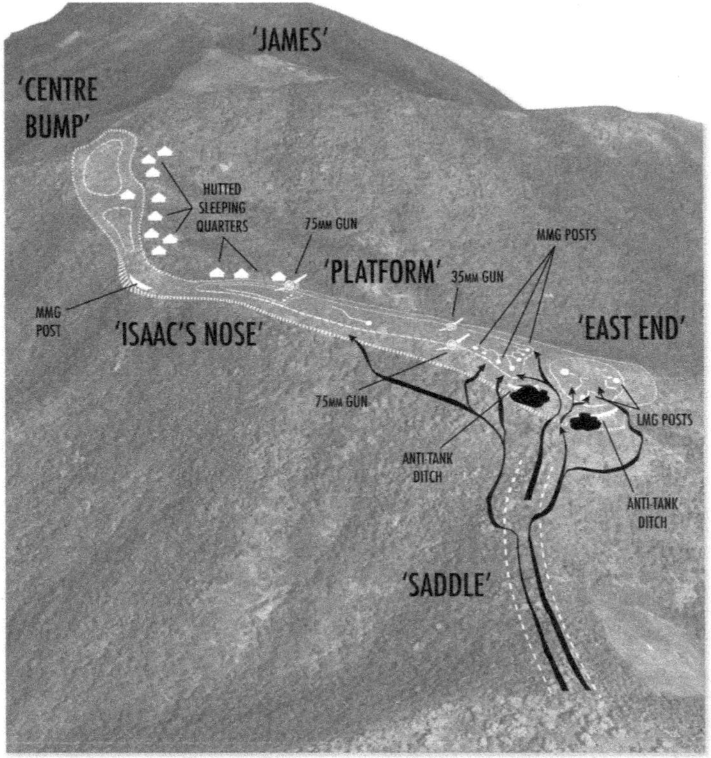

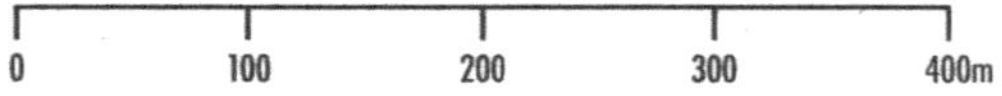

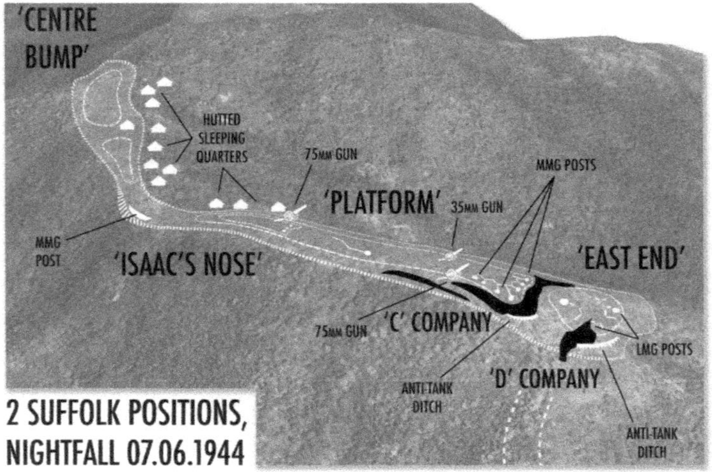

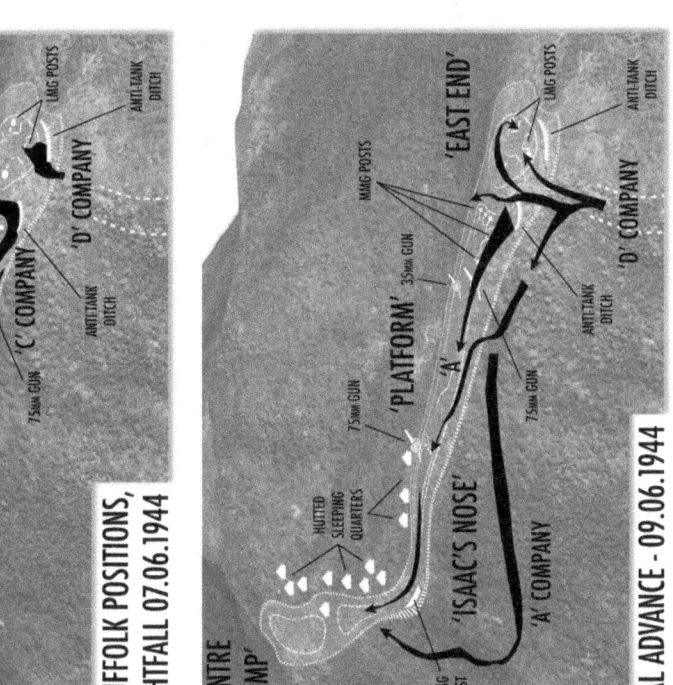

This intense fire now forced men to go to ground in the nearest possible cover, as Lance Corporal Ruffles continues:

> Again came Jap MG fire, and I dived into the nearest Jap bunker. It was occupied only by a dead Jap, crouched over in one end, his helmet down over his eyes. There were strips of machine gun ammunition beside him, but no gun. His comrade must have taken [it]. The fire was heavy and now mortars came down across the land I had just crossed, so I seemed stuck where I was. Now I waited until I saw others get up and move forward. Following behind, it was smoky and I couldn't see an officer anywhere. I didn't know at the time but he had been killed. Corporal Fern now pushed forward on the right with a few men and I joined them heading for an area of ground that looked taller than that over which we had crossed. We made for it, but suddenly we were fired upon from the rear and we realised that we'd gone too far and the enemy had got round behind us. We ran to our left, making for an area of low ground and here we lay and waited.[12]

Though they had a toehold on Isaac, it was clear to Major Forrest that they could not advance to take the Platform until the tank could knock out the other bunkers on the East End, since their enfilading fire barred any further advance onto the Platform. Whilst he was concerned by the fragility of their position, he was not at this stage unduly worried, since he hoped that with assistance the tank could extricate itself and advance to deal with the bunkers.

As was so often the case, the radios that had been sent forward had refused to work, so Major Forrest could not call upon the artillery to pound the East End. Likewise, getting a message back via runner would have been a dangerous and time-consuming affair. Instead, he decided to monitor the situation from the front in the hope of finding a weakness in the enemy's defences which he could exploit to continue the advance.

Unbeknown to the men around him, Major Forrest had been wounded. Later it was recorded that he had 'sustained slight wounds in the leg, but remained at duty'. In fact, his right leg had been badly peppered by shards from a Japanese rifle grenade that burst almost beside him on the Platform. Though in great pain, he remained with his Company in their frontal positions, still harassing the enemy.

Covered by the stricken tank, the first of the walking wounded and a couple of stretcher cases now made their way back across the Saddle under fire to the Regimental Aid Post. The MO, Captain Schwatz, was busy attending to cases, but the site of the R.A.P. was in a precarious position on Harry, as the Padre recalled:

The doctor and his staff had a very busy time attending to the wounded. The R.A.P. was situated half-way up Harry and it was under Mortar fire at all times. The stretcher bearers (heroes all) brought the wounded from the battlefield to the R.A.P. Often a blood transfusion had to be given on the spot – all were given injections. The men were made as comfortable as conditions permitted and as soon as possible they were carried to ambulances waiting on the other side of the river. It was a tremendous job carrying a wounded man on a stretcher down such a steep hill as Harry, but there was no other way. Volunteers were called for, and many came forward to help. As Chaplain it was my job to comfort and pray with the dying, to take down and forward any messages to the next of kin, to see that men were comfortable, and to get them cigarettes and tea. Then there was the sorrowful task of burying those who had fallen. Often they had to be buried just where they fell until such time as bodies could be removed to a central cemetery.[13]

Seeing that the tank was providing partial cover for the wounded to retire, Major Forrest now decided to send a runner back to Harry to request further armoured support.

A second tank was duly brought up to assist. Passing over the Saddle, it moved just to the right of the tank still stuck in the ditch at the Platform's edge, but sadly it fared little better. Moving right towards the East End, it struck a tree stump and, despite much revving, was unable to dislodge itself.

Now, late in the day, the Japanese turned their attention to the area of the Saddle, giving 'C' Company at the edge of the Platform a brief respite from their heavy fire. They had paid the Saddle little attention for a couple of hours, but as the Sappers were now hard at work laying another trackway of tree trunks up behind the stricken tanks, to assist in their recovery and in the advance of further armour onto Isaac, the Japanese had become alerted to their efforts there.

The Sappers, helped by men of the Battalion, swiftly felled trees and brought them forward. They worked feverishly right up under the lip of Isaac itself to lay a firm track some six yards wide. Two men were wounded and one Sapper was killed performing this task, but their work continued under now increasingly heavy machine-gun fire from the Platform just to the left-hand front of the first stricken tank.

Still out in front, 'C' Company were unable to advance until they had the support of the tanks, but in one final valiant effort, the third platoon of 'C' Company, who had crossed over to the feature last, now broke cover from their positions around the 'Saddle's Mouth' near the tanks and advanced onto the ground between the East End and the Platform.

This platoon, under the command of Lieutenant Haygarth, made good progress and soon linked up with the remains of Lieutenant Yonge's men, who had in their initial advance reached the east side of the Platform, north of the East End.

Just as they were preparing to move forward in another 'run', Lieutenant Haygarth was wounded by a grenade, along with several of his men. Knocked over and briefly stunned, when he came to he realized he was wounded in the chest and legs. Lying in the open, he ordered his men to continue the advance, before in a remarkable effort he got to his feet and, with the help of another wounded comrade, stumbled back over the Saddle. Weak from loss of blood, they took some time to make their way back, but seeing them from positions on Harry, two S.B. teams went out onto the Saddle to help them.

'C' Company were still scattered in their various scrapes, captured foxholes and bunkers on the Platform and also to the west close to Isaac's Nose. Lance Corporal Ruffles recalled those hours:

> The fire soon died down and we were joined by others. Behind us, about twenty yards away, was a ditch and more men were crouched in it. We began to dig in but had no shovels. We scraped down through the grass and shrubs and waited.[14]

In an attempt to strengthen his forward positions and to unlock the stalemate on Isaac, Lieutenant Colonel Menneer now sent two platoons of 'A' Company forward. One platoon he sent to the left, down into the dip to the left of the Saddle and up again to the area in front of Isaac's Nose. This platoon was to deal with that position from below to try and stop the Japanese firing across into the Saddle basin. The other platoon he sent forward past the tank still stuck at the end of the Saddle to head towards the Platform:

> As it appeared that C Company was unable to advance until a track could be got up to the crest, a platoon of A Company under Lieutenant Tomkinson was sent forward with orders to work round to the left in order to get on to the crest between the East End and the Platform. They succeeded in this, linking up with the third platoon of C Company which was in position on the shoulder of the right mound, ensuring that no fire could be brought to bear inside the basin when the track was being built. This platoon, under Lieutenant Haygarth, worked forward on to the crest with the platoon of A Company on their left. However, as soon as they got to the crest they came under MMG fire from the direction of Isaac's Nose. Lieutenant Haygarth was wounded and his platoon lost a number of men

killed. C Company platoon withdrew behind the crest and A Company's platoon was ordered to re-join their Company on the Saddle.[15]

By 1600 the Sappers had completed the track, and now a third tank proceeded onto the Saddle from Harry. However, it was not to be a case of 'third time lucky', for this tank suffered a mechanical breakdown which prevented it from getting any further than the end of the Saddle.

With the armour a 'dead duck', as one soldier later called it, and the route to Isaac well and truly barred to armoured support, at 1700 a frustrated Lieutenant Colonel Menneer decided that nothing more could be done with the tanks; he therefore sent a platoon of 'D' Company forward over the Saddle with picks and shovels to move around the disabled tanks and assist 'C' Company in digging in and strengthening their positions on the edge of the 'Platform' prior to their being relieved.

If they could deepen their positions here and bring up reinforcements and supplies in the darkness, he felt that they could use the western edge of the feature as a F.U.P. to launch further attacks onto the Platform and the East End the following day.

During that first day's fighting, casualties suffered by the Battalion were Lieutenant Yonge and eight men killed, and Lieutenant Haygarth and twenty-six men wounded. 'C' Company, which was already weak following the attack on Pyramid, was now even weaker:

> The fighting strength of C Company had been reduced to little more that 40 [men], the Company Commander too [Major Forrest] had been slightly wounded in the leg and these men were tired and exhausted, having been fighting hard since the morning and constantly under fire. Unfortunately, at no time during the day had this company been able to dig themselves in, as throughout the day and in fact from hour to hour it was hoped that the tanks would be able to get into the crest so that the assault could continue. Many casualties would undoubtedly have been saved if the Company Commander had been able to foresee that the tanks would be unable to reach the crest that day, so that his company could have dug themselves in with their entrenching tools on the topmost positions reached.[16]

With 'C' Company's positions now consolidated on Isaac, men of 'D' Company came forward at 1800 as planned to relieve them, as Lance Corporal Ruffles remembered:

How long we waited I do not know but others have told me since that it was at least a few hours. As we waited a sergeant appeared from behind us and told us that we were being relieved shortly. Not long afterwards men of A Company came over and crawled up to our positions. We crawled back over the edge of the hill and back into the *nullah* and re-joined the track running back to Harry. We spent the night on George and someone told me that Major Forrest had been wounded. [17]

'C' Company were now withdrawn from Harry onto George for a 'well deserved hot meal'. Exhausted from the assault, these men collected their thoughts. Despite being assisted by armour, Lance Corporal Ruffles recalled later that in the din and 'fog of battle' he could not recall its presence or effect: 'Everyone else remembers there being tanks in our attacks, but I cannot remember them. When the bullets are flying, you focus in on just your own little bit of the fighting and everything else seems a blur.'[18]

However, back on Isaac, both 'A' and 'D' Companies were working hard to improve and strengthen their positions:

A Company at once got to work to improve and dig complete company positions; tools and wire were already forward on the tanks and by nightfall the company was completely dug in and wired. During the night both Japs and ourselves were hard at work, the Japs being heard digging and chopping wood. Harassing fire was brought down on many occasions during the night but it is doubtful whether it had much effect as each time the flash of the gun was seen or the pop of the mortars was heard, the Japs shouted out a warning to take cover. On our side of the hill, the Sappers were busy working on and improving the track on the new alignment. Logs were cut in the Harry area and these were carried forward and placed in position.[19]

By first light on 8 June, everything was ready for another attack, just as rain again started to fall.

The new plan was for 'A' Company to move forward onto the Platform immediately after an airstrike, which was planned to commence at 1100. Then, with further assistance from the tanks, they would attempt to capture the whole of the East End, driving a wedge between the Japanese remaining there and those on the Platform. If both features could be taken, then over 60 per cent of the area would be in the Battalion's hands and reinforcements could be massed on the East End for a final assault on Isaac's Nose and the Centre Bump.

The airstrike was to have been signalled to start by smoke being fired onto Isaac by the Mortar Platoon – then positioned on Harry – but just as they were about to commence firing, the Japanese fired their own mortars into 'C' Company's positions on George, generating so much dispersed smoke across all of the Battalion's forward positions that there was a very real possibility that friendly fire incidents could occur due to confusion over the intended target. The airstrike therefore had to be cancelled.

In a quandary as to how he should proceed in the absence of aerial support, Lieutenant Colonel Menneer decided that the infantry attack would still go ahead with, he hoped, help from another tank:

> A Company's attack went in as arranged, the leading tank moving up the new track without difficulty. As the tank surmounted the steepest and most difficult part of the new track, and started working up along the crest, it was met by a volley of small arms fire. The infantry were moving up some 20 yards in the rear of the tank, which had got ahead of them to that extent owing to the speed with which it climbed. When the tank came well on to the crest of the left mound, a large cloud of white smoke and phosphorus was seen to burst on its tail and a heavy explosion was heard. The tank immediately stopped, began smoking and after a time was seen to be well on fire.[20]

The tank's commander, Lieutenant Cole of 3rd Carabiniers (Prince of Wales's Dragoon Guards), managed to escape with another crew member, although both were badly burned. The remaining members of crew perished inside the burning hulk. Observers believed that it had been hit by a Japanese 75mm gun dug in on the reverse slope of Isaac's Nose which may have been brought up specially to knock out the tanks. Now mortar fire was brought down on its position and soon its fire was silenced.

Trooper Malcolm Connolly of 3rd Carabiniers recalled the preparations and their journey forward behind their commander:

> After two days of preparation in the most vile weather, two troops of tanks with grousers (grousers are devices intended to increase the traction of continuous tracks, especially in loose material such as soil or snow) on their tracks made a notable climb on to the top of a feature called George. It was here that the attack was due to start. One Troop went forward supported by Gurkhas. The Troop sergeant was hit with a sniper's bullet but was quickly replaced. The tanks continued to make their way along a narrow ridge to another feature. It was a slow business; the tanks, though under intense fire, managed to destroy several bunkers.[21]

Near to Tac HQ on Harry, Private Ernie Bates also recalled the action:

> I witnessed, being near by the C.O., the attack on the bunkers going in and across the valley between Isaac and our hill, saw a Grant tank (I did not at the time know the type). Firing started and suddenly the tank was on fire, and we saw two figures scramble out of the tank, their clothing well alight.[22]

Despite scoring a couple of hits on bunkers on the Platform, the tank had done little to overcome the enemy's fire before it was hit, and no great advance could be made by either 'A' or 'D' Company from the positions they had consolidated the night before.

Just after noon, with the action on the Saddle clearly visible, the airstrike could now be launched in the hope of allowing the infantry to press on to take the feature. However, to avoid any doubt as to which hill should be attacked, the 25-pdr which had been hauled up onto George would now put down red smoke onto Isaac to pinpoint the positions for firing. However, as with the best laid plans, no sooner had the shells found their targets than a breeze rapidly dispersed the red smoke over all of Isaac; and so when it came, the airstrike was spread over a much wider area than had originally been requested: 'Their bombs dropped wildly, many falling very near our own troops. Some bombs however, landed on the objective and on East End and a later examination showed extensive damage done.'[23.] Swiftly, before the dust settled, 'A' Company advanced:

> A Company attacked again and were able to get on to the crest between the East End and Platform. However, just over the crest were a number of trenches and fox-holes and as our men approached they came under heavy MMG fire and a shower of grenades was thrown out on them. They withdrew below the crest. It was now late in the afternoon and A Company were ordered to consolidate the further ground gained, on the left and to dig in just below the stockade and wire protecting the Jap positions.[24]

Leading his men forward, having crossed over with them the previous afternoon, Major Browne recalled the action:

> Heavy cloud hung over the whole area on the morning of the attack, thus making it impossible to knock out enemy 'bunkers' beforehand. C Company moved up with the tanks but could not get onto the top, and neither could the tanks get up the final slope at the top, as the Japs had dug it out a bit. They tried every dodge to get over the top but failed to

do so, and eventually had so many casualties that we were ordered to take over from them. Nothing further was possible that day, so we dug in as high up on the Jap position as we could, just out of sight of them on the reverse slope, some posts being as near as 30 to 40 yards. The Jap force was as strong as ourselves and no further forces could be deployed, so we had to get the tanks up somehow. Artillery and mortar ammunition was very short. The night was therefore spent in laying a log track up into the enemy position, and they must have been too frightened to interfere. The next day we made three separate attempts to get up. On the first attempt we made one tank get up, only to catch on fire and block further progress by the threat of explosion. On the second attempt there was to have been an air strike, but we had to cancel it when the Japs imitated our target indication back on our positions. An attempt to rush the position failed.[25]

Finally, the end looked to be in sight. One platoon of 'A' Company now rushed forward and took over part of the East End, whilst the other two pushed forward over the Platform towards Isaac's Nose. Pausing only briefly to catch their breath, one of these platoons was now pushed by Major Browne to the left near Isaac's Nose and forwards to the north end of the Centre Bump. They bypassed Isaac's Nose by moving below the position and dropping down the hillside under it, then came up some fifty yards further on. However, when they emerged level with it they met with heavy fire from bunkers on the Centre Bump and also from Japanese positions on the Motbung Spur away to the north-west. For the moment they stayed put, resting on the slope.

To break the deadlock and to give supporting fire to those now attacking the Centre Bump, two teams of Battalion machine gunners were now crossing onto Isaac with their precious Vickers guns. They set them up in a captured pit on the southern end of the Platform and started to engage the Centre Bump and, more crucially, Isaac's Nose to their left flank. Behind them came the Mortar Platoon, passing a recovery crew who were working on the burnt-out tank, trying to make it ready for recovery as soon as possible. The mortars set up their 'tubes' on the southern edge of the Platform and started to pound the rear of the Centre Bump.

In addition to the move forward of the machine-gunners and mortar men, 'D' Company now prepared to move up and make one final push to the east to finally overcome the positions on the East End. They already had one platoon forward over the Saddle who were to take over 'A' Company's forward positions near Centre Bump, and their other two platoons now made for the Platform. The relief was completed by 1800, and later, in the darkness, they pushed eastwards to overcome the now isolated enemy positions on the East End:

D Company was ordered to continue pressing throughout the night by any means to get a footing on the crest of East End. Now that the positions of certain fox-holes covering the crest between East End and Platform had been located by the platoon of A Company and which positions were immediately above the positions in that area now occupied by D Company, it was decided that a patrol would creep over the crest at about 0200, throw in grenades and attempt to take by storm these positions. If they were unsuccessful they were to attempt to dig a gap into the crest at that point. Another patrol was to move round and work round to the right of East End and attempt to get on the crest in the vicinity of the bunker which had been knocked out by Lance Corporal Shanks.[26]

However, no sooner had the left-hand platoon of 'D' Company set off than they met a hail of grenades as they neared the crest of the Platform. They could make no further progress, and it was clear that the Japanese were very much alert in their positions at its northern end and beyond at the Centre Bump. Digging was heard throughout the night, and when they were harassed by the Battalion's mortars, there was much of the usual shouting from the Japanese. The platoon of 'D' Company on the right was more successful:

The patrol on the right made better progress and by first light [on 9 June] were established on the right mound of the East End. However, as the patrol got on the crest the Japs were seen to be evacuating the position. A number were shot as they got away, some falling over the *khud*. East End was quickly cleared and D Company were ordered to continue west towards Isaac's Nose. More Japs were seen getting away to the north but it was impossible to keep up with them and many long shots were fired. It appeared that the positions in the area of the East End which were closely invested by D Company during the night were held to cover a withdrawal of the whole Isaac feature. The Jap positions in the Platform and Isaac's Nose area gave evidence of an ordered withdrawal, while those on the East End were hastily abandoned, leaving a large quantity of equipment, ammunition (including 60–75mm. shells) documents and two large silk flags, also forty cup discharger bombs, eleven hand grenades, 900 rounds of MMG ammunition.[27]

Early on 9 June, another airstrike was arranged to try and knock the Japanese off the reverse slopes of the Centre Bump, but when it arrived it was a little too close for comfort for 'A' Company in their forward positions:

A further air strike with coloured smoke indication was then laid on. The planes wore only meant to strafe a very limited area, but to my horror they began dropping 500 lb bombs indiscriminately on the target area. The bombs were being released well behind us and it was a miracle that there wasn't a disaster. Four bombs landed within 50 yards of the leading men and chewed the Japs up very thoroughly, but they also shocked my men so completely that we could not follow up the advantage. Three men had to be evacuated, with mental breakdowns – probably chiefly due to the lack of sleep.[28]

However, as soon as the airstrike had finished, another tank started rolling across the Saddle onto Isaac, heading for the Platform. Minutes later, a loud explosion was heard and the tank started to 'brew up'. The Japanese had scored a direct hit on it with a trench mortar, as Trooper Connolly recalled:

Isaac had to be attacked again so once again tanks under the command of the 2 i/c of the squadron went in, but the climb up proved very difficult. The troop leader, now commanding the tank with the best engine, successfully climbed on to the ridge but as he started to turn to go along it the tank was hit and burst into flames.[29]

Just after noon, Major Browne and 'A' Company were in the area between the East End and the Platform when they met with heavy machine-gun fire and a concentrated grenade attack from positions further north on James.

Then came a report to Major Browne that the Japanese had been seen vacating their positions on the reverse slopes of the Centre Bump. Seizing the initiative, he pushed 'A' Company onwards to the north, and they were soon beyond Isaac's Nose. The Japanese were now seen running away down the slopes of the far side, though a core of fanatical fighters remained in their foxholes on the eastern side of the Platform and continued firing. Fighting would continue here into the early evening, when the enemy's resistance was finally broken:

Towards evening we made one more attempt to rush the position with all the local support, but failed. More than thirty men had been wounded and the company strength was down to about 45, so B company relieved us, and we went back about 100 yards. The next morning the Japs, bar a few men, had gone. Their position has been extremely strong, with strong rooted bunkers and every sort of weapon. We would have called it impregnable.[30]

Though Major Browne recalled two years after the action that their attack had 'failed', they had in fact routed the enemy and forced him into retreat, although admittedly no one was sure in the darkness exactly what the Japanese were doing.

At dawn, the forward elements of the Battalion fully expected that a determined Japanese counter-attack would come in retaliation, and they 'stood to' as usual in anticipation of it; but as the sun came up and the mist started to clear, the Japanese could be seen again openly packing up and retreating away from the Centre Bump through the dense country beyond in the direction of James. The Battalion's snipers were fully 'occupied' during their withdrawal.

'D' Company were, however, still in action trying to clear out a fanatical group of Japanese holding out at Isaac's Nose. They had returned there overnight following the Machine Gun Platoon's raking of the position the previous day. Once Isaac's Nose was silenced for a second time, 'D' Company pushed onwards to take over all of the Centre Bump, where they found more abandoned accommodation huts, shelters and large quantities of ammunition and grenades that the Japanese had abandoned in their flight. After three days of determined fighting, Second Suffolk had finally taken Isaac.

Gallantry had been shown in the actions to take the position, none more so than by Captain, acting Major Forrest of 'C' Company. Wounded during the initial advance, it was only after he had seen his men safely withdrawn to Harry that he went for medical attention to his own wounds.

The 'gallantry and skill with which 'C' Company was commanded merited high praise', and for his actions at Isaac, Major Peter Forrest was awarded a Bar to his Military Cross. His second citation for the award concluded:

> Throughout the day, Captain Forrest's Company, inspired by his coolness and dogged persistence, remained and held a footing within a few yards of the crest and continually under fire, his indomitable courage and endurance were an inspiration to his whole company and were largely responsible for the subsequent capture of this key feature.[31]

Major Peter 'Jungle' Forrest was commissioned into the Suffolk Regiment two months after war was declared, having previously served in the ranks of the 4th Battalion. He took a draft of new recruits out from the Depot in late 1940 to join Second Suffolk, then still at Razmak. After Isaac he did not return to the Battalion, and after recuperating from his wounds he was sent home to serve with the 8th Battalion, proceeding with them to Jamaica in 1946.

After a period of Staff work and secondment to the King's African Rifles in Nyasaland, he retired in 1963 and emigrated to Australia, where he became a school bursar. Lance Corporal Lionel Ruffles remembered him with much affection: 'Major Forrest was our officer and very good he was too. A good sportsman, he seemed to beat us at everything! He had been with the Regiment since the early days of the war.'[32]

Major John Fisher-Hock, a contemporary of Forrest's who knew him in the post-war years, recalled later: 'For those who knew him the abiding memory must be of his insouciant manner and constant refusal to take himself or almost anything too seriously!'[33]

Gallantry, too, was seen in Lance Corporal Robert Shanks' selfless advance to knock out a Japanese bunker single-handed. For his actions that day he was awarded the Military Medal. His citation noted his unfailing courage:

> During this time, Lance Corporal Shanks ran forward alone and threw a grenade into the bunker and silenced it. Lance Corporal Shanks, by his fine leadership, and complete disregard for his own safety, was an example and encouragement to his men, who held their positions under fire throughout the day.[34]

Whilst digging-in commenced, the advance elements of 3/2 Punjab passed through the Battalion en route to attack James in the north, the final hill of the range that remained in enemy hands.

Despite all the promises that the armour would 'win the day' as it had at Nungshigum, the battle for Isaac showed once again that it was only the infantryman on the ground who could take positions such as these:

> Thus, after three days fighting, our operation against these vital features was crowned with success. The ultimate success was solely due to the dogged perseverance of the Battalion (not forgetting the supporting tanks) due to the fact of what seemed at the time a continual run of bad luck. After so many attempts on the part of the tanks to shoot into the position, which only ceased when it was realised that the Jap gun made further attempts with tanks useless until that gun was silenced, it was realised that we must take the position without any further aid from them. Courage and perseverance eventually drove the Jap from his still strong position.[35]

Recalling the action, Private Clifford Price was also disappointed by the failure of the armour:

> We were full of confidence that they would do the job and the infantry would not have to go in, but in the end it was all a bit of a failure. One broke down, one blew up and one was lost over the side. We then knew

we would have to go in and take the position. After two days of fighting, we were called over to relieve the forward troops of the battalion who had been fighting there. We could see that the Japs had not wished to lose the position. Their dead were all around and many had fallen. When we got around to the rear of the positions we could see that they had constructed numerous pits and traps to catch our men, but thankfully we had stopped short of these positions. [36]

The Battalion's losses over the three-day battle to take Isaac were ten men killed and forty-five wounded. One of those killed was Private Branton Eade of 'C' Company. He had lived all of his life in the small Suffolk village of Rishangles, before being called up in 1940.

Badly wounded in the assault on Platform, Private Barnet Chenovitch was evacuated by the Company Stretcher Bearers but died on his way to hospital from the Advanced Dressing Station. He was a young Jewish lad from Hackney in London and had been posted to the Battalion from the East Surrey Regiment earlier that year.

Another man killed on Isaac was Private James Mackie. Called up in 1942, he had served first with the Black Watch, before being drafted to the Battalion just before the battle for the Pimple. He lived with his grandparents in Dundee and before he was called up had worked in the Pitalpin Jute Mill.

Lieutenant Michael Yonge, who was killed whilst attacking a troublesome bunker, was a devout Catholic. Yonge (pronounced 'Young') was educated at Beaumont College, Windsor and Trinity College, Cambridge. A fine athlete, he wrote several poems for his school magazine, and his parents chose a line from one for his headstone. Thus his epitaph was by his own hand.

In July 1956, Michael's father, Major Edward Yonge, who had served in the Indian Army during the Great War, wrote to the Regiment to obtain a copy of the Regimental History. The then Regimental Secretary, Lieutenant Colonel H.R. Hopking, sent him a complimentary copy together with a letter of appreciation about his son:

I commanded the Battalion when we moved into Burma in October 1943 until a short time before the above action [Isaac] took place, and of course knew Michael well. He was a first class officer, with great powers of leadership, popular with his brother officers and respected by his men. He was indeed a very great loss to the Battalion.[37]

An old soldier wounded whilst taking Isaac was Sergeant George 'Smoky' Barnes. He had enlisted into the Regiment in January 1931 and had served with

Second Suffolk for seven years before leaving the Army in 1938. Recalled to the Colours in September 1939, he was posted to the 1st Battalion and went with them to France the following month as part of the B.E.F. Then, having been evacuated through Dunkirk, he was posted back to Second Suffolk in 1943. After convalescing from the wounds he received at Isaac, he was discharged in October 1945. It was his section that Lance Corporal Shanks would take command of when Barnes was being evacuated for treatment.

Another man slightly wounded was Private Richard 'Dicky' Horsecroft, who was 'peppered' when a Japanese discharger shell burst close by him. Another old soldier, he had joined the Battalion in 1937 at Mhow. He was famous for his tattoos and for one in particular, which displayed a fox being chased by hounds right across his back – the tip of the fox's bushy tail just visible as it disappeared between his buttocks. Despite having several shards of shrapnel removed from his shoulder, the 'artwork' was unaffected.

Private Norman Youngman was also wounded at Isaac. He had been pushing forward with 'C' Company when he was struck by a shard from a Japanese discharger shell that burst above him. It tore through his right arm and, though badly wounded and weak from loss of blood, he made his own way back to the Regimental Aid Post to receive treatment. Whilst convalescing he learnt to write with his left hand, sending regular letters home to his mother.

Looking back a year later, the Padre recalled:

> After a short rest (if one could call it a rest with the rain pouring down) we were assigned a new hill feature, or rather three hills named George, Harry and Isaac. A river had to be crossed and a very steep 1500ft hill had to be climbed. This was George; then down a very steep bit and up to Harry; then along Harry, down again and up to Isaac. We found the Japs had withdrawn from Harry and George and had dug in on Isaac. It was gruelling work getting supplies to Harry via George. The engineers slung a suspension bridge across the river which saved a wide detour to a ford. The mules and their drivers were kept at it night and day.[38]

After the battle for Isaac, Lieutenant Colonel Menneer emphasized to his superiors that reconnaissance and intelligence were essential before attacking positions such as Isaac. While his predecessor had resigned in protest at not being given adequate time to assess the situation that confronted him, Lieutenant Colonel Menneer had had that crucial time to fully reconnoitre the objective he was being asked to take, and he noted the usefulness of this in a memorandum to his Brigadier:

> By careful and continual observation and by energetic patrolling it is essential to build up as complete a picture as possible of the Jap layout. This requires time. From the picture thus obtained artillery and mortar fire can accurately be brought to bear with good effect. Haphazard shooting in an area is largely a waste of ammunition as is also most H.F. [Harassing Fire] at night. Air strike and air strafing are most effective provided the indication is accurate. The 75mm and 70mm gun may be found at the top of the most precipitous feature. The 75mm can fire at very short range and may be mistaken for a mortar.[39]

By far the greatest number of casualties were caused by enemy discharger bombs exploding overhead, but unlike their counterparts fighting in Europe, the men did not go into action carrying heavy digging tools such as picks and shovels.

Instead, it was crucial that they used their smaller, two-part entrenching tools to dig in as quickly as possible: 'In the event of a check, infantry must immediately start digging with their entrenching tools, if they are to avoid casualties from discharger bombs and grenades of which the Jap has always an abundant supply and makes free use when in close contact.'[40]

Good communication with the armoured support was also essential, and it was noted that in this case it had worked well, despite the failings of the armour in the actual assault: 'It is essential for the Company Commander and the Troop Commander to be on the same net with 48 Set. This worked well throughout this operation.' But the CO was firm in pointing out that if tanks charged on ahead, the infantry experienced some difficulty in keeping pace with them: 'Infantry must always closely accompany the tanks – and the tank must, if it is to have this essential protection, regulate its speed accordingly.'[41]

The requirements of this constant, unrelenting jungle warfare had changed the appearance of the Battalion beyond all recognition. Men crawled back into their cubbyholes to sleep, worn out from attacking yet another hill. With water still strictly rationed, the rugged appearance of the Battalion persisted, as the Padre recalled: 'Owing to the fact that every drop of water had to be brought up by mule, the men had not shaved for days, their clothes were covered in mud, they were tired from lack of sleep, but where could one find a more reverent congregation?'[42]

Aertex battledress blouses worn for weeks on end changed from jungle green to a dirty black colour. Ingrained sweat and a lack of regular laundry services meant that it was often worn to destruction and then discarded. Private Toby Rash later recalled their dishevelled appearance: 'We looked more like scarecrows, not a bit like soldiers.'[43]

The old soldiers, too, who had served with the Regiment before the war saw how quickly the appearance of the Battalion had changed over the time they had been in combat. CSM 'Tommy' Warren had gone home six weeks earlier, but recalled how even at the time of his departure the appearance of his comrades had altered: 'The smart, polished Suffolk soldier of the plains of India was no more. Here stood the new Suffolk, the rather grubby, slightly tattered product of one year's living in the jungle.'[44]

The action at Isaac would forever be etched on the minds of those who served there, and though there were many who chose to forget those harsh days of fighting, others looked back upon the action with pride at what had been achieved.

The Battalion had, indeed, cause to celebrate its success at taking Isaac. Their Divisional Commander wrote to Lieutenant Colonel Menneer congratulating him on his Battalion's efforts: 'Your success was due to your determination to succeed.'[45]

Chapter Eleven

Silchar Track

'I had command of two companies with a ration strength of 13 men'

The evening of 9 June found the Battalion split over various hills. Two platoons of 'A' Company were dug in on East End, with one platoon on the Platform. 'B' Company was on Harry, 'C' Company on George, and 'D' had two platoons on Isaac's Nose with a third on the Centre Bump.

For 'D' Company, it had been a restless night. The eerie calm of the early hours was punctuated by a short sharp burst of fire from their Company's positions around 'Isaac's Nose'. The men were roused to stand to, but no enemy attack came. It later transpired that seeing a wild pye-dog snarling at him through the darkness, Private Cook, the Company Cook, had opened fire to deal with the beast: 'He became very unpopular, not through his cooking, but by discharging his Sten at a Pye Dog when performing his first and only stag duty, at midnight.'[1]

The following morning, the Brigadier came up to Battalion HQ and was taken onto Isaac by Lieutenant Colonel Menneer. Whilst he talked with men here, 'A' and 'C' Companies continued their consolidation. Patrols were sent out but returned reporting that no enemy had been sighted. In the evening orders were received for 'A' Company to move off the East End the following day, back to Adam via Harry and George.

Despite the battle now moving north, there remained the ongoing task of trying, under enemy observation and sporadic sniper fire, to bring in the dead for burial. While the Battalion naturally prioritized the recovery of their own men, the enemy dead still remained in considerable numbers on the reverse slopes of the Centre Bump. Captain Coward, conscious of hygiene, tried to alleviate the problem of decomposing enemy corpses by getting hold of some lime to spread over them:

> I was much involved in the final taking of Isaac where we lost a lot of good men in frontal attacks up an unkindly steep hill, which the Japs defended well from well placed dugouts. A Grant tank had blasted the bunkers before being set alight and burning out. We stayed on the terrible hill for 4 or 5 days. The smell of death – rotten bodies, flies. I asked Battalion HQ

to send lime in the hope of improving things. Battalion sent to Brigade. Brigade sent to Division. Division to Corps. Corps to Fourteenth Army, who sent it to Army Group! Three days later a team of medics came and asked for the 'safe' side of the hill and told me after much consternation that I should ask my Battalion HQ to get in 'some lime!'[2]

As the Battalion prepared to move, amended orders were now received. 'A' and 'D' Companies were to remain on Isaac to clear up and complete its defences, whilst one platoon of 'B' Company was sent to follow a stream, the Ithol Lok, northwards in search of the enemy.

In parallel, one platoon of 'A' Company now left their positions on the Centre Bump and moved off on a spur to the right, close to the village of Motbung. As 'D' Company took over positions from 3/2 Punjab on the 'Third Step' – the name given to the rearward-facing slopes of the Centre Bump – 'B' Company returned from patrolling the stream reporting that they had seen six Japanese and had engaged them with their 2" mortars.

Around 1700, the Guerrilla Platoon set out to follow 'B' Company's route up the Ithol Lok. It was suspected that this area was being used as an enemy line of communication to positions near James, and they were keen to sever any remaining telephone cables there.

As darkness fell, Major W. M. W. Cooper arrived to assume the role of Second-in-Command of the Battalion, Major Vallance now moving to command one of the rifle companies. Major 'Morris' Cooper was a regular officer with the King's Own Royal Regiment (Lancaster). He would later command its 7th Battalion in India in 1947 and its regular 1st Battalion in Germany in 1949.

On 11 June, the CO left for a conference and the Padre held a service on Adam, after which 'A' Company were relieved by the Dogras. The Brigadier returned and visited Isaac again to view the land to the north where 9 Brigade were then operating.

Returning to the Battalion after having just recovered from another bout of malaria, Private Idris Jones was now detailed to join the Pioneer Platoon. In between, he had been offered a commission but he had refused, noting that 'all the young officers were killed almost as soon as they had arrived.'[3]

He recalled the 'déjà vu' of his rejoining 'interview':

Asked once again about my trade, I explained that I was a qualified Bren gun carrier driver. I was told that a Bren gun carrier platoon has been formed, as part of Battalion Headquarters. Along I went to join this new platoon but there was not a Bren gun carrier to be seen.[4]

Considerable quantities of enemy weaponry and equipment had been found in and around Isaac, and as the defences of the site were recorded, this was stockpiled for visiting 'top brass' to inspect. 'D' Company alone recorded the following captured arms and equipment from their positions around the Centre Bump: '40 discharger cup bombs, 11 Jap hand grenades, 60 85mm shells, 960 rounds MMG, also medical equipment'.[5]

Just as 'A' Company were relieved on Adam by the Dogras, news came to Battalion HQ that the main Imphal-Kohima road was now clear to the north as far as the village of Safarmaina, since it appeared that the enemy had pulled back in force from the Molvom Ridge north of James.

Early on 13 June, Lieutenant Colonel Menneer, together with a small reconnaissance party, set out for new positions astride the Imphal-Kohima road to the west. The Battalion would once again be situated in the area of the old Ordnance Depot, but as heavy rain was falling, their move was delayed by twenty-four hours, since the tracks were all now impassable:

> The Battalion then withdrew from Isaac. Unfortunately, before the forward Companies could get down with all their kit we had several days of continuous heavy rain. The river rose and the bridge was carried away, which meant the men had an awful time getting across the swollen river. To retain one's feet on the steep slopes was practically impossible; it was sheer guts that kept them going.[6]

To make matters worse, the heavy monsoon rainfall had caused the suspension bridge that the Battalion were to use to cross the Imphal Turel to become partly submerged and completely impassable for mules. Because of this, the move to the new positions had to be delayed by a further twenty-four hours.

Early on 15 June, the Battalion's heavy kit was transported across the river at a spot to the south of their intended crossing where the Sappers had erected another suspension bridge. Here, using a cradle, the kit was conveyed across in company blocks, but it was a highly laborious process and took much longer than expected. As this was being completed, the rain continued to fall.

Later that day, however, the Battalion were safe in their new positions, where many wondered if this was the beginning of a long-overdue period of rest:

> Surely we would now be pulled out for a long rest. We had been continuously in the front line from early November – exactly seven and a half months. According to the Jungle Warfare booklet we should have been pulled out for a rest every six weeks, but apparently that was modified in India! With

light hearts we returned to Kanglatongbi and were given the luxury of sleeping in very dilapidated huts.[7]

The CO now completed the reshuffle of his officers that he had started a few days previously. Major Vallance was to take over command of 'D' Company, releasing Captain Coward to return to command of 'B' Company. Captain Hildesley now took over as Second-in-Command of 'A' Company, with Captain Thursby assuming his previous position as Adjutant.

Raymond 'Jimmy' Hildesley had been commissioned into the Regiment in July 1939. Decreed to be too young to join the 1st Battalion in France as part of the British Expeditionary Force, he was instead sent to join Second Suffolk in India. He was one of just a handful of men of the Battalion who made it through the entire campaign without being wounded, invalided or posted to another unit. He was later Adjutant to the 4th Battalion before retiring from the Army in 1959 to join the Colonial Service in Tanganyika.

That day, too, the Battalion's new Medical Officer arrived. Captain Halford took over from Captain Swartz who had reported sick a few days before. Doctor M. J. Swartz, was a Canadian from Cranbrook, British Columbia, who had volunteered for service with the Canadian Army in 1940. He had been serving with the Battalion since August 1942 and was known for his at times impenetrable accent; but for him, trying to interpret the broad Suffolk accent was also very difficult, and his trademark 'Aw eye say?' was often uttered when he couldn't understand what had been said to him. To everyone he was known simply as the 'Doc'.

Lieutenant Colonel Menneer now received tentative orders for another move in two days time to a position just south of the village of Safamaina. The men were tired but they could not be spared from duty. They desperately needed some form of relaxation and a chance to unwind, but they could not leave the front line. Instead, the entertainment would have to come to them, and on 18 June a travelling show arrived whose cast included Noel Coward. Private Idris Jones remembered:

> As I recall, I saw the show before the road to Kohima was opened. After a particularly nasty fight with the Japanese on hills named 'Isaac and James' where a number of men were killed and wounded, the Battalion took a breather. Noel Coward and his Troupe entertained officers and men before they started off on their next venture.[8]

The show was well received, as Captain Bryan Coward recalled:

> Noel Coward came to Konglakuchi [Kanglatongbi] and gave a really first class show – the sort people in London and Las Vegas would have paid hundreds of dollars to see. Next day, having that awful duty of censoring chaps mail, I read, 'Dear Mavis, we has a show by Noel Coward last night, it was quite good for a one man show.' Talk about pearls before swine! Incidentally, I am not related to Noel.[9]

The following morning, the movement orders were confirmed. The Battalion was to move north again along the Imphal-Kohima road, a distance of some 3–4 miles between the villages of Safarmaina and Molvom.

Whilst the main road was clear of enemy, it had been badly bombed and was impassable to marching troops. It was also suspected that the enemy was still holding out in small pockets on either side of it past the village of Motbung, so the Battalion would have to advance using tracks and mountain paths, searching out and destroying any Japanese who remained. In their wake, the Sappers could follow and repair the road for vehicles.

For the first part of the journey to their new position named 'Cold Harbour' a suitable track had been found, which was deemed suitable for mules, and at 0600 on 21 June the Battalion set off. The mules found it heavy going, and the Guerrilla Platoon went ahead clearing the way and sending out patrols to check the flanks, but the enemy seemed to have melted away.

Pausing around halfway, the Battalion rested overnight, and the following morning, the CO went forwards to meet with 3/2 Punjab, whom the Battalion were to replace at Cold Harbour. Within two hours, 'A' and 'B' Companies had arrived and were detailed off to their allotted assembly areas. The weather had been bad throughout their advance, as the Padre recalled:

> Rumours of the advance of this Division [2nd British] towards Imphal were very rife, but nothing was certain. Our Brigade received orders to make an encircling movement and get behind the Japs about milestone 110. The weather was too awful for words when the order was given to proceed. We moved forward in the pouring rain along a little track, or rather we slid forward because the mud was like ice. I can still see those men carrying the 3-in. mortars. They were supermen that day as they worked together, each carrying his allotted piece. Towards evening we reached our objective and bivouacked for the night. We were on a hill which overlooked the road in the direction of Kohima.[10]

At first light on 22 June, Battalion observation posts spotted movement from the north:

At daylight someone, through glasses thought he could see armoured cars moving down the road. This must be the 2nd Division – what a cheer went up – our troubles were over. About 10 o'clock there was the news that a party of 3/2 Punjab, belonging to our Brigade, had met the leading armoured car of the 2nd Division. At about 11 o'clock, there was the historic meeting of the Corps and the Divisional Commanders at Milestone 109.[11]

Now reports came by wireless that tanks from the 2nd (British) Infantry Division had been seen on the main Imphal-Kohima road near the village of Kangpokpi, and an hour later, advance elements of the Dogras had linked up with the troops pressing down from the north.

The Battalion was now hastily mobilized. At 1230 they moved off to yet more new positions, which they reached after a four-hour uninterrupted march. The march wasn't easy, however. The men were fatigued after the previous days, and many were now beginning to suffer from dysentery, as Captain Coward recalled:

I remember the march from Isaac to Milestone 109 – I doubt if anyone who took part in those actions could forget! When we joined the Dogras (1/17th) on that march we were all suffering from dysentery which made this march, mostly at night and in single file, a long and particularly unpleasant one as you can well imagine. As soon as the road had been opened, practically all of us were hospitalised in Imphal and when I rejoined 2 Suffolk I had command of two companies with a ration strength of 13 men.[12]

Private Idris Jones also remembered that march:

The trek took us along jungle paths flanking the road. It was monsoon weather at its worst. Drenching rain alternating with periods of hot sunshine which dried our mud-caked equipment. It took nearly two days to make the detour. Thankfully no Japanese troops were sighted or challenged. The advancing echelon of 2nd Division was met by this group of 123 Brigade at Milestone 109 on 22nd June. The Imphal-Kohima-Dimapur Road was open again. Japanese forces had withdrawn from the area and were on the run.[13]

Major Browne, still in command of 'A' Company, recalled the rapidity of their recent moves:

The next operation was another 'left-hook' through the jungle to get behind the Japs, and eventually link up with 2nd Division, coming down from

Kohima. Although we did quite a bit of walking, we didn't have to fight on this operation, as 2nd Division arrived more quickly than expected. It was most encouraging to hear their guns coming nearer and nearer down the road and even better to see them.[14]

However, the strain of the past weeks was now taking its toll on the Battalion. Sickness rates were up, but at this critical time, when they had the Japanese on the run, men could just not be spared:

We carried out a very exhausting move carrying everything in rain, and through mud down into the valley. The men were worn out. Eighty per cent, including myself, had chronic diarrhoea, and the majority of these were really hospital cases: but they couldn't be spared while they could walk. The company strength was made up to about 60.[15]

The following morning, Lieutenant Colonel Menneer received verbal orders to move to yet another new position on the east of the Imphal-Kohima road, and upon arrival there the Battalion spent the reminder of the day digging in and strengthening their positions. These substantial advances heartened the men. After the confined hilltop fighting of the previous weeks, such leapfrog moves reassured them that they might finally have the Japanese in retreat.

The Padre recalled that:

The following evening, the C.O. was asked to come over to Brigade Headquarters. We thought it was a bad omen and so it was. We were to be ready at daylight to be moved by lorry convoy to Burra Bazaar. It was like beating a willing horse, and the Battalion was willing, even though it was feeling the strain.[16]

Fatigue and exhaustion, however, continued to take a toll on their fighting efficiency. Back on basic rations again, as supplies ran short, their strength was being rapidly being sapped by further bouts of illness.

Patrols of 'B' Company now pressed east, and a link-up was achieved with the Dogras in the early afternoon. During their patrolling, they found several unoccupied Japanese positions but no enemy. Orders were then confirmed that the Battalion was to withdraw from the northern sector of the Imphal front and was to be sent south to a 'quiet' sector of the front beyond Imphal:

We thought a rest was due, indeed a necessity, but no. Almost immediately we were ordered down the Tiddim road, but once there had a fairly peaceful time in reserve, and were at last able to get some drugs for our tummies. It was also an inhabited area, and we were able to buy a few eggs, and a very limited quantity of fruit and vegetables. The worst of the sick were sorted out and the remainder, with the help of the improved rations, were getting into better form but were still nothing like fit.[17]

The Battalion was moved south of Imphal by lorry to a small village ten miles down the road to Tiddim called Buri Bazaar in an area then occupied by the 17th (Indian) Division. Moving off at 0600 on 24 June, the men travelled in company blocks, with the Admin Company leaving last of all. The mules, as usual, followed behind at their own speed.

Arriving some two hours later, the various companies were allotted two peaks to occupy, with the Battalion coming briefly under the command of 50 (Indian) Parachute Brigade before moving off again the following morning to occupy a lonely wooded outcrop of hills named 'Starling Box'.

Starling Box was a defensive position around three small hills to the north side the Imphal-Tiddim road close to the village of Buri Bazaar. The Battalion occupied the main peaks, whilst down in the fields below, tanks and carriers were safely parked in guarded, wired-off enclosures.

The two main peaks held 'A' and 'C' Companies, with platoons of 'B' and 'C' Companies and Battalion HQ on its slopes. To the north-west, two platoons of 'D' Company occupied the smaller, but steeper 'Naga Hill' overlooking the flooded paddy fields to the north, beyond which was the town of Imphal some ten miles away.

On 25 June, reconnaissance patrols now ventured to the village of Sadu further to the south past the larger village of Bishenpur, but returned later that evening reporting that no enemy had been sighted; in parallel to these actions, parties went south along the main road to assist in the clearing of mines.

That afternoon, orders came for a standing patrol to be sent back to Buri Bazaar in search of any enemy who might have returned there. Despite commanding the heights over the village, it was difficult to see any movement within the village itself, so a patrol of 'C' Company were sent forward with orders to fire one green Very light if any enemy were sighted. Finding no enemy, the patrol headed further south to relieve a patrol of 'B' Company at a small bridge some 200 yards further down the road towards Tiddim.

In stark contrast with their counterparts in the 1st Battalion, who were fighting bitterly to take the Château de la Londe in Normandy, Second Suffolk spent the last few days of June in continuous but uneventful patrolling and the relief of various other units nearby who were dispersed on numerous small hills in the locality. Daily came the reports 'No Enemy Sighted', and in their sector at least, the Japanese seemed to have melted away. It was perhaps in many respects, a good thing, for day-by-day men were continually falling ill, and replacements were not forthcoming. They would have had great difficulty taking on the Japanese in any large-scale combat, since their overall strength at that time was greatly impaired.

July opened for the Battalion with a reversion back to 123 Brigade in 5th (Indian) Division and the news that, the following day, they were to expect a visit by the Brigadier and some 'top brass' who would be coming to inspect the Battalion's positions around Starling Box.

On 2 July, after the Tiddim Road had been reopened, the Supreme Commander, Lord Louis Mountbatten, came to visit the Battalion again. On this, his second visit, he was presented to Major Forrest and Captain Lee Hunter, as none of those he had previously met in Burma eight months before were left to greet him: Sergeant Bates had died of wounds, Corporal Stewart and Private Brighty had been wounded and Private Crossland was sick. The others were all in forward positions or had been repatriated since the battles for the Pimple.

The *Suffolk Regimental Gazette* gave a cheerful report of the occasion: 'We were recently again visited by Lord Louis Mountbatten, who spoke informally in his usual inimitable style. We felt it quite typical that he should come and see us as soon as we had opened the Imphal-Kohima road. This visit was, as usual greatly appreciated by all ranks'.[18]

After Mountbatten had left, a church service was held for those who wished to attend, and later Major Cooper returned from Imphal in his jeep bringing with him a radio set and some board games. Despite the continual rain, the afternoon was spent relaxing under canvas.

Orders were received the following morning to move 'B' Company further south to Kaji Khul, and Lieutenant Colonel Menneer and Major Vallance set off to reconnoitre the new positions. In conjunction with this move, a standing patrol was to be sent to Leimaram to relieve the Royal West Kents in positions there.

As 'B' Company were preparing to set off to their new positions, another order was received cancelling their move and ordering them to stay put. The CO now issued orders that as the front was moving away from them to the south, they were now to spend their day in 'weapon training, zeroing, current affairs talks and recreational training'.[19] Most, however, just wanted to sleep.

The following morning, 'B' Company patrolled towards Kaji Khul as was the original plan two days earlier, but now the CO was summoned to attend a conference at Brigade HQ, where the future plan of operations in the south was outlined to him.

The next phase of the advance was to be in the south-west, below the Silchar track which ran from Bishenpur west over the mountains to Silchar itself. The

Battalion were now to take and hold the hill villages of Kokaden, Mayuron, Chario and Khulen that lay on its southern side. These small hamlets, nothing more than clusters of huts, sat on a series of wooded hills overlooking the track to the north. The Battalion's positions in the north-west looked down upon these features across a hilly, wooded terrain. In the centre, a banana plantation stood out as a dark square on the green hillside, and to the south stood a small hill known as 'Truemans'. Beyond this, past the plantation, and halfway to the villages, was another hill, 'Whiteway', and to the north beyond these villages was a final hill, 'Bulmer'. All were named after famous breweries of the time.

The Silchar track ran along a valley, then wound its way through the foothills, up and over the top and down the other side. At its eastern end it was overlooked on either side. Past Kokaden, the track rose above 5,000ft as it crossed the highest point of the hills north of Kungpi.

A combined advance was to be made to the north and the west, to squeeze a pocket of Japanese resistance that remained in these hills along the southern side of the track. The Battalion was also given the difficult task of advancing across to the hills over the barren, featureless paddy fields in the bottom of the valley, then up numerous steep tracks and paths to take and clear the villages, before finally effecting a link-up with elements advancing from the west. Cover for their advance was minimal.

On 5 July, the Intelligence Officer accompanied the CO on a journey to their new area, where they met with a forward liaison officer from 63 Brigade (17th Division), who took them to a spot named 'Point 2614', from where they could observe the topography of the area.

Accompanying them was the Intelligence Section with Private Whetnell, who now sketched the panorama in front. His absence from the ranks did not go unnoticed; many surmised that something was up and that they would soon be going onto the offensive again: 'The Intelligence Section has disappeared into the blue on some job, taking with them their many thousands of maps and, of course, Pte. Whetnell, plus his artist's brush.'[20]

Upon their return, Private Whetnell's sketch was copied and distributed to Company Commanders for the forthcoming advance. Armed with this information, a reconnaissance patrol set off that evening with the task of finding a suitable 'covered route' to get to the villages unseen.

That day, too, the Brigadier issued further revised orders that the Battalion would now move onto the hills to the north of the Silchar track, in preparation to cross it and then advance from the north towards the villages on the hills in the south. This order was welcomed, for it meant the Battalion no longer had to move across the flat, open paddy fields.

The Battalion's move was to be part of a larger advance by 161 Brigade from the north and 32 Brigade (20th Division) from the west. Lieutenant Colonel Menneer planned to send 'B' Company south over the track to Whiteway, and he now took their Company commander, Major Coward, forward to Point 2614, where he outlined the plan and showed him the position of Whiteway.

Early on 8 July, a reconnaissance patrol returned with valuable information as to the enemy's dispositions. They reported that they had proceeded northwards from a track towards Whiteway but that the shelling of a nearby hill had caused them to go to ground on a smaller outcrop just to the south of it, from where they could safely observe Kokaden village.

They saw smoke rising from a Japanese cookhouse on a slope north of Bulmer and an active bunker on a hillside away to the north-west. A possible route was observed from the south-west which they described as 'muleable', but they noted that the country was very open. The route to their present hill was very steep and certainly 'not practicable for mules', so another route would have to be found. A standing patrol now left to keep the area under observation for another twenty-four hours in advance of the Battalion's move.

At 0900 on 9 July, the Battalion marched off in column south down the Tiddim road from Starling Box towards a forward position near the village of Potsanbam. After a few enemy shells landed in their area, 'B' Company set off again alone, reaching the then unoccupied Whiteway a short while later.

As they established themselves here, a message was received by wireless that they were to 'stay put' until 13/14 July, but they had not taken enough supplies with them for such a long period of occupation and reported that they would need to be relieved within 12 hours when their supplies were exhausted. Lieutenant Colonel Menneer therefore ordered them to remain on Whiteway and arranged for a patrol of 'A' Company to make their way out to relieve them as soon as possible.

Moving towards the junction of the Silchar track, this patrol spotted a Japanese patrol of fourteen men but managed to quickly outflank them without making contact. The Japanese were moving westwards in what was thought to be a retreat, although they had left a pair of sentries astride the opening of the track to ambush any Allied troops moving west along it.

Retreating to their start positions, this patrol set off again by a different route and arrived at Whiteway at noon. In parallel, Lieutenant Colonel Menneer now decided that he would move Tac HQ and the remainder of 'A' Company into a small hamlet called Chote (Chothe) down in the rice fields below the hills, when 'B' Company were relieved from Whiteway.

The Guerrilla Platoon now went out to investigate the land to the north of the Silchar track between the positions of 'RK Ridge' and 'Toulang Wood'. They worked up to a spur between these two positions where they could overlook the track, but saw no enemy. An abandoned cookhouse was found in the bamboo, together with large quantities of unhusked rice. Half-constructed enemy trenches were also discovered close by, and it looked as though the Japanese had only recently vacated these positions.

'B' Company had a similar experience. A patrol which had struck west from Whiteway found more abandoned positions, but an hour later, they reported back that they had spotted friendly troops in positions north of the Silchar track in an area that had previously been occupied by the Japanese, and soon it was confirmed by the Guerrilla Platoon that RK Ridge was in Allied hands.

The Japanese were now retreating south and were being harassed by fighter-bombers and artillery along the way. As the Battalion remained on their various peaks overnight, their role in the advance was temporarily thwarted; they sat frustrated and inactive in the hills, although poised ready to be called forward if required.

The following days were to be spent in patrolling towards 'Garsides' – another hill to the south-west of Whiteway. 'C' Company sent out a reconnaissance patrol towards the hill but they were fired upon from enemy positions along a spur to the west. Going to ground, they were unable to ascertain what strength of enemy remained there. Whiteway was now left unoccupied, the area having been thought to be free from the enemy; but when a standing patrol returned once again, they were fired upon. Withdrawing swiftly, it was clear that they had been under observation from a Japanese position nearby which they had not spotted. It was believed, however, that this was just an isolated pocket of resistance that had remained after the main Japanese force had retreated.

During the night, 'A' Company moved further west onto another hill still some distance from Whiteway, and at 0630, 'B' Company returned to Whiteway and began digging in without opposition. With the position finally declared secure, Sergeant Bunce now took a patrol out from Whiteway towards 'Op Hill' in the south.

To reach Op Hill they would have to pass through the bottom of a valley, where 'Matthews' Hill occupied the left flank and Garsides Hill, the right. They had not been out long when fire was brought upon them from Matthews, and quickly finding cover, they observed six Japanese on the feature with at least two bunkers on the hillside below it. They retired swiftly, and at 0815 the following morning, a patrol of 'C' Company set out to establish if the enemy were still in occupation and reported back that they were – they remarked that they had managed to get close enough to hear them talking.

Whilst they kept this position under observation, another patrol now set off for Op Hill via a different route skirting around Matthews to the east. Not long

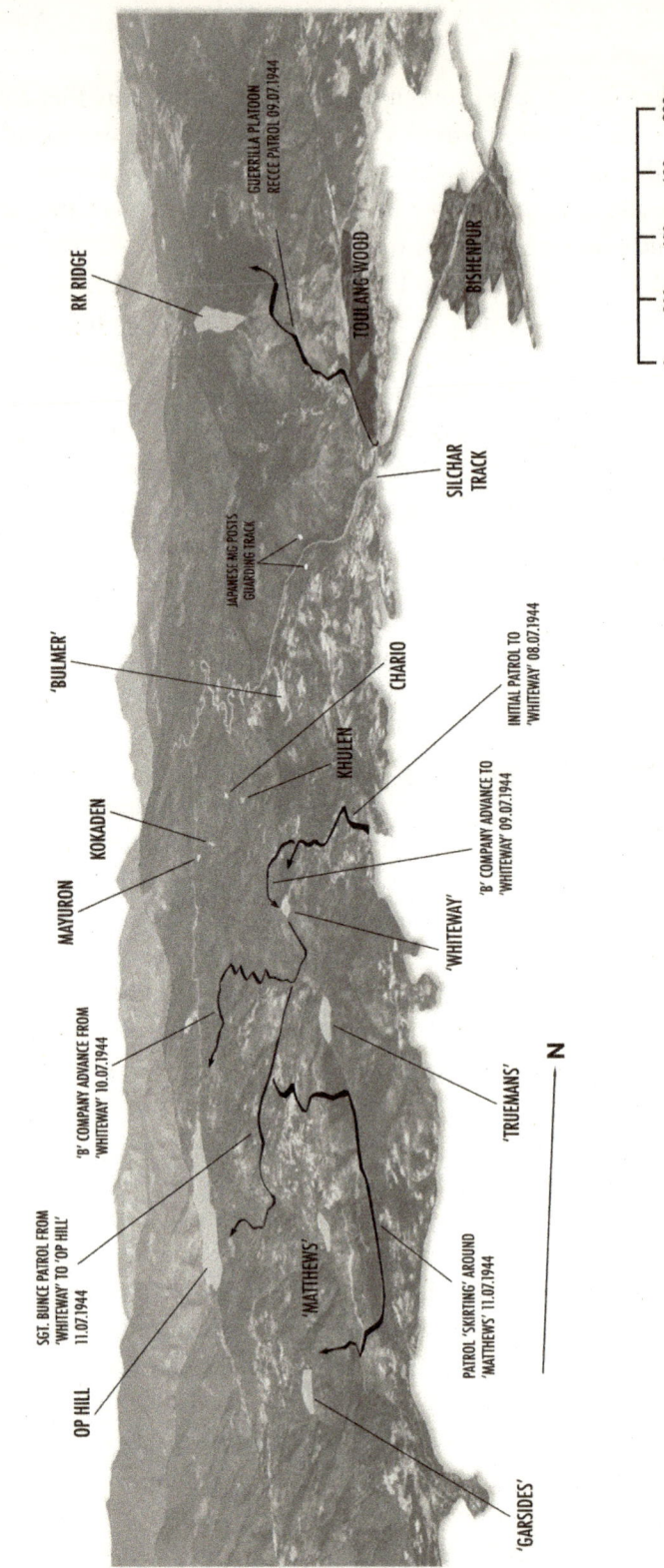

afterwards, they met another pocket of enemy dug in on a spur to the south of Op Hill and heavy fire was brought upon them. One man was wounded but was able to walk back unaided. Before retiring, the patrol made careful notes of the enemy's defences on the spur which consisted of just a single coil of wire stretched across, with five or six shallow slit trenches on its far side.

On 14 July, 'B' Company on Whiteway observed more enemy movement on Matthews, and harassing fire was brought upon the position in the afternoon. Lieutenant Colonel Menneer now felt it was safe enough to bring the mule column forward to Whiteway carrying the Battalion's heavy stores, machine guns and mortars.

The following morning, another patrol set out for Matthews and found it still occupied by the enemy: 'Captain Calver and nine B.O.R.s [British Other Ranks] patrolled to Matthews, saw 6 Japs in foxholes on western slopes. NCO opened fire with a tommy gun and killed one Jap. Enemy then threw one grenade and opened fire with rifles. Patrol moved back to Whiteway.'[21]

Lieutenant Colonel Menneer now decided to send 'C' Company forward to occupy Whiteway jointly with 'B' Company, allowing a platoon of 'B' Company to move south to take and hold Matthews.

The CO followed in their advance to observe Matthews for himself, and having reviewed the situation, decided that he would now send 'C' Company south to it the following day. He believed, based on his appreciation of the position, that it was being held by only about ten Japanese who were using it as an observation post, unlinked to any other positions in the locality.

At first light on 16 July, another patrol headed to Matthews and reported back that it was now unoccupied. Taking advantage of this, Lieutenant Colonel Menneer sent one platoon of 'C' Company forward to occupy the hill immediately.

As the Divisional Commander visited Battalion HQ, news came that the Allies had taken Kha Aimol, a hill village in the south, Op Hill and with it over a hundred enemy bunkers and vast hauls of equipment. The enemy had been encircled and forced south from the Silchar track. They were now in full flight, being chased south towards Tiddim.

Again the Battalion front became a sideshow as the action raced away from them. The following forty-eight hours were spent in patrolling to various hills in the locality, checking that the enemy had indeed fled and that no pockets of resistance remained. Great hauls of captured arms and equipment were taken. Periscopes, rifles, 2,500 rounds of small arms ammunition and over fifty grenades were found, together with much intelligence. As 'A' Company were ordered south to Shunu Sipahi, orders were received for another move, as Private Idris Jones recalled:

Our stay in Bishenpur was short and we soon moved forward onto the Tiddim Road, with the prospect of more fighting to come. I had now left battalion headquarters and joined C Company. Operating in section-sized patrols, we harried the retreating Japanese. For some reason I always seemed to be the 'get-away man' trailing a few yards behind the rest of the patrol. The NCOs must have thought that I was fleet of foot![22]

The Battalion was now called forward to rejoin the advance now pushing south towards the village of Moirang on the edge of Loktak Lake. Moving out in advance of the main column, the Guerrilla Platoon made it into the village at first light on 19 July and, searching as thoroughly as possible, established that the enemy had already left.

They fired green Very lights to signify that all was well and that the remainder of the Battalion should move forward. 'D' Company advanced first and soon reported that the village of Thamnapokpi en route to Moirang was clear of the enemy; but 'B' Company, moving up by a parallel route, encountered well-concealed Japanese snipers in the village of Ngangkha Lowai, which slowed their advance. Having dealt with them, they moved on and established a defensive position south of Moirang.

The Guerrilla Platoon continued to fire green lights from Moirang, waiting for the Battalion to arrive. 'B' Company's advance had again slowed, and now they reported that the track south of Ngangkha was covered by snipers, which had halted their advance. These last pockets of the enemy needed silencing, which took some time, but just before noon 'D' Company reported that they were now close to the village. Lieutenant Colonel Menneer ordered them to get into Moirang as soon as possible to establish a firm base there before it got dark and effect a link-up with the Guerrilla Platoon.

Whilst a 'C' Company patrol operating from Ngangkha killed another Japanese sniper and managed to bring in an enemy mule with papers and intelligence in its saddlebags, 'B' Company's advance had ground to a halt after renewed encounters with snipers.

However, leading from the front, Lieutenant Colonel Menneer was now in the thick of the action with 'D' Company advancing towards the village. Armed with a tommy gun, the War Diary recalled his heroic actions as they came up against Japanese positions on the outskirts of the village:

> Commanding officer was with D Company and had fired a LMG (light machine gun) at this Party and had killed three Japs. Japs went into bunker positions in this area. 2 platoons of D Coy attacked bunker positions but were unable to make progress owing to automatic fire. Killed three Japs.[23]

Though they did not know it at the time, this was to be the Battalion's last encounter with their Japanese enemy:

> Near the village of Moirang the Battalion had their last brush with the enemy. 'D' Company, commanded by Major K. E. J. Henderson, entered the north end of the village during the afternoon and one of his patrols brushed a party of 10 to 20 Japanese who attempted to get into a position. After several of the Japs had been seen to fall, a two inch mortar was directed on them, and a fighting patrol went out to finish them off. During the night the remaining Japs attempted to slip out and rejoin their comrades, but walked into 'B' Company; only two escaped.[24]

Upon entering the village, 'D' Company received accurate and sustained automatic fire from a position that had not been spotted by the Guerrilla Platoon. This resulted in Private Mortlock being killed and two others wounded. A sniper was also still active, with Major Henderson and four other ranks being wounded by his fire, as he later recalled:

> I was commanding the leading Company of the Battalion at a village called Moirang where we found a pocket of the enemy. As I was looking through my field glasses to see exactly where we had to attack them, I felt a sharp pain in my right hand. One of their snipers had spotted me and that was that. Although I did not realise it at the time, this in fact had the most profound effect on the whole of my subsequent life. One or two inches one way would probably have been fatal – one or two inches the other way and I would have never met Joan.[25]

'Joan' was Joan Heath, a qualified and experienced physiotherapist who had volunteered to serve in a military hospital overseas. Having been flown back to No. 14 British General Hospital at Bareilly, the pair began a romance that would see them wed in London in July 1945. Kenneth later worked for the Norwich Union Insurance Company, rising high in its senior management before retiring in 1974.

Whilst 'D' Company consolidated in Moirang, 'B' Company reported that Ngangkha was finally clear of the enemy and that they were moving south towards Moirang to effect a link-up. Passing an abandoned enemy tank, they were fired upon by a concealed pocket of the enemy. A nearby artillery unit, however, swiftly silenced their fire. They made it to a road junction where they dug in for the night, some little distance from Moirang itself.

The advance to Moirang had, however, pushed some men to the limit of their endurance. Exhausted, and with sickness on the rise, some couldn't go any further. Around Milestone 35, recently promoted Corporal Ernie Bates found he just couldn't go on. He had caught tick typhus and was now evacuated by air back to hospital in Chittagong.

Bates, who sailed to India in 1940 on the Troopship *Lancashire*, joined Second Suffolk at Razmak, where he recalled with much disappointment that they had to exchange their 'new' two-month-old battledress for 'old' service dress; but when up in the cold hills they were very glad they had, for it was much warmer.

Ernie was typical of a high proportion of men in the Battalion who after four years of Foreign Service were due for repatriation to the UK. Illness soon claimed more men, one of whom was Private Idris Jones who, having recovered from malaria just a month before, now suffered a bout of dysentery:

> By this time, along with many others I was again suffering from dysentery. While carrying a full load of mortar bombs, I had to fall out of the line of march to relieve myself, by which time battalion headquarters was far out of sight. I therefore thumbed a lift and found myself driving past the still-marching Suffolks. There were consequences, though. I was placed on a charge by Sergeant Major Duffy. It was a charge now happily forgotten and, though found guilty, nothing came of it. Many years later I met Sergeant Major Duffy at a Suffolk Regiment reunion and reminded him that he had once put me on a charge. He smiled: 'You weren't the only person I charged during my service.'[26]

From Moirang, patrols now moved south and south-west, pushing the enemy back; the villages of Okshungbung and Kumbi were declared free of the Japanese the following day. As 'A' Company moved towards the village of Toroglaobi they were fired upon, but continued. At first light on 21 July they reported that this village was also free of the enemy. The Japanese flight in the small hours was evidently a hurried one, for they left behind stocks of arms and equipment on a scale not seen by the Battalion so far in the campaign:

> Much Jap equipment collected south of Okshungbung including 3 Jap LMG's, 6 Bren guns, 2 T.S.M.G., 8 grenade dischargers, 2 3" Mortars, 1 Damaged Bn [Bren] Gun, 126 Jap rifles, 1 flame thrower complete, 3 periscopes, 1 rubber suit, 3 tanks, 1 tractor, 3 mule saddles, 20 Jap bayonets, 200 grenade[s], 40 boxes discharger bombs, 10 boxes 3" mortar ammunition,

6 boxes MMG ammunition, 6 cases magnetic mines, 6 cases 37mm shells, 50 75mm shells, 100 lbs amanol, 1 Jap pistol, 2 motorcycles.[27]

Major Browne also recalled the swiftness of the advance, and the advantages of lines of communication that now extended from Imphal to all parts of the front:

> Things were a bit more lively. It was now that men began to reap the benefit of a road L of C, for the Jap positions were given a very heavy pounding indeed, which helped them to make up their minds to start for home. About 15,000 rounds of 25-pounder and 3,000 of medium ammunition were shot into a very small area. Besides bombing by the R.A.F. the battalion were in the lead for the start of the chase down the road and met no serious check. We took up positions while another formation went through.[28]

As the Battalion now occupied new positions south of Moirang, Lieutenant Colonel Menneer went off to 9 Brigade HQ to ascertain the overall situation, and then moved on to 123 Brigade HQ to receive his orders. 9 Brigade were south of Milestone 30 on the Tiddim Road and had met no opposition for the last mile of their advance, but they could not proceed as fast as they would have wished, for in their flight the Japanese had destroyed all the road bridges behind them.

The Padre, too, recalled the swiftness of that advance and the massive artillery and aerial support that now accompanied it:

> Then came a night when all the guns opened up on the Jap positions; somewhere in the region of 9,000 shells were fired that night. At daybreak the R.A.F. dropped bombs and strafed the Japs, and then we were ordered to advance. The Jap resistance had been broken. Those who were alive had fled. All around were Jap dead, burnt out tanks and lorries, and field equipment of all sorts. The Imperial Jap Army had had enough. They were not the supermen they had claimed to be; they had met more than their match. Henceforth for them it was retreat, retreat, retreat. For us it was advance, advance, advance.[29]

For the Battalion however, there were to be no more advances. As reconnaissance patrols pushed towards Tarun Khunou on 24 July, stagnation returned as the front moved further and further away from them. Early on 28 July, the Battalion moved off to new hilltop positions north-east of Churachanpur on the Tiddim road, taking over positions previously held by 2 West Yorks. They were now 33 miles south of Imphal.

With the enemy gone, Second Suffolk's fighting war came to a gentle conclusion here. In view of their inactivity, Lieutenant Colonel Menneer decided he would now reduce the strength of his companies on their respective peaks to one platoon each, and with the remainder he advanced south-east further along the Tiddim Road. On 30 July they reached a forward position at Milestone 40, sending patrols out to the nearby villages of Khopuibung and Saikot, but the locals reported that the Japanese had pulled out three nights previously. The enemy had gone.

Major Coward, who had recently been on leave in Calcutta, now returned with a number of red and yellow roses that he had managed to procure in advance of 'Minden Day' when, as was the immemorial custom, roses would be worn in the headdress of all ranks. Upon his return, he noted the visibly changed state of the Battalion and the sharp increase of sickness in the ranks:

> At the end of the campaign north of Imphal, Numshigum, Isaac etc., the Battalion was commanded by Major Menneer and the rifle companies by Peter Forrest, Peter Hill, Browne and myself. The Battalion suffered severe casualties both in battle and health (mainly dysentery) and with the reopening of the Kohima road most of us spent time in hospitals.[30]

'Minden Day', 1 August, was the annual commemoration of the Regiment's principal Battle Honour, and it was celebrated as usual with as much festivity as could be mustered, despite the various elements of the Battalion being dispersed on their respective hills.

The day started with officers serving the men 'gunfire' – tea laced with rum. For those back at Battalion HQ there were 'proper' celebrations that included midday tombola and an evening concert, but for those out in their foxholes on the hills it was a day much like any other:

> Minden Day was celebrated as best it could be. Festivities were curtailed this year owing to operations, but in spite of this we all had beer, played tombola and had a good feed. The Rifle Companies were all on separate peaks of the forest-clad hills that surround the town of —. 'D' Company being a two-hour walk from Battalion HQ, 'HQ' Company and Admin were down in the foothills. After taking a week to get companies onto their peaks, using umpteen mules and porters, everyone was only too glad to get a well-earned day's rest. The morning was marked by a visit of our Corps Commander [Lieutenant General Sir Montagu Stopford], accompanied by the Divisional Commander and our Brigadier. He shook hands and spoke to 'selected' personnel, having a long conversation with

Sergeant Harry Cropley on that important subject, food, and congratulated Sgt. Brown, M.M. and Cpl. Peck M.M., both of the guerrilla platoon. He congratulated us on our red and yellow roses; they looked remarkably smart on a bush hat.[31]

The menu, too, was something of a welcome change, ably conjured up by the always reliable Cook Sergeant Cropley and his staff. Lunch was a cheese fritter and pickles, bread and butter and a rice pudding. The evening meal consisted of roast New Zealand lamb, baked potatoes and onions. For desert, a peach and pineapple pie had been concocted from tinned fruit out of the ration packs, and for a very lucky few there was a bottle of beer.

One soldier was later to remark: 'What a bloody meal! I wish they would have some more Minden battles',[32] and the *Suffolk Regimental Gazette* noted wryly: 'We hope next year we shall be able to celebrate Minden Day in traditional style.'[33]

The fluidity of the southern front at Imphal gave the men renewed hope that soon the Japanese might be completely defeated, but now rising illness rates were becoming a major issue. Orders were received on 6 August to move back to Company strength on their respective hills, and to institute proper daily routines to reduce the spread of various illnesses.

Tented Cook Houses and Dining Halls were to be erected, and the age-old routine of bugle calls was reinstated. Training was commenced, but hygiene was now of paramount importance, with new latrines being dug and made fly-proof. The construction of a new, semi-permanent tented camp was visible proof that for the foreseeable future the Battalion were staying where they were.

Typhus was now becoming a major concern; the long grass that surrounded their hills harboured the almost invisible mite that spread the disease. The Adjutant now issued orders to relinquish the relaxed dress of the previous months to try and combat its spread. Major Browne also recalled these conditions, and the dreaded mosquitoes:

> This was a very wet area indeed and not a good spot to live. Anything that wasn't raised in the air was in water. Leeches were all too plentiful, and the mosquitoes were unique. They could bite through almost any clothing and didn't confine their activities only to night. About ten would be biting at any given moment if conditions were favourable, but fortunately they were not malarial.[34]

It came as a shock when two days later, Sergeant Brown, the man who had won the Military Medal before the action at Bamboo Hill, died of typhus. His loss was bitterly felt. Originally from the Royal Berkshire Regiment, he lived in

Elm Row in Shadwell, London and was one of the very first men to volunteer for the Guerrilla Platoon when it was formed.

Active patrolling would now continue for the next two weeks, during which time, sickness rates increased dramatically. By mid-August the Battalion was no longer of operational strength, and a report compiled on men reporting sick in the previous month detailed that illness, diet and fatigue were all now taking a massive toll.

This report noted that of a total Battalion strength of just over 700 men, 264 had been evacuated from the Regimental Aid Post in the past seven days. Diarrhoea and dysentery accounted for 103 cases, fever, mainly malaria, for fifty, infections and jaundice for thirteen and vitamin deficiency, a further nine. Only five casualties were evacuated during that period as a result of wounds received in action.

With the monsoon continuing, the rivers had swollen, preventing the mules from getting any rations forward. Instead, the Battalion was to be re-supplied by air, a novelty they could have only wished for in earlier difficult positions. On 13 August, three days' worth of rations were dropped to them:

> These planes had enabled all our forward operations to be maintained. During the rains the troops had to carry a minimum of three days' rations, being put on to half rations when this minimum was reached; yet the longest period during which no supplies could be flown was only five days, while the 'dropping' became increasingly accurate; so that it was said that 'P for Peter' could drop the manifest on to the office table.[35]

The new Medical Officer, Captain McCloud, having just taken over from Captain Halford, who had himself fallen ill the previous week, now wrote a memorandum to Brigade HQ regarding the worsening situation:

> The striking feature in the Battalion's health is the number of men suffering from long standing diarrhoea and dysentery which has caused besides loss of numbers, much loss of efficiency from debility. There is besides evidence of vitamin B deficiency in a relatively mild form. This accumulation is attributable to the difficulties of treating and preventing such cases during the recent campaign, to a period of inadequate diet and other hardships. It is my opinion that it will take some weeks before hospital treatment, improved diet and rest produce a real change in the health and strength of this unit.[36]

As if to reinforce this point, the following day, Lieutenant Colonel Menneer was admitted to hospital with jaundice and would not return for several weeks. Command now passed to Major Browne as the most senior 'Regimental' officer still serving. He was the Battalion's third commanding officer in four months.

Private Idris Jones also recalled the loss of fighting efficiency within the Battalion in connection with a rumour that spread through the ranks that they were to be removed from the front:

> The battalion was ordered to move forward to recapture Manipur Bridge on the Tiddim Road. The rumour mill suggested that the CO complained to the brigade medical officer that his battalion wasn't sufficiently fit to undertake this task. They had been in action for many months and desperately needed a rest.[37]

On 20 August, the then Intelligence Officer, Captain Gray, fell ill, and it was three days before his successor could be appointed. Lieutenant Ellis undertook to compile the Battalion War Diary for the final days of August.

The Battalion was now the exact opposite of their counterparts in the 1st Battalion in Europe, suffering the highest sickness rate in their Brigade, and the decision was made to withdraw them from front-line service to further assess their overall condition.

Whilst they continued in training, they were inspected by the Assistant Divisional Medical Officer, who decreed that their training could continue; but by 26 August, the anniversary of the battle of Le Cateau thirty years earlier, the sickness rates had risen further, and with close to 40 per cent of its ranks suffering from one form of illness or another, the Battalion had to be reorganized into a two-company unit.

With such depletion of its manpower, the Battalion could no longer be considered fit for duty, and the Brigadier delivered the news that they were being withdrawn from 123 Brigade and would not be accompanying it on the next phase of the offensive in the south.

Major Browne now broke the news to all officers. The last entry in the War Diary for August recorded: 'The Commanding Officer held a conference at which he stated that the main reason for this Battalion not accompanying the Brigade on the coming operation was the under strength of this unit. 33 Corps H.Q. had decided that another Bn. would temporarily replace this Bn.'[38]

The Padre described those final days that he would spend with the Battalion:

> The Battalion, however, did not go all the way. The strain was telling on the men and their efficiency as infantry was impaired. Towards the end of

August they were pulled out and sent back to Imphal for a long-overdue rest. So ended my time with the men of the Eastern Counties – an experience I would not have missed for anything. They nobly upheld the honour of the XIIth Foot; their names will be written up on the pages of history.[39]

The underlining of the word 'temporarily' in the Battalion War Diary was perhaps a last defiant gesture to indicate to history that, as soon as they were fit enough, they would be back at the front. But in reality, for the 'Battalion in the East' the fighting war was over.

Chapter Twelve

Tomorrow is a Lovely Day

'No flags, no fuss and no fanfares'

For Second Suffolk, their replacement in 123 Brigade by 2/1 Punjab was the final nail in the coffin of their front-line participation in the Burma Campaign.

For nine months in 1943/44 the Battalion had fought the Japanese tenaciously to take and hold a series of hilltop objectives, each of strategic importance to the overall advance. They had at every stage of their war been robbed of experienced men and materiel for the war in Europe. They had taken, in comparison to other units serving on that battlefront, comparatively few fatalities in combat, but suffered in their last months the most appalling rates of sickness. Despite such setbacks, and the difficult and arduous terrain they were forced to fight in, they still achieved much; although their actions did not always meet with success, they helped, without a doubt, to pave the way for others to triumph where they had failed.

For the second half of September the Battalion became Line of Communication troops falling under 256 Area, before returning to 123 Brigade in early October, but they were never to be front-line troops again. In their absence, the 5th (Indian) Division had pushed the enemy far south of Tiddim and had now earned a rest before their next major offensive; but despite being part of their ranks once more, Second Suffolk would now be restricted to rear area duties only.

Morale amongst its fitter ranks was, however, still high. Mrs Monier-Williams, wife of the Battalion's former commanding officer, had remained in India while her husband accepted a staff position at home. She maintained contact with the men of her husband's old Battalion, sending them, where possible, copies of local Suffolk newspapers that she had been sent by her family at home.

To men of the Battalion these small links with home were crucial in keeping up morale, and the papers were eagerly read by all who borrowed them. She received a reply from CSM Randall, who had only just returned to the Battalion himself after service with another unit, thanking her for all she had done. He wrote that he was pleased at 'being at home with all the old faces' but also about how the Battalion had changed in the short time he had been away:

Out here in the jungle it is most difficult to get any news of the Regiment and the country, and the papers have been a great joy. You will have probably seen that Forrest, Lee Hunter and Watt have been awarded the M.C. and we have four M.M.s and more to come I hope. The old Battalion is not quite the same old faces, some keep leaving us for home, but the old fighting spirit is still with us.[1]

For the next major Allied offensive, Imphal was to be the supply base. It was therefore crucial that the Fourteenth Army's lines of communication should be well protected, and now the Battalion took on the job of traffic control without much of a struggle. In the following three months the Battalion watched in awe as supplies were stockpiled around them for the great offensive ahead, supplies they had only dreamt of when they occupied their various jungle peaks in Burma, rationed to just half a bottle of drinking water a day.

Despite their natural resentment at this logistical miracle, the *Suffolk Regimental Gazette* reported continually high morale in the Battalion's ranks and spoke of the 'new generation' of 'veterans' that the Battalion now possessed:

So great are the changes, in fact, that the new generation of 'old sweats' has come into its own and can now spin yarns of their campaigning without being shouted down. Instead of 'Razmak' and 'Jhelum' we now hear tales of 'Bamboo', 'Isaac' and treks into the jungle with full equipment, ostensibly to outflank and cut off the Jap, but often believed to be intended to test our morale and endurance, which always seemed to win through in the end. However, in spite of the 'lines of bull' put out by the old campaigners, the results can now be seen and history alone will show what part the Old Dozen has played during the last twelve months on the Burma Border.[2]

Major Browne also recalled his last days commanding the Battalion at Imphal:

We moved from here to take up a holding role in the area of the mountains – a welcome change from the valley once one was up. My highest post was almost 5,000 feet up with a wonderful view all round, but hardly good enough for the climb involved. Eventually we concentrated down in the valley for a short rest and training. The long strain was telling badly on the men and the hospital admissions were up to 60 and 70 a week, mostly general debility, and with some malaria, dysentery, and scrub typhus. Eventually we were down to six fighting officers, with myself in command, and two companies of eighty men each (instead of four of 130 each). Then I caught jaundice, but the prospect of evacuation over the Assam L of C was so discouraging that I stayed where I was. The Brigadier decided that the battalion could not be used on operations for a time, and before long we went back into a rest area at Imphal, where we were fairly comfortable. The sight of the first white woman for eight months was quite a disappointment. One thought they were all beautiful! On 3rd November I set off on leave and jumped a lift in an American aircraft bound to Dacca. My fate was not to return, thank goodness.³

Still under the command of XXXIII Indian Corps, the Battalion were now engaged on traffic duties between Kalewa and Shwebo to the south-west of Imphal across the Burma border. Private Clifford Price recalled those last few months there before their replacement by 7 York and Lancs:

We spent Xmas 1944 there and although dinner was not too appetising, we did have gunfire served by the officers and senior NCOs. Those who could drive collected new 6x6 Dodges (Lend-Lease?) from a vehicle depot a few miles out on the Kohima road. The battalion was loaded and we set off across the Imphal Plain, over the hills east of Palel (Hara-Kiri corner) and spent the first night in the Kabaw valley. Early the following morning, trucks were being refuelled from 45-gallon drums by the light of a hurricane lamp and Pte. (later C.S.M.) Arthur Foster's truck went up in flames. After a display of exploding grenades, ammunition and petrol, plus the hilarious sight of Pte. Foster trying to rescue his rifle and kit from the truck, we carried on eastwards to Kalewa, where we crossed the Chindwin via the Bailey bridge and halted at Kiang, just off the bridge on the eastern bank of the Chindwin where we were informed we were taking over Line of Communication duties from Indaneyi to Pyinggaing (known as 'Pink Gin'). Small contingents were spread over the length of the road, controlling traffic, guarding strategic points, *nullah* bridges etc. Admin and transport were based in Kiang during this period. We handed over, I think, to 2 Borders and headed eastwards in R.I.A.S.C. trucks, crossing the Shwebo plain via Yeu and Shwebo, and halted before reaching the Irrawaddy, where after some delay we were routed south to an airstrip at Ondaw (not Indan). After spending the night there, during which we had a short foray with a Nippon DP (displaced persons) patrol, we flew out soon after dawn in USAAF Dakotas to Chittagong.⁴

As the campaign in the Far East continued without them, more and more men of the Battalion were returning home on repatriation. Private Charles 'Whistler' Pryke arrived back in Bury St Edmunds in January 1945, having served almost five years overseas. He had served throughout the campaign, and his arrival home was quite an event, with his local newspaper sending a reporter to hear his story:

> Pte. Pryke had gone to buy some meat for his favourite meat pudding, and the things he wrote about most in his letters home were that he longed for English brewed tea, meat pies and cool atmosphere. 'Twenty-eight days' leave in England is certainly a change after serving in the Arakan', he said on his return. 'Nine times I have been attacked from malaria.'[5]

Pryke was full of praise for his Indian comrades: 'The Indians are fine soldiers, and will fight with you, and for you, through thick and thin. They call us "The White Gurkhas".'[6]

Before joining the Regiment, 'Whistler' had worked in his local branch of the newsagents W.H. Smith, and at the local sugar beet factory. His younger brother, Frederick, was a prisoner of war, having been captured at Singapore in February 1942, and his two sisters were both employed on war work in local factories. The article also explained the reason for his nickname: 'He is noted for his whistling, which he has continued with success in the army, winning several prizes at talent competitions.'[7]

At the end of January, the remainder of the Battalion were moved deeper into Burma, where they remained for some weeks, being briefly attached to 'ROB Force' – a special, short-lived unit under the command of Brigadier Gordon Roberts who were responsible for seeking out remaining pockets of Japanese resistance in Burma. On 10 March they were moved across India to new positions around the city of Lahore, where in the final months of the war the native population were clamouring to be rid of British rule and it looked as if a major civil disturbance might be imminent.

Whilst the Battalion reverted to khaki drill, having shed its jungle green just a week or so after arrival, it was clear that the old order had passed. A Battalion that had been famed for its pre-war sporting prowess, superb marksmanship and smartness of dress and drill had disappeared. The new Battalion that emerged was very different to the one which had left India eighteen months before.

The stark reality of their weakened state was evident. The Battalion had left India 743-strong, but their ranks now held a total of just 387 officers and men, just over 50 per cent of their strength when they entered the Second Arakan Campaign. 'A' Company's strength stood at 108 men, 'B' Company at 141, and 'HQ' and Support Companies combined at 138. They would never reach full strength again.

In men who had been used to basic subsistence rations, new, richer foodstuffs from Indian Depots, combined with an abundance of fresh meat and vegetables, caused many digestive illnesses. Men in Lahore often had to be put onto strict diets of liver and milk for several weeks on end, as Private Tom Dunnett of 'HQ' Company, who had by then returned to the Battalion, recalled: 'The liver was to replace lost blood and the milk was to line my stomach.'[8]

As 1945 continued, the routine of training, civil duties and sport carried on for the Battalion, but all the time, men were leaving for home. 'L.I.A.P.' and L.I.L.O.P. were letters that many muttered. They stood for 'Leave in advance of Python' and 'Leave in lieu of Python' – 'Python' being the code name given to the scheme whereby those who had served overseas for longer than four years were now due leave before returning home. It was the same for officers. Four were repatriated on the same day in August 1945, causing much chaos and a hasty reshuffling of roles.

A high spot which broke the tedium of training and anti-riot duties came when the Battalion Colours were retrieved from Lahore Cathedral. They had been deposited there in 1943 when the Battalion was posted to Burma, and whilst it was a momentous event to get them back again, there were pitifully few old soldiers of Second Suffolk still serving with the Battalion who had been present when they were lodged there for their safekeeping.

As autumn wore on, some lucky men had the opportunity to record a few seconds of film to be broadcast to their loved ones at home. 'Calling Blighty' featured a special edition for men from the Manchester area in October 1945, and Privates Donald Saxon of 'A' Company and Arthur Partington of 'HQ' Company were seen on screen recording short messages to their families.

Now came a change of command. Lieutenant Colonel Menneer was replaced by Lieutenant Colonel H. W. Dean, who returned to command the Battalion he left as Adjutant in 1941. Lieutenant Colonel Kenneth Menneer, who now departed, had done all that was asked of him and his Battalion:

> The Regiment owes a debt to Menneer of the 4th Suffolk. He learnt his wartime soldiering with the First Battalion, returning from Dunkirk with them, and serving under Lt. Col. F.A. Milnes at home. Then for a short time he was Second in Command to Lt. Colonel Victor Oborne and to Lt. Col. R.E. Goodwin. He succeeded Lt. Colonel H.R. Hopking O.B.E., in Burma and during the War he was probably longer with the Second Battalion than any other officer.[9]

'Sweat' Dean came from a long line of Suffolk soldiers; his father also served in Second Suffolk, and his son, Tom 'Dixie' Dean, served with 1 Suffolk in the 1950s.

Lieutenant Colonel Dean had been recalled to Europe in 1941 to be given command of a Battalion of the Duke of Cornwall's Light Infantry (D.C.L.I.).

He had been taken prisoner with them in the Western Desert but had made a spectacular escape from Italian captivity, reaching Switzerland safely. Having been repatriated, he was sent back to take command of his old Battalion in India.

However, upon his arrival he found just a handful of men left with whom he had served. In fact, he recalled that only five men still serving with Second Suffolk in August 1945 had been with him when he left it in 1941. It was an almost identical story in 1918, when at the Armistice, Second Suffolk had just seven men still serving in its ranks who had gone overseas with the battalion in August 1914.

The year 1946 began as 1945 had ended, with endless sport and training to keep the Battalion occupied, interspersed with the occasional marriage. Major Browne returned from a period at Tactical School and became Second-in-Command, at which point it was noted that it was 'the first time for a long while that we have had a "Twelfth Foot" skipper and mate at the helm.'[10]

Men were now leaving at such a rate, for home and for service with other units, that training had to be carried out in co-operation with their comrades in 2 Royal Norfolk Regiment, who were also based in Lahore and suffering comparable losses from their ranks. The Mortar Platoon had been run down to such an extent that by the New Year it contained just seven men, and the trend looked set to continue as British rule in India appeared certain to come to an end:

> Our old friends continue to go at an ever-increasing speed, and there are very few left who were with the Battalion in the days of the Arakan and Imphal. We are fortunate that not all have gone, and we wish that the Army in India could be sufficiently attractive to tempt more to stay. To those who are short of houses and servants, and who find rationing too harassing, we would say come, but as for the rest, India is very different from what one understands of the pre-war life.[11]

Those who had served their time were now pleased to be going home, even if their 'return' transport was not exactly luxurious. Private Cyril Wilkinson reflected later on his departure from India:

> My repatriation took place in 1946. I was with 'D' Company at Amritsar, God-forsaken hole on the edge of a windswept plain, the heat was terrible, we all suffered septic prickly heat, we revelled in the Camp cinema, and the barracks echoed to the singing and whistling of the music from the 'Desert Song', and of course some magnificent games of football were played. I stood laden with kit on the docks at Bombay, looking for a troopship, but

there she was squat below the level of the quay, just masts sticking up, the 'HMS PERSIMMON', an American-built lease lend, utility all welded assault infantry landing ship. She was a rough old tub, and I remember that a lot of us lay on the deck made of bitumastic which had softened in the sun and had got stuck to our K.D. [Khaki Drill]. We were too ill to worry, and I remember an Army Padre coming up and saying, 'Stick it out lads, remember every mile is a nautical mile nearer home.' At the time we couldn't care less what we were on, she was going in the right direction. Years after, I often thought what a way to bring home lads who had suffered so much in Burma.[12]

As 1947 opened, the fate of the Battalion now hung in the balance. It had been announced the previous year at home in a Government white paper that the second battalions of all infantry line regiments were to be reduced to a cadre and placed in 'suspended animation'. With the planned progression to Indian Independence being scheduled for the following year, British battalions were being removed from service in the sub-continent as swiftly as possible.

On 5 February the axe finally fell, with Lieutenant Colonel Dean receiving a private, personal letter from the Commander-in-Chief India, Sir Claude Auchinleck, informing him of the likely fate of his Battalion:

Dear Dean,
I am writing personally to give you early warning of the probable placing in suspended animation of your battalion by the end of next May. This decision has been taken by the War Office in conformity with the policy explained by the Secretary of State in the House of Commons on the 24th October 1946. I fully sympathise with you on the temporary loss to the Army of a battalion of your regiment but you will realise that the reduction in the strength of British Infantry has necessitated this step. I must ask you to treat this information as confidential and personal to yourself until you receive executive orders.[13]

Trouble flared up again in the following weeks as the Indian nationalist cause gathered momentum. The Battalion was engaged on difficult riot control duties when 'flag marches' were organized throughout their area, but their steady, unflappable manner in these turbulent times brought praise from their Brigadier. However, with the date for Independence now brought forward to August that year, the situation in India was deteriorating rapidly, as Private Clifford Price recalled:

During the summer of 1947 the Battalion was on exercise in the hills at Dinah (towards Rawal Pindi) when it was urgently recalled to Lahore which we reached after a hard night's drive. Some of the Battalion went to Amritsar, the scene of further trouble. We returned to Ferozepore and within a few weeks practically all the Battalion had been posted to various units and the few remaining regulars, myself included, returned to Bury St Edmunds.[14]

With their fate confirmed, seven officers and 225 other ranks were now posted to join 1 Essex, with a further five officers and 230 other ranks joining 2 Royal Norfolk. Thus, with a minimal cadre of just the CO, his Second in Command, Major Dewar, the Adjutant, Captain Boddington, and two officers, Major Hildesley and Captain Skitmore, to carry the Colours home, on 7 May the final parade of the Battalion in India was held; then, on 30 May 1947, the Adjutant wrote the last lines in a Battalion Log which had been kept since the early 1850s. Of those officers, only Major Hildesley had served throughout the entire Burma campaign. The final volume of Regimental History noted the ambivalent mood at that time:

> By then the 2nd Battalion had to intents and purposes ceased to exist. Its demise was felt deeply by those who had been a part of it, perhaps for almost all of their service, and yet the sense of corporate shock, which might have been expected, was scarcely apparent. Perhaps it was too soon after the experiences in Burma which inevitably led to a desire to enjoy life come what may, or was it that there were by then in the Battalion so many officers and men from other units and arms of that service that the family feeling had, to a degree, evaporated? There was, too, reluctance to accept that British rule in India was about to come to an end, and that would leave no role for the Battalion in any case.[15]

In June the cadre came home to Suffolk for redistribution. It was the first time that it had been home to the county since 1925. In the twenty-two years between it had seen service in Gibraltar, China, India and Burma and had added 'Burma 1943–45', 'North Arakan' and 'Imphal' to a proud list of Battle Honours of the Regiment.

Those last remaining men of the cadre, still proud to have belonged to the 'Old Dozen', were now to join the 'First Dozen' to get on with the next job at hand: keeping the peace in a fragile post-war Greece.

Their memories of the jungle faded into history, and many never gave a thought to recording them. It was those happy days in India before, and again afterwards, that remained uppermost in their thoughts. The jungle was the grim, bitter interlude between these two highlights, and many now chose to forget it.

After a special farewell parade at Bury St Edmunds, the Colours were lodged in the Officers' Mess at the Depot and the Battalion's silver and property redistributed. By then its ranks held fewer than fifty men.

In the end, it fell to Major 'Ossy' Leach to take the cadre out to Greece, and after just ninety-four years, Second Suffolk was soon to be no more. Following a journey by lorry, boat, train and lorry again, they finally reached Athens: 'We arrived in time for tiffin, and after being vetted were sent to our various Companies. So passed the amalgamation of the 2nd Battalion Cadre. No flags, no fuss and no fanfares.'[16]

The 'Old Dozen' had passed quietly into history.

Epilogue
They Meet in Twos and Threes

'The Regiment is equally proud of what they achieved'

The aim of this work has been to provide a factual 'warts and all' account of the Battalion's part in the Burma campaign, relying as its backbone upon the words of those who were there. Though no one has written of their campaign since 1946, when the third volume of Regimental History was compiled, this book, in common with that volume, is written with the aim of maintaining untarnished the proud history of the Suffolk Regiment.

It is fair to say that Second Suffolk have been forgotten by history for over seventy-five years, with their counterparts in the 1st Battalion taking the limelight from them at almost every opportunity. Second Suffolk's jungle war was every bit as tough as that which was fought in Europe, and what their jungle war lacked in scale it made up for in ferocity.

With a Battalion strength never exceeding 750 all ranks, excluding illness, they were to suffer over 220 men wounded in action and almost 100 killed, as they waged an active and relentless war against a savage enemy.

Despite its ferocity, the Regimental History struggled severely to find first-hand accounts of the campaign, and its author, Colonel W. N. Nicholson, relied almost exclusively on two short personal accounts by Majors 'Gordon' Browne and Peter Hill written just after the war had ended. Colonel Nicholson wove these accounts into his own narrative, but in the preceding text you will have read excerpts from the original manuscripts.

Colonel Nicholson also relied heavily on snippets of information that were published periodically in the *Suffolk Regimental Gazette*, but at least he was honest in his appraisal of the condition of the Battalion as it entered front-line service on the Imphal front:

> Everything in comparison favoured the First Battalion; they had a solid core in the quality of their leaders, and could absorb all who came. The First Battalion's physique remained magnificent, whereas sickness had greatly undermined the strength of the Second Battalion. There was no reserve in India of tried, experienced officers to fill senior gaps. The Second Battalion entered the next phase of the Burma Campaign very heavily handicapped.[1]

Second Suffolk's war was a bitter one: 'This was a war fought against an enemy who gave no quarter even to wounded men, over country in which communications – even those between platoons – were extremely difficult to maintain.'[2]

Here, miles from home, there were no great advances to meet the enemy. Here, there were no trucks to bring them from the line to rest. Here, no reporters came calling to ask for their stories. Theirs was a relentless but private war that went on day after day, week after week. Rest, if it came, was measured in hours, never in days.

Though their written legacy is minimal, and their photographic archives are slim, their story without a doubt deserves to be told. This book, it is hoped, will fill a long overdue need for a factual account of their campaign. It is also hoped that it will go some way to readdress the imbalance of attention between Second Suffolk and their brothers, First Suffolk, who have in the years that followed received considerably more recognition for their wartime service than other Battalions of the Regiment.

One of the first to recognize this huge disparity was Brigadier Bill Deller, President of the Suffolk Regiment Old Comrades Association. An officer of the post-war years, who would later serve with many former Second Suffolk officers, he was always acutely aware that the 1st Battalion's war in Europe always monopolized the media's attention, and he was quick to promote the service of Second Suffolk as well as the other Battalions of the Regiment who fought in the Second World War:

> It always strikes me as sad that those who fought in Burma, the Far East and in North Africa and Italy in other Battalions of the Regiment do not have the demonstrations of gratitude for what they achieved as do those that fought in Europe with the 1st Battalion. Many who served with 1 Suffolk agree with this sentiment. Those who served elsewhere should know that the Regiment is equally proud of what they achieved in difficult conditions, often without the resources that were available in Europe. This was not a one-battalion regiment.[3]

Men of Second Suffolk who served in the Burma Campaign and who remained close to the Regiment after leaving its service were always few in number. The wartime composition of its ranks, with long-serving men being continually repatriated and precious few younger reinforcements coming up to replace them, meant that the bond was always stronger with the old guard than it was with the new.

When these old soldiers were to be found, it was in small groups, sometimes just in pairs. Usually seated around an old parade ground in deck chairs, or sharing a drink at an old comrades meeting, there were never many of them, certainly not the great gatherings of their comrades who served in the 1st Battalion.

These men had many stories to tell each other with a common theme, but unlike their contemporaries who fought in Europe, their battlefields were inaccessible for any form of pilgrimage; for the men of Second Suffolk there were no grateful inhabitants of liberated towns to welcome them back for a '*Vin d'Honneur*'. Nor were there any film crews clamouring to record their stories. These men and their war were still forgotten, and rightly, that sense of rejection cut deep. Their friendship with one another was important, for most shared that feeling.

In 1984, the focus of remembrance fell upon Normandy and the veterans of the 1st Battalion. Perhaps too bluntly, the Regimental Newsletter noted: 'Consistent with the lack of publicity and recognition afforded them at the time, less likely to be remembered are the exploits of the 2nd Battalion as part of the "Forgotten Army" at Imphal 40 years ago'.[4]

A mention, the following year, of the presentation of a flag captured at Bamboo Hill to the Regimental Museum by Cyril Wilkinson brought the Battalion back into the news, albeit very briefly, but there were precious few like him who troubled to remember their time in Burma.

However, Wilkinson can rightfully claim the honour of keeping the memory of the Battalion alive, for over the next ten years he regularly contributed pieces to the Regimental Newsletter and kept up a spirited correspondence with any Second Suffolk comrades he came across. He was later described as 'indefatigable' in his correspondence. It was he, together with Burma veterans Tommy Warren, Jack Woodard, Dickie Moss and later, Ernie Bates, who throughout the 1990s ensured that that Second Suffolk's jungle war was not forgotten, even though they only ever merited a paragraph or two, whilst their comrades in 1st Suffolk had page after page of reports devoted to their pilgrimages to Europe.

The major anniversaries of VJ Day in 1995 and 2005 drew attention to the war in the Far East, but now it was their comrades in the 4th and 5th Battalions, who had been prisoners of the Japanese, that took the media's attention. And by 2015 it was too late; virtually all of that generation have sadly passed, never to return.

Second Suffolk's war may not have been as spectacular as that of some of their contemporaries. They may not have been showered in awards. But it says much for the self-effacing modesty of the Suffolk soldier that he was never bothered about medals and was concerned more with getting the job done than chasing glory.

They may not have been mentioned much in the official histories or the books that have been written since, but now their story has at least been told. One would have wished to have more material to include here, but if this work produces more stories and accounts that call for a future revised edition, then it will have served its purpose.

For those brief few months in 1943/44, the men of Second Suffolk fought loyally against a ruthless, emboldened and at times fanatical enemy. Though their war was shorter than others', it was in no way less important than that being fought elsewhere in the world at the time. They more than played their part in defeating a regime that was every bit as unpleasant as the one that was being fought in Europe; and now, eighty years on from their service in the East, those last surviving veterans of Second Suffolk, and the relatives of those who are no longer with us, have much cause to be proud of their actions – actions that were never at the time, or since, publicly appreciated.

As Lance Corporal Lionel Ruffles modestly said: 'There were no heroics from me. I just did the job I was trained to do.'[5]

Stabilis

Appendix I
'The sort of man who wins wars'

The account below was written by ex-Bombardier, later Captain George Hawley MM, 28th (Jungle) Field Regiment, Royal Artillery, to ex-Private Cyril Wilkinson of 17 Platoon, 'D' Company, Second Suffolk in August 1985.

Mr Hawley started corresponding with Mr Wilkinson as a result of a small notice the latter had placed in the Long Eaton Advertiser *on the 40th anniversary of VJ Day. Mr Hawley was amazed to hear of a soldier of Second Suffolk, for he had not met another since his encounter with them in Arakan on 25 January 1944. He wrote to Mr Wilkinson stating that he 'held the Suffolk Regiment in high esteem; it was they who nominated me for my Military Medal.'*

After a meeting between the two men later that year, Mr Hawley produced a battered Japanese flag that had been taken during the Suffolk attack on Bamboo Hill. This flag had been sent to Bombardier Hawley's mother by Major General Harold Briggs, then commanding 5th (Indian) Division.

Mr Hawley gave Mr Wilkinson the flag, saying that it rightly belonged to Second Suffolk, especially all those who fell on Bamboo Hill, and in turn, Mr Wilkinson travelled from Nottingham to Bury St Edmunds to present the flag to the Regimental Museum.

'When people start talking about Generals and Field Marshals winning wars', said the gunner captain as we sat in mess the other evening, I always say, 'Nonsense – it's the lance corporals and corporals commanding forward sections who do most to win wars.'

Then I always tell them this tale.

The gunner, who had seen quite a bit of service before being commissioned, went on:

It was in the Arakan in 1944. My Regiment had hurriedly been sent up to the front to take part in its first action. I was F.O.O. [Forward Officer Observation] and had been told to range my guns on a Jap-held hill called 'Bamboo Hill'. The unit holding positions opposite this hill was a battalion of the Suffolk Regiment.

Eventually I found myself on a small isolated hill where my O.P. [Observation Post] was to be set up. There was a Lance Corporal there who greeted me. I asked him who was in charge. He said he was. I enquired how many men he had got. He told me he had got a machine gun and six riflemen. He told me they had been there a week with his section in this exposed position.

'There the blighters are', he added, pointing to a little pimple of a hill, but they were ready for them up here. 'Now down in the bottom there every afternoon at about three o'clock, there's a little bastard down there lights up a fire and starts cooking.'

He wished to settle this chap – 'Will you have a shot at him, sir?'

I told him I had come to range my guns on Bamboo Hill.

'Now where is Bamboo Hill', I asked.

'There it is', he replied pointing to the little pimple he showed me before. 'There it is, just 240 yards away.'

I asked him how he knew the distance so exactly. He knew all right. He'd been here long enough to know. He went on to tell me to watch out as any minute there would be some planes over to attack the Jap position on the hill.

I knew nothing about this episode. Sure enough, two or three minutes later the planes were heard, and thus down they came to drop their bombs. Cocky little chap, he was, full of confidence, and he seemed to know everything of what was going on.

I was trying to get through by line but there was some trouble in getting it laid. I got the wireless up but couldn't get through. The afternoon was drawing on. Then, whilst trying to fix up communications, I felt a jab in my arm. There was the Lance Corporal. He was pointing down the valley to where this little spiral of smoke rose from the jungle. He begged me to get my guns onto it.

Eventually I managed to get my line through and was able to start ranging, but I was interrupted by mediums plastering the hill. The shock of the big shells disturbed the camouflage of the Japs. There could be seen, as the Lance Corporal said, a horseshoe trench on top of this hill. Half an hour after the mediums had stopped, the trench was camouflaged and hidden from view again. I finished my ranging but unfortunately, I was never able to fulfil the Corporal's request. I just couldn't quite get the guns onto the cook.

Now, I've never forgotten that Lance Corporal. He was the best of men there was. Competent and confident. Nothing would shake him as he commanded that small party of soldiers on an Arakan hilltop.

Three days later, from that same position, I watched that Suffolk Battalion storm 'Bamboo Hill'. They lost two company commanders before the day had started, but they went for 'Bamboo Hill' and took it.

Appendix II

The missing of the battle for 'Pimple'

There has for many years been some mystery surrounding the men killed during the attack on the Pimple; they were buried, but their graves have subsequently been lost.

In October 2020, a group of local Indian diggers of the 'Imphal Campaign Foundation' climbed the steep slopes of the Pimple to search for the remains of the five missing men who have no known grave and who are commemorated on the Rangoon Memorial to the Missing.

Despite finding personal items such as combs, belt buckles, ammunition in charger clips, and various webbing strap ends, they uncovered no human remains. The event was recorded for ITV News, and their broadcast also contained an interview with the granddaughter of one of the missing men, Private David Tod.

In other videos posted online, the diggers looked to be working from the sketch maps in the Battalion War Diary for April 1944, and in particular, the diary entry below from 18 April:

> Padre buried the bodies of the following men: recovered after the capture of the Jap positions on NORTH face of PIMPLE:- C Coy men – Pte. BLAKE reported as Missing-Believed killed on 11.4.44, Sgt. STEELE, Cpl. JAMES, Ptes. DOWELL, EBBAGE, TORRENCE, PIGDEN – reported as Missing-Believed killed on 13.4.44 – D Coy men – Ptes. DEFUE, MOTT, NARDUZZO, BENNETT, TOD, and Cpl. GOUDIE W 3053489, Pte. KNOX F 14541024, Pte. SAVAGE R 14515513 – who were reported as Missing-Believed killed on the 15.4.44 – A Coy men – Pte. MACE – reported as Missing-Believed killed on 13.4.44.

The assumption made by the diggers was that these men were laid to rest upon the Pimple itself, but the excerpt above mentions only that they were 'recovered after' and not that they were 'buried upon' the Pimple.

When one examines the Concentration Report for the graves of Sergeant Steele, Corporal Goudie and Privates Bennett, Dowell, Ebbage, Knox, Pigden, Savage and Torrence, it details that they were exhumed from their original grave on 18 November 1944 and their remains were reinterred in Imphal

War Cemetery. Crucially, however, the report gives the map reference of their 'Original Grave Site' as being '491734'.

If it is reasonable to assume that all sixteen men recorded above in the War Diary were buried together in the same communal grave, then how were the remains of nine men subsequently recovered, when five were not, even though they must have been buried close together?

To confuse matters further, the entry against the original location of the grave of Private Dowell is given as '12 miles N.E. Imphal PT4057, 83L/NW 491734'. 'Point 4057' was known on maps of the time and was named by the Battalion as 'The Mound', but 491734 is not the same location. In the Battalion War Diary, the map reference for the Mound is given as '492729', with the Pimple being '495731'.

By using further map references given in the Battalion War Diary for the other key features in the locality that were associated with the battle, such as Ring I (494739), Ring II (492735) and Ring III (492733), one can locate the position of the original grave at '491734' as being some way off to the northwest, being equidistant from Ring II and Ring III, but as the crow flies, it is some 1,200 metres from the summit of the Pimple.

This original grave site is in many ways a practical one: it made sense when expanding positions such as the Mound and the Pimple, which would require deep habitation and the building of further defensive features such as trenches, dugouts etc., that a grave located on its summit would most likely be destroyed should the enemy subject the position to an artillery bombardment or a possible infantry counter-attack. It was also not sensible, for hygiene reasons, that living men should share such a small area of ground with the bodies of the dead from previous attacks.

Creating a cemetery at '491734' was a feasible long-term solution. This location was in the bottom of a valley below Ring II to the north-east and Ring III to the south-east. Protected by the hills above, the hard work of bearing the dead from the battlefield to the cemetery could be completed in relative safety, since the Battalion held the heights above and could cover the Burial Parties and the Pioneers at work below; and from here, once the battle had moved on and it was safe to do so, the fallen could be taken once more to a larger concentration cemetery.

However, the mystery still remains of how these five men – Corporal James and Privates Blake, DuFeu, Narduzzo and Tod – were not recovered, having clearly been buried at the same time as all those men mentioned above in potentially the same grave.

One should remember, however, that of the seven men of 'C' Company who attacked the Pimple on 12/13 April, their patrols and attacks were launched from the area of Ring III across to the south-east, before they retired north to Ring I; and also that the eight men of 'D' Company who launched their attack on the Pimple on 15 April from Ring II advanced across the same ground as 'C' Company had done two days earlier. This would explain why the dead were collected and then assembled close to Ring II at '491734'.

Today, with the advent of satellite technology, one can examine the site from all angles, and by overlaying the original 1:25,000 maps to which the War Diary and Imperial War Graves Commission reports refer, one can, with some accuracy, plot the various hill positions given above from their six-figure map references to find the location of this original grave.

Perhaps in the years to come there may be scope for the Commonwealth War Graves Commission, or the local diggers at Imphal, to visit '491734' and excavate the area in the hope of finding the remains of the five missing men of Second Suffolk who may still lie there. After eighty years it is only right that the bodies of these men should be 'brought in from the cold' and be given a fitting resting place alongside their comrades.

Appendix III
Honours and Awards

MILITARY CROSS & BAR
Captain P. B. Forrest
Captain D. Lee Hunter

MILITARY CROSS
Lieutenant T. S. Watt

MILITARY MEDAL
Corporal R. J. Brown
Lance Corporal J. R. Peck
Lance Corporal F. G. Salter
Lance Corporal R. Shanks

MENTIONED IN DISPATCHES
Lieutenant W. S. Gilbert
Captain D. R. Gray
Captain K. E. J. Henderson
Lieutenant M. C.M. Arrindell
Lieutenant J. R. Tomkinson
Sergeant J. E. Bates
Sergeant D. F. A. Steele
Lieutenant T. S. Watt

It should be noted that, through the fortunes of war, Major P. B. Forrest and Captain D. Lee Hunter were both awarded their second Military Crosses before their first ones were officially gazetted.

Captain (Temp. Major) Peter Forrest was gazetted with the award of his first Military Cross in October 1944, for his actions commanding 'C' Company at 'Isaac' on 7 June 1944. Four months later, his second Military Cross was gazetted in February 1945, but this award was for his active patrolling in Arakan between November 1943 and February 1944, and specifically for his actions to take the 'Pimple' on 15 April 1944. Both recommendations for the award were submitted by Major K. C. Menneer.

War Substantive Lieutenant (Acting Captain) Douglas Lee Hunter, was gazetted with his first Military Cross in July 1944 for his actions on a Guerrilla Platoon raid of 10 May 1944. Seven months later, his second Military Cross was gazetted in February 1945 for his actions in Arakan between November 1943 and February 1944. Major K. C. Menneer submitted the former recommendation for the award, but his predecessor, Lieutenant Colonel H.R. Hopking, submitted the latter.

Appendix IV
Roll of Honour

The following Roll of Honour is compiled from three known sources of information: the Battalion War Diary, the Commonwealth War Graves Commission's burial registers and the periodic casualty lists printed in the *Suffolk Regimental Gazette*. Though all sources contain errors, and in some cases duplications, the Roll below is the first complete list of men who died whilst serving with Second Suffolk in Burma and in India.

It only includes men serving with the Battalion who died between 10 September 1943, when the Battalion commenced training for service in Burma, and 31 August 1944, when they were withdrawn from 123 Brigade as a fighting unit.

TRAINING IN INDIA
Killed on Exercise
5831722   Boyden, Pte. J. S.   5827106   Hunt, L/Cpl. H. G.
5391524   Thompson, Pte. D.

ARAKAN
Killed in Action
5781623   Grimes, Pte. L. W.

Died of Wounds
5830159   Barnard, L/Cpl. L. B.   5832726   Mower, Pte. C. E. J.
14372313   Ward, Pte. W. T.*   14522875   White, Pte. P.

Missing in Action
871791   Hadlow, Pte. B. R.*   14328571   Thulbourn, Pte. D. S.
14370806   Watt. Pte. P.*

Died in Accident
6147851   Bissell, L/Sgt. A. F.

'BAMBOO'

Killed in Action

85613	Richards, Major P. E. V.	5950365	Anstee, Pte. J. H.
5891905	Brooks, Pte. K. S.	6028957	Eden, Pte. J.
5438517	Edlin, BEM, L/Sgt. E. D.*	5837097	Grace, Pte. J
6020044	Hopkins, Pte. S.*	5836588	Jeffs, Pte. O. G.
5827199	Jennings, Pte. C. K.	5393078	Lee, Pte. G. B.*
5833829	Long, Cpl. E. B.*	5126446	McCormack, Pte. J. A.*
7907038	Moody, Pte. H. D.*	5109973	Palmer, Pte. G.*
5836929	Price, Pte. T. H.		

Died of Wounds

87474	Gray, Captain D. R. (R. Norfolk Attd.)		
5833764	Barfield, Pte. J.	5827034	Bloomfield, Pte. W.
15001338	Da Costa, Pte. V. A.	5830523	Thurston, Pte. C. D.

IMPHAL

Killed in Action

14523393	Haynes, Pte. D.	5782683	Wigger, Pte. W. J. C.

'PIMPLE'

Killed in Action

14563495	Bennett, Pte. D. C.	5827015	Blake, Pte. G. E.*
5507588	DuFue, Pte. H. J.*	14345619	Ebbage, Pte. L. W.
14534020	Fallowfield, Pte. W. G.	3053489	Goudie, Cpl. W. G.
6295654	James, L/Cpl. C. G.*	14541024	Knox, Pte. F.
14601163	Mace, Pte. R. H. J.	3066850	Matthewman, Pte. E. C.
14545245	Mott, Pte. C. G. D.	5393263	Narduzzo, Pte. S.*
14525004	Pigden, Pte. G. F.	14515513	Savage, Pte. R.
5826128	Steele, Sgt. D. F. A.	14595719	Tod, Pte. D. *
14357349	Torrance, Pte. A. H.		

Died of Wounds

5771526	Bates, Sgt. J. E.	5782770	Davidson, Pte. C. A.
14595779	Dowell, Pte. B. N.		

'RING I'

Killed in Action

7891493	Doyle, L/Cpl. J. W.	14386239	Pittard, Pte. W. E.
6020100	Reeve, Pte. A. J.	5680944	Young, Pte. G. E.

Roll of Honour

Died of Wounds
5570884   Perkins, Pte. H. J.

SEDANG (IRIL VALLEY)
Missing in Action
5831771   Foster, Pte. D.*

ADVANCE TO 'PYRAMID'
Killed in Action
5784468   Buck, Pte. J. A.   14558140   Coleman, Pte. J.
14406605   Hook, Pte. H. J.

'PYRAMID'
Killed in Action
117112   Anslow, Captain D.R. (E. Surrey Attd.)
308932   Stephens, 2/Lieut. C.W. (R. Berks Attd.)
5836573   Anderson, Pte. R. A.   14533949   Collinson, Pte. L. W.
14588316   Hewat, Pte. J.   14217359   Lucas, Pte. P. W. H.
14577051   Mynott, Pte. R. E. J.*   14559089   Neighbour, Pte. A. C.
14520008   Page, Pte. S.   14559094   Parker, Pte. G. H.
5831024   Pettitt, L/Cpl. R. G.   14341707   Robinson, Pte. B.
5117729   Stanton, Pte. F. W.   5833656   Studd, Cpl. R .J.
6351373   Terry, Pte. D. J.   5392094   Thould, Pte. D. F.
5835590   Whitehand, Pte. S.

Died of Wounds
5833309   Lockey, L/Cpl. R. C. G.*

Died in Accident
4626346   Salter, M.M., Cpl. F. G.   14577127   Sewell, Pte. C. V.

ADVANCE FROM 'PYRAMID'
Died of Wounds
14258543   Dearsley, Pte. H. F.

ISAAC
Killed in Action
165647   Yonge, Lieut. M. J. J.
5437874   Bax, Pte. S. T.   5833724   Bryant, Pte. E. G.
5827609   Dean, Pte. C. E.   5832567   Eade, Pte. B. E.

5829771   Hammond, Pte. D. J.
14219160 Mackie, Pte. J. C.
14327571 Illand, Pte. T.
7935624   Phillips, Pte. R.

Died of Wounds
6150664   Chenovitch, Pte. B.

SILCHAR TRACK
Died of Wounds
5832671   Jennings, Pte. E. R.

MOIRANG
Killed in Action
5833061   Mortlock, Pte. K. G.

Died of Illness
5345948   Brown, MM, Sgt. R. J.

* No known grave

Notes

NB: GB554 references are to documents held in the Suffolk Regiment Archives at Bury St Edmunds.

Chapter One
1. Henderson, Kenneth E. J., *Lucky Man*, Private, 2004
2. Bevan, W.S. 'Recalling days in India', *Castle*, No. 40, June 1987
3. Cooper, Ashley, *The Khyber Connection*, Bulmer Historical Society, 1985
4. *Memoirs of an Unknown Suffolk Officer*, Private, c. 2020
5. *Suffolk Regimental Gazette*, No. 479, Bury Free Press, May/June 1948
6. Warren, Tom, 'Toady Picquet – NW Frontier of India', *Britannia & Castle*, No. 68, Private, 1987
7. Ibid.
8. Nicholson, W.N., *The History of the Suffolk Regiment, 1928–46*, East Anglian Daily Times, 1947
9. *Old Ipswichian Journal*, Issue No. 6, Summer 2015
10. *2nd Battalion Log 1842–1947* (GB554/C1/3)
11. *Suffolk Regimental Gazette*, No. 442, Bury Free Press, January/February 1942
12. Nicholson, W. N., *The History of the Suffolk Regiment, 1928–46*, East Anglian Daily Times, 1947
13. Ibid.
14. *Suffolk Regimental Gazette*, No. 451, Bury Free Press, September/October 1943
15. Coward, Bryan, 'Wartime memories of the Royal Norfolks', Interview, Bedford Museum, 2005

Chapter Two
1. *Suffolk Regimental Gazette*, No. 453, Bury Free Press, January/February 1944
2. Wilkinson, Cyril, *Britannia & Castle*, No. 72, Private, 1989
3. Brown-Moffet, W. *Reflections of a Chaplain; Suffolk Regimental Gazette*, No. 470, Bury Free Press, November/December 1946
4. *Suffolk Regimental Gazette*, No. 453, Bury Free Press, January/February 1944
5. Nicholson, W. N., *The History of the Suffolk Regiment, 1928–46*, East Anglian Daily Times, 1947
6. Ibid.
7. Brown-Moffet, W. *Reflections of a Chaplain; Suffolk Regimental Gazette*, No. 470, Bury Free Press, November/December 1946
8. Nicholson, W. N., *The History of the Suffolk Regiment, 1928–46*, East Anglian Daily Times, 1947
9. Wilkinson, Cyril, *Britannia & Castle*, No. 91, Private, 1998
10. Henderson, Kenneth E. J., *Lucky Man*, Private, 2004
11. Wilkinson, Cyril, *Britannia & Castle*, No. 91, Private, 1998
12. Bates, Ernie, *Britannia & Castle*, No. 93, Private, 1999

Chapter Three

1. Brown-Moffet, W. *Reflections of a Chaplain; Suffolk Regimental Gazette*, No. 470, Bury Free Press, November/December 1946
2. Wilkinson, Cyril, *Britannia & Castle*, No. 79, Private, 1992
3. Duncan, Murdo, 'My War', transcription of taped reminiscences, c.1985
4. *Suffolk Regimental Gazette*, No. 454, Bury Free Press, March/April 1944
5. Ibid.
6. VJ Day 50th Anniversary Special, *Evening Star*, 1995
7. *Suffolk Regimental Gazette*, No. 454, Bury Free Press, March/April 1944
8. *Battalion War Diary* TNA (WO 172 4922), 1944
9. Duncan, Murdo, 'My War', transcription of taped reminiscences, c.1985
10. Archer, Jeremy, *The Final Curtain, Burma 1941–45, Veterans Stories*, Pen & Sword, 2022
11. Ibid.
12. Gray, Rod, 'My Story', 2014 (GB554/Y1/721)
13. Wilkinson, Cyril, *Britannia & Castle*, No. 79, Private, 1992
14. Letter to Cyril Wilkinson from Bill Skeels, 23 July 1998
15. Airmail letter from Private Cyril Mott (GB554/Y1/584)
16. Brown-Moffet, W. *Reflections of a Chaplain; Suffolk Regimental Gazette*, No. 470, Bury Free Press, November/December 1946

Chapter Four

1. Wilkinson, Cyril. *Britannia & Castle*, No. 88, Private, June 1987
2. Wilkinson, Cyril. *Britannia & Castle*, No. 67, Private, June 1986
3. Ibid.
4. Nicholson, W. N., *The History of the Suffolk Regiment, 1928–46*, East Anglian Daily Times, 1947
5. *Battalion War Diary* TNA (WO 172 4922), 1944
6. Brown-Moffet, W., *Reflections of a Chaplain; Suffolk Regimental Gazette*, No. 470, Bury Free Press, November/December 1946
7. Cooper, Ashley, *The Khyber Connection*, Bulmer Historical Society, 1985
8. *Battalion War Diary* TNA (WO 172 4922), 1944
9. Dell, Cyril, *Bunkers in Burma*, Private 1946 (GB554/Y1/827)
10. Ibid.
11. Sheets, Millard, *Life Magazine*, 5 June 1944
12. Ibid.
13. Ibid.
14. Duffy, Kevin, *Britannia & Castle*, No. 66, Private, 1986
15. Ibid.
16. *Battalion War Diary* TNA (WO 172 4922), 1944
17. Ibid.
18. Ibid.
19. Sheets, Millard, Transcript of Interview, University of California, Los Angeles, 1976
20. Jones, Idris, *Our Appeal: Remembering the Forgotten Army*, Burma Star Foundation website (www.burmastarmemorial.org), 2023.
21. *Suffolk Regimental Gazette*, No. 454, Bury Free Press, March/April 1944
22. *Battalion War Diary* TNA (WO 172 4922), 1944
23. *Suffolk Regimental Gazette*, No. 454, Bury Free Press, March/April 1944
24. Ibid.

25. Ibid.
26. Ibid.
27. Ibid.
28. *Evening Despatch*, 22 January 1945
29. Brown-Moffet, W., *Reflections of a Chaplain; Suffolk Regimental Gazette*, No. 470, Bury Free Press, November/December 1946
30. Interview with the author, Ipswich, 2000
31. *Suffolk Regimental Gazette*, No. 455, Bury Free Press, May/June 1944
32. Dilley, Roy, *Japanese Army Uniforms and Equipment, 1939–45*, Altmark, 1970.
33. Nicholson, W. N., *The History of the Suffolk Regiment, 1928–46*, East Anglian Daily Times, 1947
34. Brett-James, Anthony, *Ball of Fire, The Fifth Indian Division in the Second World War*, Gale & Polden, 1951
35. Warren, Tommy, *Britannia & Castle*, No. 65, Private, 1985
36. *Suffolk Regimental Gazette*, No. 454, Bury Free Press, March/April 1944

Chapter Five
1. Warren, Tommy, 'Imphal in Retrospect', *Britannia & Castle*, No. 63, Private, 1984
2. *Suffolk Regimental Gazette*, No. 454, Bury Free Press, March/April 1944
3. Interview with the author, Harrow, 2004
4. *Suffolk Regimental Gazette*, No. 458, Bury Free Press, November/December 1944
5. Brown-Moffet, W., *Reflections of a Chaplain; Suffolk Regimental Gazette*, No. 470, Bury Free Press, November/December 1946
6. *Suffolk Regimental Gazette*, No. 460, Bury Free Press, March/April 1945
7. Dell, Cyril, *Bunkers in Burma*, Private 1946 (GB554/Y1/827)
8. facebook post, 4 May 2015
9. Nicholson, W. N. *The History of the Suffolk Regiment, 1928–46*, East Anglian Daily Times, 1947
10. Ibid.
11. Ibid.
12. Duncan, Murdo, 'My War', transcription of taped reminiscences, c.1985
13. *Suffolk Regimental Gazette*, No. 454, Bury Free Press, March/April 1944
14. Browne, E.G.W. *Travel and Experience 1944*, Private, 1946 (GB554/Y1/303)
15. Chadburn, Paul, *Men of the Arakan*, G.H.Q., M.E.F., 1944
16. Ibid.
17. Ibid.
18. Duncan, Murdo, 'My War', transcription of taped reminiscences, c.1985
19. Ibid.
20. Ibid.
21. Ibid.
22. Ibid.
23. *Suffolk Regimental Gazette*, No. 454, Bury Free Press, March/April 1944
24. Duncan, Murdo, 'My War', transcription of taped reminiscences, c.1985
25. *Reading Evening Post*, 22 September 1988
26. *Battalion War Diary* TNA (WO 172 4922), 1944
27. Brett-James, Anthony, *Ball of Fire, The Fifth Indian Division in the Second World War*, Gale & Polden, 1951
28. *Suffolk Regimental Gazette*, No. 455, Bury Free Press, May/June 1944

29. *Suffolk Regimental Gazette*, No. 454, Bury Free Press, March/April 1944
30. Duncan, Murdo, 'My War', transcription of taped reminiscences, c.1985
31. Browne, E. G. W., *Travel and Experience 1944*, Private, 1946 (GB554/Y1/303)
32. Henderson, Kenneth E. J., *Lucky Man*, Private, 2004
33. Brown-Moffet, W., *Reflections of a Chaplain; Suffolk Regimental Gazette*, No. 470, Bury Free Press, November-December 1946
34. Browne, E. G. W., *Travel and Experience 1944*, Private, 1946 (GB554/Y1/303)
35. Laing, Sgt., Photograph caption, IWM B12460, 4 December 1944
36. Coward, Bryan, 'Wartime memories of the Royal Norfolks', Interview, Bedford Museum, 2005
37. Interview with Taff Gillingham, 2002
38. Nicholson, W. N., *The History of the Suffolk Regiment, 1928–46*, East Anglian Daily Times, 1947

Chapter Six
1. Coward, Bryan, 'Wartime memories of the Royal Norfolks', Interview, Bedford Museum, 2005
2. Nicholson, W. N., *The History of the Suffolk Regiment, 1928–46*, East Anglian Daily Times, 1947
3. Browne, E. G. W., *Travel and Experience 1944*, Private, 1946 (GB554/Y1/303)
4. Ibid.
5. Coward, Bryan, 'Wartime memories of the Royal Norfolks', Interview, Bedford Museum, 2005
6. Brown-Moffet, W., *Reflections of a Chaplain; Suffolk Regimental Gazette*, No. 470, Bury Free Press, November/December 1946
7. Henderson, Kenneth E. J., *Lucky Man*, Private, 2004
8. Warren, Tommy, 'Imphal in Retrospect', *Britannia & Castle*, No. 63, Private, 1984
9. Browne, E.G.W., *Travel and Experience 1944*, Private, 1946 (GB554/Y1/303)
10. Nicholson, W. N., *The History of the Suffolk Regiment, 1928–46*, East Anglian Daily Times, 1947
11. Squirrell, George, *Britannia & Castle*, No. 80, Private, 1993
12. VJ Day 50th Anniversary Special, *Evening Star*, 1995
13. Nicholson, W. N., *The History of the Suffolk Regiment, 1928–46*, East Anglian Daily Times, 1947
14. Dell, Cyril, *Bunkers in Burma*, Private 1946 (GB554/Y1/827)
15. Cooper, Ashley, *The Khyber Connection*, Bulmer Historical Society, 1985
16. Interview with the author, Ipswich, 2006
17. Bevan, W. S., *Topees and Red Berets*, Square One, 1995

Chapter Seven
1. Nicholson, W. N., *The History of the Suffolk Regiment, 1928–46*, East Anglian Daily Times, 1947
2. Warren, Tommy, 'Imphal in Retrospect', *Britannia & Castle*, No. 63, Private, 1984
3. Browne, E. G. W., *Travel and Experience 1944*, Private, 1946 (GB554/Y1/303)
4. Press Release, 5 April 1944, University of Texas Archives
5. Brown-Moffet, W., *Reflections of a Chaplain; Suffolk Regimental Gazette*, No. 470, Bury Free Press, November-December 1946
6. Nicholson, W. N., *The History of the Suffolk Regiment, 1928–46*, East Anglian Daily Times, 1947
7. Ibid.

8. Ibid.
9. Ibid.
10. Brown-Moffet, W., *Reflections of a Chaplain; Suffolk Regimental Gazette*, No. 470, Bury Free Press, November-December 1946
11. *Battalion War Diary* TNA (WO 172 4922), 1944
12. Bates, Ernie, 'In my old ration tin', *Britannia & Castle*, No. 81, Private, 1994
13. Ibid.
14. Nicholson, W. N., *The History of the Suffolk Regiment, 1928–46*, East Anglian Daily Times, 1947
15. Ibid.
16. Duncan, Murdo, 'My War', transcription of taped reminiscences, c.1985
17. Citation, TNA (WO 373/33/38)
18. Browne, E. G. W., *Travel and Experience 1944*, Private, 1946 (GB554/Y1/303)
19. Brown-Moffet, W., *Reflections of a Chaplain; Suffolk Regimental Gazette*, No. 470, Bury Free Press, November-December 1946
20. Letter to the author, 2002
21. Ibid.
22. Browne, E. G. W., *Travel and Experience 1944*, Private, 1946 (GB554/Y1/303)
23. Letter to the author, 2010
24. Wilkinson, Cyril. *Britannia & Castle*, No. 89, Private, 1997
25. Duncan, Murdo, 'My War', transcription of taped reminiscences, c.1985
26. Ibid.
27. Browne, E. G. W., *Travel and Experience 1944*, Private, 1946 (GB554/Y1/303)
28. Ibid.
29. *Battalion War Diary* TNA (WO 172 4922), 1944
30. Ibid.
31. Browne, E. G. W., *Travel and Experience 1944*, Private, 1946 (GB554/Y1/303)
32. Warren, Tommy, 'Imphal in Retrospect', *Britannia & Castle*, No. 63, Private, 1984
33. *Peterborough Standard*, 29 April 1945
34. Browne, E. G. W., *Travel and Experience 1944*, Private, 1946 (GB554/Y1/303)
35. Dell, Cyril, *Bunkers in Burma*, Private 1946 (GB554/Y1/827)
36. Nicholson, W. N., *The History of the Suffolk Regiment, 1928–46*, East Anglian Daily Times, 1947
37. Ibid.
38. Brown-Moffet, W., *Reflections of a Chaplain; Suffolk Regimental Gazette*, No. 470, Bury Free Press, November-December 1946
39. Browne, E. G. W., *Travel and Experience 1944*, Private, 1946 (GB554/Y1/303)
40. Nicholson, W. N., *The History of the Suffolk Regiment, 1928–46*, East Anglian Daily Times, 1947
41. Ibid.
42. Brown-Moffet, W., *Reflections of a Chaplain; Suffolk Regimental Gazette*, No. 470, Bury Free Press, November-December 1946
43. Gray, Rod, *My Story*, 2014 (GB554/Y1/721)
44. *Suffolk Regimental Gazette*, No. 458, Bury Free Press, November/December 1944
45. *Suffolk Regimental Gazette*, No. 454, Bury Free Press, March/April 1944
46. Smith, Jim, *Dekho! The Magazine of the Burma Star Association*, No. 118, 1995

Chapter Eight
1. Archer, Jeremy, *The Final Curtain, Burma 1941–45, Veterans Stories*, Pen & Sword, 2022

2. Wilkinson, Cyril, *Britannia & Castle*, No. 91, Private, 1998
3. Wilkinson, Cyril, *Britannia & Castle*, No. 88, Private, 1997
4. Bates, Ernie, *Britannia & Castle*, No. 73, Private, 1989
5. Warren, Tommy, 'Imphal in Retrospect', *Britannia & Castle*, No. 63, Private, 1984
6. VJ Day 50th Anniversary Special, *Evening Star*, 1995
7. Warren, Tommy, 'Imphal in Retrospect', *Britannia & Castle*, No. 63, Private, 1984
8. Henderson, Kenneth E. J., *Lucky Man*, Private, 2004
9. *Battalion War Diary* TNA (WO 172 4922), 1944
10. Nicholson, W. N., *The History of the Suffolk Regiment, 1928–46*, East Anglian Daily Times, 1947
11. Ibid.
12. Ibid.
13. *Middlesex Independent and West London Star*, 9 December 1944
14. Nicholson, W. N., *The History of the Suffolk Regiment, 1928–46*, East Anglian Daily Times, 1947
15. Citation, TNA (WO 373/33/300)
16. *Sunday S.E.A.C.*, Issue No. 315, 19 November 1944
17. *Suffolk Regimental Gazette*, No. 459, Bury Free Press, January- February 1945
18. *Battalion War Diary* TNA (WO 172 4922), 1944
19. Browne, E. G. W., *Travel and Experience 1944*, Private, 1946 (GB554/Y1/303)
20. Brown-Moffet, W., *Reflections of a Chaplain; Suffolk Regimental Gazette*, No. 470, Bury Free Press, November/December 1946
21. Browne, E. G. W., *Travel and Experience 1944*, Private, 1946 (GB554/Y1/303)
22. Ibid.

Chapter Nine
1. Nicholson, W. N., *The History of the Suffolk Regiment, 1928–46*, East Anglian Daily Times, 1947
2. Ibid.
3. Ibid.
4. Letter to the author, 2010
5. Moss, Richard, *Britannia & Castle*, No. 90, Private, 1998
6. Nicholson, W. N., *The History of the Suffolk Regiment, 1928–46*, East Anglian Daily Times, 1947
7. Scriven, G.J., *Called Up*, Stanley L. Hunt, 1976
8. *Old Ipswichian Journal*, Issue No. 6, Summer 2015
9. *Suffolk Regimental Gazette*, No. 458, Bury Free Press, November–December 1944
10. *Old Ipswichian Journal*, Issue No. 6, Summer 2015
11. *Evening Despatch*, 22 January 1945
12. Ibid.
13. Brett-James, Anthony, *Ball of Fire, The Fifth Indian Division in the Second World War*, Gale and Polden, 1951
14. *Suffolk Regimental Gazette*, No. 458, Bury Free Press, November-December 1944
15. Brown-Moffet, W., *Reflections of a Chaplain; Suffolk Regimental Gazette*, No. 470, Bury Free Press, November-December 1946
16. Ibid.
17. *Battalion War Diary* TNA (WO 172 4922), 1944
18. Browne, E. G. W., *Travel and Experience 1944*, Private, 1946 (GB554/Y1/303)
19. Watts, William, IWM Interview (21115), 2001

20. Nicholson, W. N., *The History of the Suffolk Regiment, 1928–46*, East Anglian Daily Times, 1947
21. Smith, Jim, *Dekho! The Magazine of the Burma Star Association*, No. 133, 2000

Chapter Ten
1. Browne, E. G. W., *Travel and Experience 1944*, Private, 1946 (GB554/Y1/303)
2. Appendix J.1. *Battalion War Diary* TNA (WO 172 4922), 1944
3. Letter, Ernie Bates to Bill Deller, 2002 (GB553/CQ0/36)
4. *Nottingham Evening Post*, 25 January 1945
5. Browne, E. G. W., *Travel and Experience 1944*, Private, 1946 (GB554/Y1/303)
6. Nicholson, W. N. *The History of the Suffolk Regiment, 1928–46*, East Anglian Daily Times, 1947
7. Ibid.
8. Ibid.
9. Ruffles, Lionel, *The Battle for Isaac*, Private, c.1995
10. Ibid.
11. Appendix J.1. *Battalion War Diary* TNA (WO 172 4922), 1944
12. Ruffles, Lionel, *The Battle for Isaac*, Private, c.1995
13. Brown-Moffet, W., *Reflections of a Chaplain; Suffolk Regimental Gazette*, No. 470, Bury Free Press, November/December 1946
14. Ruffles, Lionel, *The Battle for Isaac*, Private, c.1995
15. Appendix J.1. *Battalion War Diary* TNA (WO 172 4922), 1944
16. Ibid.
17. Ruffles, Lionel, *The Battle for Isaac*, Private, c.1995
18. Ibid.
19. Nicholson, W. N., *The History of the Suffolk Regiment, 1928–46*, East Anglian Daily Times, 1947
20. Ibid.
21. Connolly, Malcolm, *Dekho! The Magazine of the Burma Star Association*, No. 190, 2018
22. Letter, Ernie Bates to Bill Deller, 2002 (GB553/CQ0/36)
23. Appendix J.1. *Battalion War Diary* TNA (WO 172 4922), 1944
24. Ibid.
25. Browne, E. G. W., *Travel and Experience 1944*, Private, 1946 (GB554/Y1/303)
26. Appendix J.1. *Battalion War Diary*, TNA (WO 172 4922), 1944
27. Ibid.
28. Browne, E. G. W., *Travel and Experience 1944*, Private, 1946 (GB554/Y1/303)
29. Connolly, Malcolm, *Dekho! The Magazine of the Burma Star Association*, No. 190, 2018
30. Browne, E. G. W., *Travel and Experience 1944*, Private, 1946 (GB554/Y1/303)
31. Citation, TNA (WO 373/34/29)
32. Ruffles, Lionel, *The Battle for Isaac*, Private, c.1995
33. Obituary, *Britannia & Castle*, No. 106, Private, 2006
34. *Citation*, TNA (WO 373/33/92)
35. Appendix J.1. *Battalion War Diary* TNA (WO 172 4922), 1944
36. Letter to the author, 2010
37. Letter from H. R. Hopking, to E. Yonge, 12 July 1956, Private collection
38. Brown-Moffet, W., *Reflections of a Chaplain; Suffolk Regimental Gazette*, No. 470, Bury Free Press, November/December 1946
39. Appendix J.1. *Battalion War Diary* TNA (WO 172 4922), 1944
40. Ibid.

41. Ibid.
42. Brown-Moffet, W., *Reflections of a Chaplain; Suffolk Regimental Gazette*, No. 470, Bury Free Press, November/December 1946
43. Cooper, Ashley, *The Khyber Connection*, Bulmer Historical Society, 1985
44. Warren, Tommy, *Britannia & Castle*, No. 65, Private, 1985
45. Appendix J.1. *Battalion War Diary* TNA (WO 172 4922), 1944

Chapter Eleven
1. Winter, Stan, *Britannia & Castle*, No. 8, Private, 1962
2. Coward, Bryan, *Dekho! The Magazine of the Burma Star Association*, No. 132, 1999
3. Jones, Idris, *Burma Star Memorial Fund Newsletter, No. 3*, September 2020
4. Archer, Jeremy, *The Final Curtain, Burma 1941–45, Veterans Stories*, Pen & Sword, 2022
5. *Battalion War Diary* TNA (WO 172 4922), 1944
6. Brown-Moffet, W., *Reflections of a Chaplain; Suffolk Regimental Gazette*, No. 470, Bury Free Press, November-December 1946
7. Ibid.
8. Jones, Idris, *Dekho! The Magazine of the Burma Star Association*, No. 131, 1999
9. Coward, Bryan, *Dekho! The Magazine of the Burma Star Association*, No. 130, 1999
10. Brown-Moffet, W., *Reflections of a Chaplain; Suffolk Regimental Gazette*, No. 470, Bury Free Press, November/December 1946
11. Ibid.
12. Coward, Bryan, *Dekho! The Magazine of the Burma Star Association*, No. 132, 1999
13. Jones, Idris, *Dekho! The Magazine of the Burma Star Association*, No. 131, 1999
14. Browne, E. G. W., *Travel and Experience 1944*, Private, 1946 (GB554/Y1/303)
15. Ibid.
16. Brown-Moffet, W., *Reflections of a Chaplain; Suffolk Regimental Gazette*, No. 470, Bury Free Press, November/December 1946
17. Browne, E. G. W., *Travel and Experience 1944*, Private, 1946 (GB554/Y1/303)
18. *Suffolk Regimental Gazette*, No. 458, Bury Free Press, November–December 1944
19. *Battalion War Diary* TNA (WO 172 4922), 1944
20. *Suffolk Regimental Gazette*, No. 460, Bury Free Press, March-April 1945
21. *Battalion War Diary* TNA (WO 172 4922), 1944
22. Archer, Jeremy, *The Final Curtain, Burma 1941–45, Veterans Stories*, Pen & Sword, 2022
23. *Battalion War Diary* TNA (WO 172 4922), 1944
24. Nicholson, W. N., *The History of the Suffolk Regiment, 1928–46*, East Anglian Daily Times, 1947
25. Henderson, Kenneth E. J., *Lucky Man*, Private, 2004
26. Archer, Jeremy, *The Final Curtain, Burma 1941–45, Veterans Stories*, Pen & Sword, 2022
27. *Battalion War Diary* TNA (WO 172 4922), 1944
28. Browne, E. G. W., *Travel and Experience 1944*, Private, 1946 (GB554/Y1/303)
29. Brown-Moffet, W., *Reflections of a Chaplain; Suffolk Regimental Gazette*, No. 470, Bury Free Press, November/December 1946
30. Coward, Bryan, *Britannia & Castle*, No. 93, Private, 1999
31. *Suffolk Regimental Gazette*, No. 458, Bury Free Press, November–December 1944
32. Ibid.
33. Ibid.
34. Browne, E. G. W., *Travel and Experience 1944*, Private, 1946 (GB554/Y1/303)
35. Nicholson, W. N, *The History of the the Suffolk Regiment, 1928–46*, East Anglian Daily Times, 1947

36. *Battalion War Diary* TNA (WO 172 4922), 1944
37. Archer, Jeremy, *The Final Curtain, Burma 1941–45, Veterans Stories*, Pen & Sword, 2022
38. *Battalion War Diary* TNA (WO 172 4922), 1944
39. Brown-Moffet, W., *Reflections of a Chaplain; Suffolk Regimental Gazette*, No. 470, Bury Free Press, November/December 1946

Chapter Twelve
1. *Bury Free Press*, 3 November 1944
2. *Suffolk Regimental Gazette*, No. 459, Bury Free Press, January- February 1945
3. Browne, E. G. W., *Travel and Experience 1944*, Private, 1946 (GB554/Y1/303)
4. Price, Clifford, *Britannia & Castle*, No. 88, Private, 1987
5. *Bury Free Press*, 12 January 1945
6. Ibid.
7. Ibid.
8. VJ Day 50th Anniversary Special, *Evening Star*, 1995
9. Nicholson, W. N., *The History of the Suffolk Regiment, 1928–46*, East Anglian Daily Times, 1947
10. *Suffolk Regimental Gazette*, No. 466, Bury Free Press, March-April 1946
11. *Suffolk Regimental Gazette*, No. 468, Bury Free Press, July-August 1946
12. Wilkinson, Cyril, *Britannia & Castle*, No. 73, Private, 1989
13. *2nd Battalion Log 1842–1947* (GB554/C1/3)
14. Price, Clifford, *Britannia & Castle*, No. 88, Private, 1987
15. Godfrey, F. A., *The History of the Suffolk Regiment, 1946–1959*, Leo Cooper, 1988
16. *Suffolk Regimental Gazette*, No. 482, Bury Free Press, November–December 1948

Epilogue
1. Nicholson, W. N., *The History of the Suffolk Regiment, 1928–46*, East Anglian Daily Times, 1947
2. Moir, Guthrie, *The Suffolk Regiment*, Leo Cooper, 1969
3. Deller, William, *Britannia & Castle*, No. 93, Private, 1999
4. *Britannia & Castle*, No. 62, Private, 1984
5. VJ Day 50th Anniversary Special, *Evening Star*, 1995

Index

Abbott, Private S.R.B., 45
Aircraft (Allied):
　Curtiss Commando, 70
　Douglas Dakota, 72, 197
　Hawker Hurricane, 52
　'Hurri-Bombers', 94–6, 102, 120, 131
　Mitchell Medium Bombers, 52
　Supermarine Spitfire, 52
　Vultee Vengeance Dive-Bombers, 29, 47, 52, 56–7, 63, 95–6, 101, 131
　Westland Wapiti, 5
Aircraft (Japanese):
　Mitsubishi Zero, 29, 100, 115
Armour (Allied):
　Crossley Armoured Cars, 5
　Grant Tanks, 162, 172
　Lee Tanks, 38, 93–4, 115
　Stuart Tanks, 79, 115, 131
Aldren, Private, 137
Allum, Lieutenant 'Vic', 61
Amritsar, 200, 202
Anderson, Private, 137–8, 143
Anslow, Captain Denis, 55, 84, 124, 132, 137
Arras, 85
Arrindell, Lieutenant Miles, 6, 47, 79, 85, 89, 107, 136, 143
Atkins, Major 'Tommy', 6
Auchinleck, Sir Claude, 201
Australia, 77, 95, 166

Bailey Bridge, 116, 197
Baker, Private, 18
Barber, Lance Corporal Alec, 34, 70–1
Barfield, Private Jack, 44
Barnes, Sergeant George 'Smokey', 153, 168–9
'Basha's', 11, 50, 120–1, 139, 148
Bates, Sergeant James, 18, 94, 180

Bates, Corporal Ernie, 14–15, 50, 93–4, 99, 117, 148–9, 162, 188, 206
Battalion (Second Suffolk)
　'Admin' (Administration) Company, 11–12, 23, 44, 49, 179, 190, 197
　Cookhouse, 50, 56, 77, 115, 119
　Guerrilla Platoon, 11, 13, 22, 25–7, 30, 47, 52, 58–60, 63–4, 79, 89, 94, 106, 109, 116, 120–3, 139–40, 146, 173, 176, 182–3, 186–7, 191–2
　HQ Company, 12, 14, 69, 84, 108, 136, 190, 199
　Intelligence Section, 43, 47, 67, 89, 138, 146, 181
　Machine Gunners (MMG), 13, 34–5, 163
　Mortar Platoon, 5, 13, 49, 56, 58, 61–4, 66, 101, 104–105, 137, 163–4, 176, 185
　Pioneer Platoon, 12, 21, 30, 43, 105–106, 110, 141, 173, 211
　Signal Platoon, 44, 92, 117, 148–9
Batten, Private, 146
Battle Honours (Dogras), 66
Battle Honours (Battalion), 202
Beaumont College, Windsor, 168
Bedfordshire, 136
Bengal, 9–10, 12
Bennett, Private, 110, 210
Bevan, Lieutenant W.S., 2, 80
Bishenpur, 179–80, 186
Bissell, Sergeant Arthur, 49
Blake, Private, 93, 110, 210–11
Bloomfield, Private William, 29
Boddington, Captain, 202
Bombay, 1, 144, 200
Box, Lieutenant, 47, 66, 74
Boyden, Private Jack, 12
Bradley, Lieutenant, 62, 92–3, 96

Bren Gun, 5, 26–7, 47, 59–60, 66, 96, 99, 101, 104–105, 107, 117, 120–2, 144, 188
Bren Gun Carrier (Universal Carrier), 21, 74, 77, 89, 92, 101, 110, 117, 173, 179
Briggs, Major General Harold, 41, 208
Brighty, Private, 18, 180
British Army:
   14th Army, 17, 40–1, 61, 173, 196
   2nd (British) Infantry Division, 177
   Armoured Regiments:
     3 Dragoon Guards (3.D.G.), 149, 161
     3rd Carabiners *see above*
   Infantry Regiments/Battalions:
     Bedfordshire and Hertfordshire, 111
     Black Watch (Royal Highlanders), 111, 168
     Cambridgeshire Regiment, 6, 117
     Duke of Cornwall's Light Infantry (D.C.L.I.), 199
     East Kent Regiment (Buffs), 44
     East Surreys, 111
     Essex Regiment, 22, 111, 202
     King's (Liverpool), 111
     King's Own Royal Regiment (Lancaster), 173
     King's Own Scottish Borderers (K.O.S.B.), 127,
     2 King's Own Yorkshire Light Infantry (K.O.Y.L.I.), 142
     1 Lincoln, 47
     Oxfordshire and Buckinghamshire Light Infantry, 42, 111
     Queen's Own, Royal West Kent, 76, 180
     Royal Berkshire Regiment, 63, 104, 131, 144, 191
     Royal Inniskilling Fusiliers, 10
     Royal Norfolk Regiment, 8, 18, 27, 94–5, 99, 115, 122, 141
     2 Royal Norfolk, 149, 200, 202
     5 Royal Norfolk, 41
     6 Royal Norfolk, 6
     70 Royal Norfolk, 30, 85
     Royal Scots, 104, 110–11
     1 Royal Scots Fusiliers, 55
     Royal Warwickshire Regiment, 43, 111, 138
     Suffolk Regiment:
       1 Suffolk, 2, 5, 8, 10–11, 30, 42, 45, 70–1, 85, 117, 136, 150, 169, 179, 204–206
       4 Suffolk, 6, 199
       5 Suffolk, 109
       7 Suffolk, 114
       8 Suffolk, 7, 59
       30 Suffolk, 13, 66
       70 Suffolk, 114
     2 West Yorks, 65, 75, 119, 189
     4 Welch, 117
     Wiltshire Regiment, 108, 131
     Worcestershire Regiment, 96
     York and Lancaster Regiment, 68
     7 York and Lancs, 197
     8 York and Lancs, 66
   Royal Army Service Corps (R.A.S.C.), 48, 75
   Royal Artillery, 22, 31, 48, 92, 95, 98, 120, 131
     28 (Jungle) Field Regiment, R.A., 29, 46, 208
     221 Anti-Tank Battery, R.A., 148
   Royal Corps of Signals, 67, 109
   Royal Engineers ('Sappers'), 38, 40, 67, 109, 157, 159–60, 174, 176
     74 Field Company, R.E., 67, 151
British Artillery:
   25-pdr gun, 148–9, 162, 189
   6-pdr gun, 148, 150
British Small Arms (including US-made weapons):
   Grenades (No. 36), 106, 143
   SAA (Small Arms Ammunition .303), 20, 69, 134, 164
   Springfield Rifle, M1903, 11, 106
   Thompson Sub-Machine Gun (Tommy Gun), 11, 18, 33, 40, 57, 120–1, 123, 126, 144, 185–6
   'VB' (Vickers Berthier) Guns, 4–5
   Vickers (Machine Gun), 34–5, 47, 117, 163
Brooks, Private Kenneth, 65
Brown, Sergeant Richard 'Dickie', 27, 124
Browne, Major E.G.W. 'Gordon', 55, 63, 68, 70, 73, 76, 83, 97, 100, 107–108, 112,

125–7, 140–1, 149, 162–3, 165–6, 177, 189–91, 193, 196, 200, 204
Brown-Moffet, Captain the Reverend (Padre), 10, 12, 16, 23, 28, 43, 50, 69, 85, 88, 98, 113, 125, 141, 156, 169–70, 173, 176, 178, 189, 193, 210
Bruce, Private Ernest 'Ed', 109
Buck, Private, 126, 130, 210
Bullock, Private, 47
Bunce, Sergeant, 84, 92, 183
Buri Bazaar, 179
Burma (Places):
  Akyab, 14
  Buthidaung, 16, 29, 57, 63, 66
  Buywyin, 13
  Chindwin River, 197
  Donbaik, 54
  Indaneyi, 197
  Kalewa, 197
  Kiang, 197
  Maungdaw, 14, 16, 21, 29, 46, 63, 66, 84
  Mayu Range (mountains), 16–17, 20–1, 23, 58, 65
  Naf River, 20
  Ngayedauk Pass, 55
  Pyinggaing, 197
  Razabil, 20–1, 62–3, 65
  Shwebo, 197
  Tumbru, 13
  Yeu, 197
Burma (Positions):
  'Admin' Box, 20
  'Ant and Bean' Hills, 38, 65
  'Bamboo Hill', 20, 25–46, 47–9, 52, 55–6, 58–67, 70, 108, 120, 132, 137, 143, 191, 196, 206, 208–209
  'Biscuit' Hill, 64
  'Caterpillar' Hill, 28, 30–1
  'Chimney' Hill, 52, 58, 61, 63
  'Cock and Bull', 30
  'Hook', 29, 35, 38
  'Hundred Foot Feature', 64, 66
  'Leach Hill', 58–9
  'Long Hill', 25, 27–32, 34, 39, 46–9, 60–4, 66
  'Long Hill South', 52, 59
  'Mound', 29–30
  'Pampus Hill', 64
  'Parson's Nose', 65
  'Pineapple' Hill, 63, 67
  'Propeller' Hill, 63
  'Pipe' Hill, 49, 52, 55–6
  'Point 731', 21–2, 26, 29, 49, 62, 66–7
  'Point 1079', 66
  'Razabil Fortress', 63, 65
  'Red Bungalow', 20
  'Ring II', 56,
  'Right Knob', 29
  'Sausage' Hill, 49
  'Sickle' Hill, 49, 55
  The 'Wrens', 20, 25, 29, 31, 40, 63
    'Middle Wrencat', 25–7, 66, 68
    'Wrencat', 25–8, 31, 38, 47, 62–4, 66
    'Wrenkitten', 25–7, 29, 38, 60, 62–3
Bury St Edmunds, 197, 202–203, 208

Calcutta, 29, 190
'Calling Blighty' (Newsreel), 199
Calver, Lieutenant, 47, 52, 185
Cannell, Private, 108
Carr, Private, 93,
Carter, Sergeant 'Nick', 23, 144
Casey, Private, 59–60
Chaplin, Private Dennis 'Arab', 14
'Charwallah', 7, 28
Chenovitch, Private Barnet, 168
China, 2, 202
Chingdal (Chingdai), 79–80
Chittagong (Chittogram), 13–14, 16, 69, 188, 197
Churachanpur, 189
Cigarettes, 77, 79, 112, 157
Cole, Lieutenant John (3.D.G.), 161
Coleman, Private, 126, 130
Collinson, Private Leonard, 138
Connolly, Trooper Malcolm (3.D.G.), 161, 165
Cook, Private, 172
Cooper, Major W.M.W. 'Morris', 173, 180
Cotton, Private, 111
Coward, Major Bryan, 8, 71–2, 74, 85, 139, 172, 175, 177, 182, 190
Coward, Noel, 175–6
Cox's Bazaar, 13
Cranbrook, B.C., Canada, 175

Cropley, Cook Sergeant, 56, 69–70, 115, 191
Crossland, Private, 18, 180
Cunliffe, Sergeant, 130
Cunnington, Private, 18

Dacca, 197
DaCosta, Private Vincente, 44
Danvers, the Reverend G.C., 85
Dash, Private Ted 'Jack', 44, 117, 138
Davidson, Private Charles, 115
Davies, Corporal, 127
D-Day, 70–1, 85, 150
Dean, Lieutenant Colonel H.W. 'Sweat', 199, 201
Dearsley, Private Henry, 143
Dell, Corporal Cyril, 30, 51, 77, 109
Deller, Brigadier W.C. 'Bill', 205
Deolali B.B.R.C. (British Base Reinforcement Camp), 47, 116, 138
Dewar, Major Malcolm, 202
Dixon, Private, 55
Dohazri, 68, 70, 72
Dowell, Private Norman, 110, 210–11
Doyle, Lance Corporal James 'Ginger', 107
DuFeu, Private, 110, 211
Duffy, CSM Kevin, 15, 34–5, 188
Duncan, Lieutenant Murdo, 17, 20, 54–5, 59, 61–2, 66–8, 80, 84, 86, 88, 95, 102, 111
Dunkirk (Evacuation), 5, 11, 55, 108, 169, 199
Dunnett, Private Tom, 77, 199

Eade, Private Branton, 168
Earle, Private, 34
Ebbage, Private Leonard, 110–11, 210
Edlin, Lance Sergeant Daniel, 44
Ekban/Ekwan, 128, 145
Eley, Lieutenant Colonel D.R.A., 5
Ellis, Lieutenant, 47, 193
Ennion, Captain 'Tony', 6, 28, 65, 124–5, 139
Entrenching Tools, 31, 100, 102, 131, 159, 170

Fallowfield, Private William, 95
Fern, Corporal, 158

Fildes, Lieutenant, 27–8
Fisher-Hock, Major John, 167
Fletcher, Private, 137
'F.O.B.' (Forward Officer Bombardment), 46
'F.O.O.' (Forward Officer Observation), 46, 208
Forrest, Major Peter, 26–8, 38, 55, 63–4, 80, 85, 101–103, 126, 132, 137, 151–2, 156–7, 159–60, 166–7, 180, 190, 196
Foster, Private Arthur, 197
Foster, Private Donald, 122–3
Fyson, Private James 'Fitz', 117

Gant, Private, 18
Gauld, Lieutenant, 63, 79–80, 89, 124
Gewskill, 111
Gibraltar, 202
Gilbert, Second Lieutenant, 87, 101, 111
Glover, Lieutenant, 28–9
Good, Lance Sergeant, 116
Goodwin, Lieutenant Colonel R.E., 199
Gorleston-on-Sea, 131
Grace, Private Joseph, 65
Gray, Captain Douglas, 38, 41, 132
Gray, Captain Rod, 21–2, 31, 47, 59, 113, 130, 139, 143, 193
Gray, Private, 143
Great Yarmouth, 131
Green, Private, 137, 144
Grimes, Private Leslie, 27
'Grousers' (Tank Track Shoes), 161
Guanthabi, 79
Gunton, Lieutenant, 131
Gurkha Paratroopers, 97, 102
Gurkhas, 64–5, 148, 161
Gurney, Major, 31, 79

Hadlow, Private Bernard, 22
Halford, Captain, 175, 192
Haraorou, 116, 118
Hart, Private Leslie 'Jim', 108
Hart, Private William, 108
Hastie, Lieutenant, 30, 63, 66, 127
Hawkins, Private, 137
Hawley, Bombardier George (28 (J) F.R. R.A.), 208
Haygarth, Lieutenant, 158–9

Haynes, Private Denis, 85–6
Heal, Private, 27
Heath, Joan, 187
Henderson, Major Kenneth, 1, 14, 35, 69, 75, 119, 136, 187
Hewat, Private, 137
Hildesley, Captain Raymond 'Jimmy', 40, 175, 202
Hill, Major Peter, 6, 82, 86, 89, 92, 109, 131–2, 137, 139, 190, 204
Hong Kong, 6
Hook, Private, 126,
Hopking, Lieutenant Colonel H.R., 12–13, 17–18, 28–9, 41, 43, 49, 61, 65, 72, 74, 88–9, 92, 97–8, 100, 103, 105, 107–108, 112–13, 168, 199
Hopkins, Lance Sergeant 'Polly', 4
Horsecroft, Private Richard 'Dicky', 169
Hospitals:
  14 British General Hospital (Bareilly), 187
  38 British General Hospital (Assam), 95
  45 Indian Field Hospital, 55
  49 Indian Base Hospital (Kohima), 74
Howlett, Corporal E.A. 'Charlie', 120
Hunt, Lance Corporal Herbert, 12,
Hunter, Lance Corporal James 'Tich', 85

Imphal, 69–70, 72, 77, 79, 83–4, 86, 110–11, 115, 118, 176–9, 189–91, 194, 196–7, 200, 204, 206, 210–12
Imphal (Positions):
  'Charing X', 136–7
  'Everest', 120
  'Hump' Feature, 120
  'Isaac', 145–75, 177, 190, 196
    Actions around:
    'Adam' and 'Eve', 145, 172–4
    'Centre Bump', 146–8, 160, 163–6, 172–4
    'East End', 146–53, 156–60, 162–5, 172
    'F.U.P. (Forming Up Place), 147, 150, 159
    'George', 145, 148–51, 160–62, 169, 172
    'Harry', 145–52, 156–60, 162, 166, 169, 172
    'Isaac's Nose', 146–8, 150, 158, 160–1, 163–6, 172
    'James', 145, 165–7, 173–5
    'Platform', 146–7, 151–3, 156–60, 162–5, 168, 172
    'Saddle', 146–8, 150–3, 156–9, 162–3, 165
    'Third Step', 173
    'Twin Pimples', 146, 151
  'Lion Box', 129,
  'Mouse', 131
  'Pimple', 82–114, 127, 129, 134, 136, 139, 168, 180, 210–12
    Actions around:
    'Minden Way', 110
    'Point 4057 (The 'Mound'), 82–3, 85–9, 92–102, 105–106, 108, 110, 113, 115–16, 211
    'Point 4066', 109
    'Point 5074' (Nungshigum), 88
    'Ring I', 89, 92, 94–8, 100, 104–105, 107–108, 111, 118
    'Ring II', 92, 98, 100–101, 103–104
    'Ring III', 85–6, 92–3, 99, 100–103, 115
    'Saddle', 93–4, 97–9, 101, 105–106
    'Sausage Hill', 89, 92, 94, 99–102, 104–105, 107–109
    'Spur', 89, 95–6
  'Point 3813', 127
  'Point 4241', 80, 92
  'Point 4743', 124
  'Point 5521', 120
  'Pyramid', 124–45
    Actions around:
    'Baby's Bottom', 129, 131–2, 134, 136–9, 141
    'Northern Feature', 130–2, 134–5, 138–9
    'Southern Feature', 130–2, 134–5, 138–9
  'Runaway Hill', 119
  'Zebra', 131, 143–5, 148
Imphal Airfield/Airstrip, 72, 75, 100, 110, 149
Imphal Cemetery, 86, 138, 143, 211
Imphal-Litan Road, 82

Imphal-Kohima Road, 118–19, 123–4, 127, 129, 136, 138, 144–5, 174, 176–8, 180
   'Cold Harbour', 176
   Milestone 16, 127, 136
   Milestone 17, 124, 126–7, 129–31
   Milestone 109, 177
   Milestone 110, 176
Imphal-Tiddim Road, 179
Imphal Turel (River), 124, 127, 143, 174
Imphal-Ukhrul Road, 72, 82, 88
(British) Indian Army:
   XXXIII Indian Corps, 193, 197
   256 Area (Lines of Communication Troops), 195
   Armoured Brigades:
      254 (Indian) Tank Brigade, 79
      7 Cavalry, 79
   Infantry Divisions:
      5th (Indian) Division, 13, 16, 41, 46, 69, 72, 96, 144, 180, 195, 208
         9 (Indian) Infantry Brigade, 65, 75, 119, 173, 189
         123 (Indian) Infantry Brigade, 13, 25, 28, 41, 59, 65, 76, 177, 180, 189, 193, 195
            1/17 Dogra, 13, 25, 29, 31, 38–40, 47, 52–3, 55, 62–3, 66, 95–7, 115, 124, 127, 141–4, 148, 173–4, 177–8
            3/9 Gurkha, 13, 64–5
            3/9 Jats, 84, 88, 120
            2/1 Punjab, 13, 25, 62, 93
            3/2 Punjab, 13, 126, 167, 173, 176–7, 195
            3/14 Punjab, 119,
         161 (Indian) Infantry Brigade, 49, 65, 182
      7th (Indian) Division, 16, 21, 61, 69
         29 Brigade, 55, 61
      17th (Indian) Division, 179
         63rd (Indian) Brigade, 181
      20th (Indian) Division:
         32 Brigade, 182
   Infantry Regiments:
      1 Assam, 74
      4 Burma Rifles, 142
      Frontier Force Regiment, 61, 64

      4/8 Gurkha Rifles, 145–6, 148, 161
      3/9 Jats, 84, 120
      4/5 Mahratta (37 Brigade), 115
      4/7 Rajputs, 66
      1/11 Sikh (89 Brigade), 128
   Parachute Units:
      50 Parachute Brigade, 79–80, 179
         151 Parachute Battalion, 5, 80
Indian Engineers, 127, 139
Inman, Lieutenant, 28, 35
Ipswich, 12, 44, 48, 123, 143
Ireland, Private Dennis, 152
Iril River (and Valley), 83, 92, 96, 108, 115
Ithol Lok, 119, 173
Izzard, Sergeant Sidney, 116, 144

James, Corporal, 110, 210–11
James, Private Les, 14,
Japanese Army:
   51st Regiment (1st Company), 85
   112th Infantry Regiment, 47
   138th Infantry Regiment, 115
   'Jiffs' (J.I.F.C., Japanese Indian Fifth Column), 26, 48, 79, 127
Japanese Weaponry:
   50mm discharger, 132
   75mm gun, 62, 100, 146, 161, 170
   Artillery barrage 'Overs', 127
   Type 10 mortar, 39, 144,
Jasper, RSM George, 61–2, 112
Jessami, 74, 79
JIFFs, *see* Japanese Army
Johnson, Private Sid, 109
Jones, Private Idris, 21, 40, 116, 173, 175, 177, 185, 188, 193

Kabaw Valley, 83, 197
Kaji Khul, 180
Kameng, 101
Kanglatongbi, 124–7, 129, 135, 142, 144–5, 175–6
   Ordnance Depot, 124, 129–30, 139–40, 142, 174
Kashmir, 137
Kassader/Khassidar (Native Guide), 3–4
Keft, Lieutenant, 47
Kerridge, CQMS Harry 'Kate', 48
Khopuibung, 190

King's African Rifles, 166
Kirk, Corporal, 47
Knox, Private Forrest, 110–11, 210
Kohima, 69, 72–81, 129, 136, 149, 175–6, 190, 197
   'Hospital Hill', 73

Lahore, 198–200, 202
Lamboida Kut, 79, 89
Lamyenching, 83, 93
Last, Private, 108
Lawrence, Lieutenant, 34, 56, 74, 79
Leach, Major O.K. 'Ossy' (also 'Slogger'), 13, 21, 40, 46, 49, 54, 56, 99–101, 103, 106, 203
Le Cateau, 193
Leech, Private, 137
Lee Hunter, Captain Douglas 'The Monk', 11, 30, 58, 60, 63–4, 74, 79–80, 106, 109, 120–3, 137, 180, 196
Leeke, Corporal Reginald 'Reggie', 70
Lime (for sanitary use), 172–3
Linge, Private Bill, 123
Litan, 80, 82
Lockey, Lance Corporal Roy, 135–6, 139
Loktak Lake, 186
Long, Private, 137
Lucas, Private Paul, 137, 141
Lucknow, 6

Maas River, 45
Mackie, Private James, 168
Madras, 13, 108
Makepeace, Private Lawrence, 136
Malaya (1942), 26, 84
Malayan Emergency, 62
Mallett, Private Charles, 12
Malta, 117
Makhan, 124–5
Mapeo Khunou, 120
Mattin, Private 'Maxie', 44, 117
Menneer, Lieutenant Colonel Kenneth, 80, 107, 113–16, 124, 126, 128, 130, 134–6, 139, 144, 146, 148, 150, 158–9, 161, 169, 171–2, 174–5, 178, 180, 182, 185–6, 189–90, 193, 199
Mhow, 2, 14, 169
Militiamen, 7, 14, 117

Milnes, Lieutenant Colonel F.A., 199
'Minden Day', 117, 190–1
'Minden' Roses, 190–1
Mitchinson, Captain, 35
Moirang, 186–9
'Molotov Cocktail' (petrol bombs), 105–7
Molvom Ridge, 174, 176
Monier-Williams, Lieutenant Colonel H.B., 3, 5–6
Monier-Williams, Mrs, 195
Moody, Private Herbert, 31
Moplah Rebellion (1921/22), 8
Mortlock, Lance Corporal, 149
Mortlock, Private, 187
Moss, Private Richard 'Dickie', 134–5, 137, 206
Motbung (Modbung), 119, 141–2, 145–6, 173, 176
Motbung Spur, 163
Mott, Private Cyril 'Sonny', 23, 110–11, 210
Mountbatten, Admiral Lord Louis, 17–18, 94, 180
Mowle, Lance Corporal Don 'Spitter', 70–1
Mules, 10, 21, 23–4, 48, 67, 69, 72–4, 97–8, 112, 119, 124, 127, 129–30, 139–40, 169–70, 174, 176, 179, 182, 185–6, 190, 192
Muleteer (Mule Driver), 21, 24
Mynott, Private, 137, 141

Narduzzo, Private Serafino, 102, 110–11, 210–11
Neighbour, Private, 137–8
Ngangkha Lowai, 186–7
Nice, Sergeant, 48
Nicholson, Colonel W.N., 204
Nippon DP (Displaced Persons), 197
Normandy, 2, 70, 206
   Chateau de la Londe, 42, 179
   Tinchebray, 71
Nottingham, 149, 208
Nungoi, 115
Nungshigum Feature, 82, 84–5, 88, 93–5, 97, 101, 108, 115–16, 149, 167
Nurathen, 139
Nyasaland, 166

Oborne, Lieutenant Colonel Victor, 199
O'Conor, Private Michael, 42

Page, Private, 137
Palel, 74, 197
Papillon, Captain Philip, 41–2
Parade (magazine), 57–8
Parker, Private George 'Dad', 43, 137–8
Parr, Sergeant Charlie, 58, 71, 117
Partington, Private Arthur, 51, 199
Pathans, 4–5, 73
Peck, Lance Corporal Jack 'Tiny', 121–3, 191
Perkins, Private Harry, 108
Pettit, Lance Corporal, 137
Pie-Dogs (Pye-Dogs), 87, 172
Pigden, Private, 110, 210
Pitalpin, 168
Pittard, Private, 107, 118
Pooley, Lance Corporal, 144
Porters (Native), 124–5, 129, 190
Potsanbam, 182
Power, Private 'Tyrone', 4
Presland, Lance Corporal, 108
Pryke, Private Charles 'Whistler', 197–8
Purum, 119
'PYTHON' (Leave Scheme), 199

Randall, CSM, 195
Rash, Private Toby, 170
Rations, 12, 48, 112, 119, 130, 135, 145, 178–9, 192, 198
   Biscuits, 53, 77, 115, 118
   'Bully Beef', 77, 115, 118–19
   Cookhouse, 50, 56, 77, 115, 119
   'K' Rations, 119, 125
   Rice, 84, 115, 191,
   Slaughtering Party, 115
Rawalpindi, 1, 5–6, 202
Razmak, 2–5, 7, 117, 166, 188, 196
   'Toady' Piquet, 4
Reeve, Private Arthur, 107, 111
Regimental Aid Post (R.A.P.), 22, 27, 34, 38, 50, 56, 85, 94–5, 101, 110, 135–7, 139, 143–4, 156, 169, 192
Rehkat Chaung (Stream), 25, 28, 30, 48, 63, 65, 67

Richards, Major Patrick 'Dickie', 31–2, 34–5, 41–3, 65
Risebrow, Private, 55
Roberts, Brigadier Gordon, 198
'ROB Force', 198
Robinson, Private, 137
Rolfe, Private Norman, 77
Roome, Private David, 149
Royal Air Force, 85, 189
Ruffles, Lance Corporal Lionel, 18, 118, 152, 156, 158–60, 166, 207

Sachungkhok, 83
Safamaina, 119, 174–6
Saikot, 190
Saitu, 130
Salter, Lance Corporal Frederick, 38, 44, 63, 143
Sands, Private George, 63
Sangshak, 79–80
Satchell, Private Herbert, 45
Savage, Private Robert, 110, 210
Sawombung, 82
Saxon, Private Donald, 199
Sayfritz, Private, 108
Schwatz, Captain M.J., 56, 156
S.E.A.C. (South East Asia Command), 17, 83
S.E.A.C. (Forces Newspaper), 58, 123
Sedang, 120, 122–3, 139
Sejang, 84
Sengmai, 118, 123–4, 127, 130, 139
Sewell, Private Charles, 143
Shaboodeen, Khan Sahib Haji F., 7–8
Shafaron, Private, 137
Shanghai Defence Force, 1, 12
Shanks, Lance Corporal Robert, 152–3, 164, 167, 169
Sherman, Private, 137
Sherriff, R.C., 132
Shunu Sipahi, 185
Silchar Track, 180–3, 185
   Places Around:
      Chario, 181
      Chote (Chothe), 182
      Kha Aimol, 185
      Khulen, 181
      Kokaden, 181–2

Mayuron, 181
'Point 2614', 181–2
Positions:
  'Bulmer', 181–2
  'Garsides' Hill, 183
  'Matthews' Hill, 183, 185
  'Op Hill', 183, 185
  'RK Ridge', 182–3
  'Toulang Wood', 182
  'Truemans', 182
  'Whiteway', 181–3, 185
Sinclair, Private, 93
Singapore, 6, 26, 41, 95, 109, 127, 198
Skeels, Corporal Bill, 23
Skitmore, Captain, 202
Slim, Lieutenant General William 'Bill', 28, 41
Smith, Private Jim, 114
Springfield, Major G.T.O., 48
Squirrell, Lieutenant George, 6, 47, 76
Stanground, Peterborough, 108
Stanton, Private Frederick, 137, 141
'Starling Box', 179–80, 182
  'Naga Hill', 179
Steele, Sergeant David 'Herbie', 93–4, 110–11, 210
Steward, Sergeant, 84
Stewart, Corporal, 18, 94, 180
Stephens, Lieutenant Cyril, 55, 124, 131, 137, 144
Stopford, Lieutenant General Sir Montague, 190
Stretcher Bearers ('SBs'), 14, 35, 39, 101–103, 107, 110–11, 135–6, 149, 157, 168
Studd, Sergeant, 137
Stutters, Private, 137
Switzerland, 200

Tarun Khunou, 189
Terry, Private, 137
Thamnapokpi, 186
Tiddim, 179, 182, 185, 195
Tiddim Road, 178–80, 182, 186, 189–90, 193
Thompson, Private David, 12
Thould, Private, 137
Thursby, Lieutenant Pat, 35, 55, 109, 124, 141, 175

Thurston, Private Cyril, 59
Tochi Valley, 5
Tod, Private David, 110–11, 210–12
Tomkinson, Lieutenant, 38–9, 41, 120, 158
Toroglaobi, 188
Torrence, Private, 110, 210
Trimulgherry, 1
Trinidad, 12
Trinity College, Cambridge, 168
Troopships/Transport Ships:
  RMMV *Athlone Castle*, 144
  SS *Ethiopia*, 13
  HMT *Lancashire*, 188
  HMS *Persimmon*, 201
Tuffield, Private, 126–7

Ukhrul, 84
Uniform and Equipment:
  Battledress (Aertex), 9, 170
  Blankets, 57, 69, 120, 140
  Bush hat/Slouch hat, 9, 12, 18, 26, 80, 99, 141, 191
  Groundsheets, 3, 11, 50, 69
  Jungle Green, 9, 58, 170, 198
  Khaki Drill, 9, 198, 201
  Steel Helmets, 18, 99, 118
Urdu (Language), 2, 54, 124
Uyumpok, 116

Vallance, Major G.R.A. 'Rickie', 142–3, 173, 175, 180
Victor (comic), 123

Wakhong, 115, 118–19
Wallace, Corporal, 22
War Correspondents, 32, 40
  Chadburn, Paul, 56–8
  Sheets, Millard, 32–3, 39
Ward, Major A.A., 13
Ward, Private, 21–2
Warren, Sergeant Major 'Tommy', 4, 46, 48, 75, 82, 107, 117–18, 120, 171, 206
Watt, Lieutenant Thomas 'Tommy', 28, 61, 64, 76, 80–1, 89, 92, 96, 130, 196
Watt, Private Peter, 21–2
Watts, Sergeant 'Bill', 142
West Lothian, 110–11
Wheeler, Corporal, 89, 92, 108

Whetnell, Private Leslie, 43, 89, 141, 181
White, Private Graham, 135–6
Whitehand, Private, 137–8
Wigger, Private William 'Bill', 85–6
Wilkinson, Private Cyril, 9, 14, 16, 23, 25–6, 102, 116–17, 200, 206
Winter, CSM 'Stan', 9, 49
Winterton, Brigadier, 28, 35, 41
Woodard, Private Jack, 206

Worlledge, Private James 'Jim', 95
Wuppertal, 120

Yainganpokjoi (Yainganpokoi), 76, 79–81, 88–9
Yonge, Lieutenant Michael, 59, 118–19, 124–5, 128, 152–3, 158–9, 168
Young, Private, 107
Youngman, Private Norman, 111, 169

Dear Reader,

We hope you have enjoyed this book, but why not share your views on social media? You can also follow our pages to see more about our other products: facebook.com/penandswordbooks or follow us on Twitter @penswordbooks

You can also view our products at www.pen-and-sword.co.uk (UK and ROW) or www.penandswordbooks.com (North America).

To keep up to date with our latest releases and online catalogues, please sign up to our newsletter at: www.pen-and-sword.co.uk/newsletter

If you would like a printed catalogue with our latest books, then please email: enquiries@pen-and-sword.co.uk or telephone: 01226 734555 (UK and ROW) or email: Uspen-and-sword@casematepublishers.com or telephone: (610) 853-9131 (North America).

We respect your privacy and we will only use personal information to send you information about our products.

Thank you!